Dark Paths, Cold Trails

DARK PATHS, COLD TRAILS

How a Mountie Led the Quest
to Link Serial Killers to Their Victims

Doug Clark

HarperCollins*PublishersLtd*

Dark Paths, Cold Trails: How a Mountie Led the Quest to Link Serial Killers to Their Victims
Copyright © 2002 by Doug Clark.
All rights reserved. No part of this book may be used or reproduced in any manner whatsoever without prior written permission except in the case of brief quotations embodied in reviews.
For information address
HarperCollins Publishers Ltd,
55 Avenue Road, Suite 2900,
Toronto, Ontario, Canada M5R 3L2

www.harpercanada.com

HarperCollins books may be purchased for educational, business, or sales promotional use. For information please write:
Special Markets Department,
HarperCollins Canada,
55 Avenue Road, Suite 2900,
Toronto, Ontario, Canada M5R 3L2

First edition

Canadian Cataloguing in Publication Data

Clark, Doug, 1952–
Dark paths, cold trails : how a Mountie led the quest to link serial killers to their victims

Includes index.
ISBN 0-00-200078-4

1. Violent Crime Linkage Analysis System (Computer system)
2. MacKay, Ron.
3. Criminal investigation – Canada – Databases.
4. Violent offenders – Canada – Databases.
I. Title.

HV6023.8.C53 2002   025.06'3632595'0971
C2001-902527-0

HC 9 8 7 6 5 4 3 2 1

Printed and bound in the United States
Set in Sabon
Jacket author photo: Mirko Petricevic

*To the victims,
to those who love and mourn them
and to those who avenge them that
none suffered or died in vain*

The unexamined life
is not worth living.

SOCRATES

Contents

Preface

Dark Paths, Cold Trails chronicles an improbable revolution led by an unlikely revolutionary to make our world a safer place. Inspector Ron MacKay, of the Royal Canadian Mounted Police, the first non-American profiler trained by the FBI and driving force behind the ViCLAS linkage system adopted around the world, has changed policing forever. He didn't do it alone, but he led the way, his efforts a catalyst uniting a handful of like-minded pioneers whose combined efforts help save lives and money by catching serial predators sooner.

Peering behind the scenes and beyond the headlines, I have tried to detail the heroic efforts of these dedicated men and women, the extraordinary lengths to which they went to help solve brutal, bizarre, high-profile and lesser-known crimes using behavioural analysis—psychological and geographic profiling, forensic psychiatry, and serial-crime linkage.

To the surviving victims and those who mourn lost loved ones, I hope to offer the small comfort that your suffering was not in vain. There are women and children alive today, unborn generations are safer, because of the lessons learned and applied from what you suffered. It is a cherished legacy, dearly purchased and, unconscionably, ignored across most of Canada.

I urge all Canadians to demand that Ottawa and their provincial or territorial governments follow Ontario's lead and adopt the recommendations of the Justice Campbell Report on the Green Ribbon Task Force requiring their police to use existing investigative tools that have proven to reduce needless risk from serial predators.

It has happened here.

It will surely happen there.

Prologue

Alison Parrott

Ten years after the 1976 Montreal Olympics, the eyes of the world were again on Canada as Expo 86 opened in Vancouver. Canadians once more basked in the international acclaim of living in the safest, healthiest, and most peaceful country on Earth. Canada's largest city was still hailed as "Toronto the Good" where women felt safe walking alone at night, police patrolled the streets and traffic corridors, not school hallways, and "school violence" meant a playground punch-up. Even the worst bully back then drew the line at cowardly kicks and hair-pulling in a pinch; he would never show up toting a fully loaded semiautomatic assault rifle. That remained the preserve of overzealous SWAT units and the Ohio National Guard in the days before the police discovered they had a knack for negotiation.

Glancing askance across the longest undefended border on the planet, Canadians felt safe. Smug. Clearly superior to our American neighbours wracked by escalating and increasingly bizarre violence. "It's America," we'd shrug as if that explained it all. "It can't happen here."

Yet Canadians were equally seduced by the intoxicating headlines of the 1970s and early '80s that romanticized, and familiarized us with, and deadened us to, the true horror of murderous predators we'd recall by their aliases long after we'd forgotten their names—the Tower Sniper, Son of Sam, the Killer Clown, the Hillside Strangler, and the Vampire Killer. A few kept their identity—the Manson family and, of course, Ted Bundy. Feature films, television movies, and miniseries churned out sanitized versions of their horrific crimes but, contrary to Hollywood, sometimes the bad guys won. The Zodiac Killer was never caught, or if he was, it was for something else, and the Green River Killer eluded police for decades before DNA linked a suspect to several of those murders in late 2001.

Perhaps without meaning to, certainly never admitting it, the media and Hollywood glamorized violent death, not as fiction or some great war epic fought for a greater cause, but because multiple homicide was "sexy" and it sold. It was what the masses wanted, as evidenced by book and ticket sales. When FBI Special Agent Robert Ressler came up with the term "serial killer" in 1982, it became the pitch line for books and movies into the next millennium.

It was easy to forget the victims and their grieving families in all this murder and mayhem. Names and faces and deaths blurred after a while as the carnage increased, transforming America into "the land of the spree and home of the depraved." Only the "Atlanta Child Murders" reminded us of exactly who was dying. But Atlanta was an exception to the rule.

Alison Parrott was another.

In that promising summer of 1986, a phone rang, a child vanished, and everything changed forever.

Alison Parrott was 11 but considered mature beyond her years by those who knew and loved her. She enjoyed, by all accounts, a privileged, but not pampered, lifestyle. Her parents included "independence" in their nurturing priorities and were rewarded with a popular and considerate daughter who approached life responsibly. She earned her independence, never pushed or crossed the line. She began taking the subway to school in Grade 4 and always phoned home when a plan was made or changed with friends. A typical carefree kid, Alison slept over with friends, compared notes and giggles on boys they were just starting to notice, snuck onto the roof to toss water balloons. Standing four-foot-nine, weighing in at 75 pounds, she had a model's features and good looks—short blonde hair, haunting wide blue-green eyes. Her lithe frame was ideal for running and Alison was known as a runner with promise. Consistently shaving seconds off her best times, she won her first race that summer, qualified for an international track meet in New Jersey, and got her name published with the other qualifiers in *The Toronto Star*, Canada's largest-circulation daily newspaper.

About 10:30 a.m. Friday, July 25, 1986, fresh back from summer camp, Alison got a phone call from a man claiming to be a sports photographer asking to take her picture for a track magazine. Could she meet him at Varsity Stadium in downtown Toronto? Alison said she'd have to ask; the man agreed to call back in a few minutes. Lesley Parrott, her mother, worked at an ad agency about 10 minutes from their upscale home on Summerhill Avenue on the rim of affluent Rosedale. She hesitated briefly, but relented, believing Alison's teammates would be at the photo session, and reviewed the subway route with her excited young daughter—two stops south on the Yonge Street line, change trains at Bloor, two stops west, exit at St. George. That left a short walk down Bedford Street, cross Bloor Street with the lights and she'd be at Varsity Stadium, a stone's throw from Queen's Park and the Ontario legislature.

Mother and daughter said goodbye. The man called back as promised. Alison confirmed she'd be there, raced out the door, down the street and caught the subway downtown. A bank security camera videotaped her striding down Bedford.

Then Alison Parrott vanished without a trace.

Lesley reported her daughter missing as evening shadows lengthened. About 6:00 p.m. Metro Toronto Police responded promptly and surmised immediately that this wasn't a troubled kid running away or hiding out at a friend's. There was no evidence of abuse or anger or some imagined slight; this was a nice girl from a good home. The cops moved quickly, broadcasting Alison's disappearance and description to the crowd watching a lacrosse game at Varsity Arena.

Nothing.

At 10:00 p.m., her disappearance and photo were aired by CityTV.

Nothing.

Hundreds helped search the next day.

Nothing.

On July 27th, two days after she was lured from home, Alison's naked body was found curled into a fetal position in bushes of

Kings Mill Park along the Humber River, a popular area for early-morning anglers and late-night lovers. She had been bound, raped, and strangled.

The impact rippled far beyond Toronto. Across the province and throughout the country, Canadians lost their innocence, their glib naivety, the same day the Parrotts lost their daughter. Canadians went into mourning for a child they never knew, who in death became "every child." Their child became our child; their ordeal became every parent's nightmare. Worried that we would fail our children, it was a short step to sensing we had failed Alison. What had we become? How could this happen?

The grim crime details were chilling. Fear was palpable; an invisible monster was running free, preying on children. *Our children.* Alison's wide eyes bored through us, into our consciousness and conscience, from TV screens, newspaper front pages, and magazine covers. Her familiar photo—chin cupped in hand, head cocked to one side, lips pursed in an impish Mona Lisa smirk—was a portrait of innocence haunting total strangers who anguished they had somehow failed this child, betrayed her faith, abandoned her family—but had no idea what to do, how to help. A stranger had stolen Alison and total strangers shared the Parrotts' pain because, in Alison's image, we saw our own children; in her fate, their peril. That photo ensured no one would soon forget Alison Parrott and launched the police on a crusade to find her killer and bring swift justice.

Every homicide is a crime but a murdered child is an atrocity, a sin, an abomination so monstrous even the stoutest heart cracks a little. Beyond the fear, the shock, the outrage, a murdered child changes all the rules for even the most jaded homicide cops: Now it's personal! Each investigator silently vowed to go the extra mile to crack *this* case, to avenge Alison, to bring closure for her family by arresting the beast who did this.

The investigators knew going in it wouldn't be easy, might not be quick. Most murders were solved quickly because most victims knew their killer and motives rarely varied: lust, loot, or lunacy. But this time they were starting from a dead stop, confronted by a scene that offered few clues, fewer leads, and no "prime" suspects. In a major city like Toronto, such cases literally offer a million suspects—and none. It was the nature of the job.

Homicide cops are a breed apart, reputedly the toughest, most cynical clan on the planet, an elite, at times elitist, horde of avenging angels ready to swoop down anywhere at any time to mete out man's justice or God's wrath as the crime warrants. Retaining their sanity through dark gallows humour unfit for polite society, they trace their lineage to God fingering Cain for the first murder, a bust the least reverent insist wasn't all that hard: God only had three suspects and the victim knew his killer.

Alison had been lured from her home by a stranger, giving detectives myriad possible suspects and no leads. Despite the soaring trend in "stranger murders" that began in the 1970s, the method of homicide investigation was little changed from the days Centurions had patrolled Rome 2000 years ago: roust an informant and round up the usual suspects—known sex offenders and pedophiles. Playing it by the numbers, the Metro Toronto cops interviewed hundreds, believing someone knew something, someone would crack, someone would talk.

But no one did.

The police were haunted by a fear that they had interviewed the killer and let him go, that he had sat across the table from them and lied his way out the door and back onto the street. But which one? That was always the trick without an informant or an eyewitness or a confession.

Which one?

As the trail cooled with each passing hour, the odds rose that someone would get away with murder. Despite heroic efforts of the dedicated investigators on behalf of Alison and her grieving family, no one was charged with her murder. Deemed a random, isolated tragedy, she was shunted aside by new victims, fresher trails. Years passed, cops retired, more children disappeared and were found dead. Investigators privately conceded Alison's death might never be solved.

But even out of sight, she was never totally out of mind.

Eventually, an FBI "profiler" was brought in. Profiling was a new approach, a sign of desperation, and proof they'd try anything to avenge Alison. But the profile was dismissed as too general to be much help and shelved. The cops gently set Alison aside, one of many "open" but "inactive" cases to be revived and pursued when time and staff and budget allowed.

Through it all, the police never lost faith they'd catch Alison's killer. They just needed one break. A clue. A tip. A confession. A miracle. Traditionally, and cops are steeped in tradition, they would need new evidence to crack this case.

What they got was new light on old evidence from a distant torch that had sparked an improbable revolution led by an unlikely revolutionary from out of the west.

That all lay years down the road, and stargazing is a luxury homicide cops can't afford, bogged down as they are in the carnage of the here and now. And so, in 1987, a year after Alison's murder, no closer to catching her killer, her avengers trooped east to put an end to a series of savage assaults on young women. A new horror. An escalating terror. Another nameless, faceless predator on the rampage. Shunning American hyperbole, Toronto headline writers dubbed this sexual sadist simply "The Scarborough Rapist." The banality belied the monstrous nightmare that was descending. Sadly, it had descended before. Tragically, with rare exceptions, we had learned nothing. And more innocents would die.

Among the few to learn from the past, from that distant nightmare we call Clifford Olson, was RCMP Inspector Ron MacKay, the Mountie from Moosomin, the Saskatchewan farm boy. When Alison was murdered and the Scarborough Rapist began prowling, there was no clue that MacKay would alter policing forever as Canada's first psychological profiler and driving force behind ViCLAS (Violent Crime Linkage Analysis System), the most sophisticated computerized database ever devised for linking serial crimes wherever and whenever they occur, superior to anything the FBI—once the acknowledged masters—had produced, and the envy of the world.

Back then, MacKay, widely respected as a hell of an investigator, was a cop on the lam with a price on his head.

I

FBI Road Show

FBI "road shows" always drew a good crowd—a healthy mix of converts, cynics, and the just plain curious to hear what the Feds had learned about what makes bad guys tick.

In the fall of 1979, Mounties Ron MacKay and Fred Maile trooped into the year-old Justice Institute of British Columbia—the "JI"—in Vancouver with about 100 other police investigators to hear Special Agent Rick Mather from the nearby Seattle office share FBI research into "stranger" homicides. Historically, victims were murdered by people they knew; killed by family members in the heat of passion or for money, by lovers in a jealous rage or friends or associates for some grievance, real or imagined. Motive was usually predictable and easily detected, and the killer often left a clear trail. The vast majority of homicides were solved, the guilty apprehended and punished quickly. Mather had come to town to warn that all that was changing, that a new breed of killer was murdering people they didn't know, may never have met, for the thrill or to gratify some deviant sexual fantasy. Traditional motives didn't apply and conventional investigative techniques rarely worked.

That same year, the American Psychiatric Association replaced the term "psychopath" with "sociopath" and "antisocial" to describe this emerging breed of killers and rapists. Mather had come to share the FBI theory on all these alarming changes. As these killers stalked America, the number of unsolved crimes escalated dramatically. Mather was in town to sell Canadian cops on the concept of stranger homicide and warn them that the rising plague in America wasn't likely to stop at the border. That what was happening in America could happen here—*would* happen here. He faced a tough crowd, none tougher than Ron MacKay, known widely as a realist whose mulish "show me" streak meant taking nothing at face value, nothing for granted.

As the sergeant in charge of the General Investigative Section (GIS) at the North Vancouver RCMP detachment, MacKay was a respected investigator who had solved scores of rapes, murders, and other violent crimes. An occasional lecturer at the J I, he faced audiences every bit as mulish as he, endearing himself to these tough crowds by speaking their language, being one of them who solved cases with cynicism as much as clues, demanding every assumption or alibi be supported or disproved by evidence. He was a proven player in the shadowy world of homicide and sex-crimes investigators. Maile was a corporal posted to the Serious Crime Section at RCMP "E" Division headquarters in downtown Vancouver. The two western farm boys, who had never dreamed of being Mounties, respected each other as investigators and had been close personal friends since an earlier posting together as constables.

Their camaraderie extended to an off-hours police hockey league that could be competitive enough to inflate the local body count. Maile, a five-foot-nine scrapper, was one of the smallest players on the ice. Punished along the boards, he always bounced back until an opponent, a foot taller and 100 pounds heavier, crushed him into the corner boards. This hurt Maile, but it pained MacKay even more and outraged his sense of fair play. Justice was swift. The opponent survived the first open-ice collision but was carried off the ice on a stretcher after the second. Clean hits. No foul. No penalty. And no contest, since MacKay wore football pads under his jersey, further evidence of his "pragmatic" nature. As the movies warned, don't bring a knife to a gunfight. Maile had never asked MacKay to fight his fights, and MacKay may not have meant to knock his opponent unconscious, but neither was really upset at how things played out that night.

Such were the characters Mather faced in a mixed crowd of hardcore—some would argue hardass—investigators, rookies, wannabe lawyers, and public servants who wouldn't know a crime scene if they tripped over the yellow warning tape. Even a civilian could spot the difference in body language, the eyes. Keen or cynical, proven or inept, all were polite, offering Mather a fair hearing. This was Canada, these were professionals, after all. But every teacher since Socrates has faced that "special child" sitting in the back row, arms folded across chest, legs splayed into the aisle, fixed smile and blazing eyes defying the orator to "show me."

MacKay and Maile were such "special children."

MacKay had joined the Royal Canadian Mounted Police in October 1961. It was not his first choice. Growing up on the farm and attending high school in Moosomin, Saskatchewan, his head was in the clouds, his boyhood dream being to become a jet fighter pilot, swooping and soaring with the grace and dignity of an eagle on those "laughter-silvered wings" of the popular school poem "High Flight." What better way to serve his country? What glory could compare? Accepted by Royal Roads Military College in Victoria, B.C., after graduating high school, he aced most of his subjects and physical requirements, but flamed out on the mysteries of calculus, chemistry, and the French language that would be required to graduate. He was ejected, but landed on his feet and considered his options.

The Mounties were a logical second choice, with their storied history dating to the early days of Confederation and the opening of the west; paramilitary roots and the same Queen's Commission as offered by the airforce; and postings across Canada and around the world. Hoping to return to his adopted province of British Columbia—known as E Division to national headquarters in Ottawa, "Lotus Land" to the rest of Canada—he could be happy anywhere. Anywhere, that is, but Ontario or Quebec, who had their own provincial police to investigate major crimes, relegating the Mounties to the sidelines while they pursued killers and rapists. The rest of the country contracted the RCMP for those duties and young MacKay pined for action, perhaps unaware you should be careful what you wish for.

MacKay's career had begun simply enough. In the fall of 1962, the newly minted constable was posted to E Division, joining the 12-man detachment at Fort St. John. Held back for three months as a troop leader, MacKay was unsure if the "honour" did more *to* than *for* him, as it delayed his progression through a series of postings across B.C. In 1964, he joined the two-man detachment at Hudson's Hope, then went on to the 30-man detachment in Prince George a year later. In 1967, he celebrated his own good fortune and Canada's Centennial, joining the plainclothes three-man GIS as a detective.

Two years later, he added his own chapter to RCMP history, riding in what may have been the final Mountie mounted manhunt.

In late 1969, MacKay joined a dragnet for two inmates who had escaped from the Prince George regional jail. The fugitives stole a guard's .38 special and his car and fled south. They abandoned the car near a ranch in the Cottonwood River valley near Quesnel. Staff Sergeant Gord Graham, who led the manhunt, talked a rancher out of two horses and ordered MacKay and Brian Bowen, his traffic-cop neighbour in Mountie quarters, to saddle up. In the finest Hollywood tradition, the duo trailed the men's tracks for miles through the snow. They never found them—another Mountie got their men, arresting the escapees after they were spotted crossing the river on a railway trestle—but they bagged the glory and bragging rights for the mounted pursuit some say marked the end of the era of Mounties riding into action on horseback.

In 1970, MacKay was transferred to North Vancouver GIS, a 20-man unit in a 120-man detachment. He was promoted to corporal two years later while working drugs, returned to GIS, joined the Vancouver Drug Squad, then returned to "North Van" GIS in 1973 and took charge of the 10-man Capilano Zone two years later. In 1976, MacKay oversaw training, auxiliary police, crime prevention, community relations, and, interestingly, the Emergency Response Team (ERT) as the Mounties called their SWAT unit. A year later, he was promoted to sergeant and put in charge of GIS operations and major crime investigations for North Van. Now married, with a young family, MacKay had put down roots in B.C. He had no desire to move or seek promotion to the commissioned officer ranks that would require a posting "elsewhere in Canada." Besides uprooting his family, it would mean leaving the action on the streets, a place he excelled. Nothing, he thought, could drive him from his Pacific paradise or shatter his plans for the future. Not even Mather's dire warning that, as the Bob Dylan rock anthem declared, the times they were a-changing.

Settling into their seats at the J I that fall day in 1979, MacKay and Maile had no axe to grind with Mather or the FBI. The agent, despite his expensive suit and shades, seemed like a nice guy. They just felt this gifted orator would be as comfortable talking to a pew of church elders as he was addressing an auditorium of grizzled homicide and rape investigators who had seen and heard it all, for whom life held few surprises.

Guided more by instinct than faith, governed by the rules of evidence, many cops steadfastly retain their belief that pure evil exists. Toiling in a dark underworld, bearing witness to the grief and suffering of society's most vulnerable—traditionally women and children—wherever and whenever they fell prey to monsters, they sustain their sanity with gallows humour unfit for polite society. But polite society never sees what they see, hears what they hear, smells what they smell. Polite society sleeps well at night, free from the nightmares that haunt those who protect them, from the duty to rap on a door in the dead of night to tell a stranger their loved one is dead, as are their dreams and hopes for the future. Nor do we have to sit at the table across from monsters who wreak havoc, destroy all in their path, look the cops in the eye, lie to their face, and walk out the door for lack of evidence.

No formal training academy or FBI road show could adequately prepare you for life on the street. The most enduring lessons were learned the hard way—by experience in the field. You learned quickly how best to save others, yourself, or your career, and that the only thing more threatening than a domestic dispute was an officer from headquarters on your step, announcing "I'm here to help."

Experience had also taught MacKay and Maile when to lower their expectations to avoid disappointment. How could FBI college boys help real cops? They didn't even have a mandate to investigate rapes and murders in their own country unless some fool abducted his victim across a state line. Why were *they* interviewing high-profile killers and assassins? With little expectation of being educated, MacKay and Maile hoped to at least be entertained. Mather didn't disappoint.

The FBI had always been conscious of its image under J. Edgar Hoover and little interest was shown in Special Agent Robert Ressler's novel ideas about behavioural research based on interviews with imprisoned killers and assassins. When J. Edgar died in 1972, Ressler sped into action almost before the eternal director's body was cold, first interviewing Sirhan Sirhan, who gunned down Bobby Kennedy during his 1968 presidential campaign, then others, seeking to learn what made them do what they did the way they did it. Unorthodox and unsanctioned, Ressler knew that it is better to beg forgiveness than seek approval in a bureaucratic quagmire like the FBI. When he showed what he'd learned, his bosses weren't happy with his go-it-alone strategy but couldn't dispute his tactics or results: his "profiles" shed new light on criminal behaviour.

Ressler never claimed, nor has anyone ever claimed, that profiling would solve a case. It is another investigative tool, like the crime lab matching a fingerprint or a Black Lab sniffing out a fugitive, to help cops catch bad guys. Profiling could help focus particularly complex or bizarre investigations and maybe shed new light and warm the trail of a cold case. With formal approval and funding, Ressler and other agents took his findings on the road to FBI bureaus and outside police agencies. Profiles weren't evidence, and so might not be admissible in court, but they had proven their worth. If nothing else, they stimulated discussion and could help break down the walls separating police jurisdictions and ease turf wars. Thus Mather came to Canada.

Everyone in the J I auditorium that day had read the headlines and seen the TV footage as a plague of violence engulfed America in the 1970s. Vicious new killers and heinous crimes were on the rise: Charles "Tower Sniper" Whitman; the Manson family; Son of Sam; the Atlanta Child Murders; John "Killer Clown" Gacy; the Hillside Strangler; Ted Bundy. The plague was concentrated in America, but not confined there. Britons were terrorized by the Yorkshire Ripper and appalled to find a woman accomplice in the bloody Moors Murders. But this was Canada. No tower snipers. No stalkers doing the bidding of their talking dog, no *femmes fatales* wielding the hammer. There was just no evidence that these psychopaths were a threat to Canadians.

Undeterred, Mather classified this new generation of killers and rapists into "organized" predators, who carefully planned their crimes and hid their tracks well, and the "disorganized," who exploded on the spur of the moment with no plan and little or no effort to hide their victim or their tracks.

The second type, striking from ambush in a frenzied blitz attack, often, as a final degradation, masturbated on their victims, living or dead. Mather called it "loping his mule," and a low appreciative chuckle rumbled through the J I auditorium. Realizing he'd hit a responsive chord, Mather invoked the phrase repeatedly during his presentation, unwittingly adding a lesson in "overkill" for his audience.

Even MacKay and Maile had to admit they'd learned something new. Nevertheless, retreating outside for a smoke at the break, the two Mounties were still unconvinced there was any way to apply profiling to policing in Canada. It sounded more like a parlour game, perhaps useful in the States but not here. Most Canadian murderers knew their victims. They weren't strangers, not monsters. They still killed for money, for gain, for love, not insatiable, deviant sexual fantasy. Everyone knew that. Butting their cigarettes, they went back inside to watch an FBI filmed interview with "Hillside Strangler" Kenneth Bianchi.

Over two years, between 1977 and 1979, Bianchi, a personable young man, and his older uncle, Angelo Buono, had kidnapped, tortured, and murdered five prostitutes in the Los Angeles area. During interrogation, Bianchi had confessed, ratted out his uncle, then convinced medical experts, and apparently some FBI agents, that he suffered from a "multi-personality disassociated reaction." His split personality, it was argued, made him unaccountable for his crimes. The film allegedly showed the young killer switching personalities under hypnosis.

MacKay and Maile had used hypnosis on witnesses, seen it work and not work. Watching Bianchi in the film, they were convinced he was faking his "condition." Right then, in their eyes, the road show went off the rails. FBI credibility sank and the notion of profiling tanked. Walking out of the J I, MacKay and Maile did not feel they were any better equipped to solve murders than they had been trooping in.

But if they saw no Canadian application, there were Canadian connections.

Bob Ressler was a rising star at the FBI for his early interviews with high-profile killers and assassins, but even he considered his friend Russell Vorpagel a true Bureau legend. Each had independently profiled the Sacramento "Vampire Killer" the previous January when police asked their help to find who was killing families in their homes and apparently drinking their blood. Their profiles were identical, almost word for word, in describing what "type" of person the police should look for:

> White male; aged 25–27 years; thin, undernourished appear-
> ance. Residence will be extremely slovenly and unkempt and
> evidence of the crime will be found at the residence. History of
> mental illness, and will have been involved in use of drugs. Will
> be a loner who does not associate with either males or females,
> and will probably spend a great deal of time in his own home,
> where he lives alone. Possibly receives some form of disability
> money. If residing with anyone, it would be with his parents;
> however, this is unlikely. No prior military record; high school
> or college dropout. Probably suffering from one or more forms
> of paranoid psychosis.

Vorpagel had specified the killer's age as 27 and suggested the police look for the killer close to his crime scenes: "Lives within a mile. Aware of houses in the area. Not too disabled to drive or use an automatic pistol. Weird looking. Disheveled."

Though unsure how the two FBI agents came to these conclusions, the police went looking and found, with the help of a tip, Richard Trenton Chase, who matched every major point in the profiles, right down to his age, 27, and was a classic "disorganized" offender. He was sentenced to death.

That case went a long way to legitimizing the burgeoning art of investigative behavioural analysis, popularized as profiling.

Chase died of an apparent drug overdose in prison, but not before Ressler had interviewed him. Chase, believing he had been injected with acid from a rabbit bite and that his blood was turning to sand, said he bled his victims and drank their blood to replace his own. When his "voices" told him to take a life, he'd walk down a street close to home, rattle doors until he found one open, enter, and kill everyone he encountered. Ressler asked why he didn't just kick in the first door if it was locked. "Oh," Chase replied matter-of-factly, "if the door is locked, that means you're not welcome."

Chilling. A basic childhood lesson had decided who lived or died in northern California in January 1978.

Few, if any, in the J I crowd listening to Mather a year later had heard of the Chase case. It's a safe bet none knew of its Canadian cousin: the case of the "Montreal Vampire" captured in Calgary, Alberta, in 1971. Wayne Clifford Boden had been seen driving with a Calgary woman the day she disappeared. Traced through his car registration and linked to the murder by a broken cufflink found under the woman's body, Boden was responsible for a series of killings dating to 1968—a full decade before Chase had begun killing. Each victim appeared to have been raped, strangled, and hideously chewed à la Hannibal Lecter, yet she had died with a "serene smile" on her face—except one who no longer had a face. Boden confessed to all the murders except hers. All, it seems, had died when his sadistic tendencies flared during consensual sado-masochistic sex; he was a true lust killer.

Russ Vorpagel, the FBI legend lionized by Ressler, provided a stronger, more visceral Canadian connection in the classes of cops and deputy sheriffs he taught up and down the California coast. As the FBI Behavioral Science Unit coordinator in Sacramento, he was well known and respected, and the first profiler called in on the Chase Vampire case. His one-week courses did not teach his students how to be profilers, but enough to know when to call a profiler for help. At six-foot-four and 260 pounds, his presence was as impressive as his accomplishments as an expert sex-crimes investigator and former Milwaukee homicide cop who clasped a law degree in one hand and dismantled bombs with the other.

For decades, working well into retirement and the new millennium, Vorpagel opened every class by reciting Canadian John McCrae's "In Flanders Fields" over slides of contrasting images— the serene majesty of Arlington National Cemetery intercut with graphic shots of mangled bodies and grim crime scenes. Eulogizing the Canadian hero and his epic 1915 tribute to the countless thousands slaughtered in the mud and blood of the Western Front during World War I, it's doubtful he would note that McCrae worked so close to the front lines that the wounded men literally dropped into his entrenched aid station or wryly observe that American troops who joined the conflict late were called doughboys because it took them three years to rise. But no historic omissions could alter his penchant for prophesy. As his students studied the images, he studied the students, watched them fidget and grow restless, and often unerringly predicted who would ask the question on all their minds: What did military history and a World War I poem have to do with homicide investigative technique?

On cue, Vorpagel would flash a vivid closeup onscreen of horrific abdominal wounds inflicted on a victim of the Manson family and recite some chilling stats: 25,000 Americans murdered every year, 2,000,000 since the end of World War I. Then he'd warn his students never to forget their "thin blue line" was battling a ruthless foe who took no prisoners, murderous predators who left only death and destruction, broken bodies, and shattered dreams in their wake. It was, he intoned, war. And a conflict they dare not lose.

• • •

The war came a year later to Vancouver.

MacKay survived unscathed but Maile became a target in the crosshairs.

Neither had ever heard of Clifford Olson.

2

Olson

Fred Maile, a farm boy raised near Beaverlodge, Alberta, which is about 300 miles northwest of Edmonton, grew up with no intention of being a Mountie. He was one of about 120 students at Beaverlodge High School. Like many teenagers, he hadn't given his future much thought until approached by his principal, Stewart Little, just prior to graduation. Was he, Little wondered, going to finish school, hang around, work the farm, marry the girl next door? Maile flashed that easy smile, part of the "Aw, shucks" rustic charm that endeared him to so many, and pointed out there was no girl on the next farm—which struck him suddenly as very sad. In truth, Maile *had* planned to stick around, work the family farm, and run it one day. He hadn't figured out the girl-next-door problem but felt that would sort itself out. Little persisted, urging his young charge to "Go. Leave this place. See the world. Make it a better place. Take your best shot. You can always come back and run the farm."

It got Maile thinking. Pondering his options, he recalled a recent job fair at the school and the interesting presentation by Mountie recruiter Mike Eastham. Why not? But enthusiasm was tempered by the Mounties' rejection of a bright, handsome, athletic schoolmate Maile considered a poster-boy candidate. What chance did he have if the Mounties shot down a prospect like that? Maile trailed the other guy in every category, not to mention missing a fingertip he'd lopped off while sawing wood on the farm. It seemed pointless.

Then again, he thought, God hates a coward. Maile applied. Against all odds, and his expectations, he was accepted and reported to Training Depot in Regina.

In the fall of 1979, at about the time Mather addressed the J I,

Maile was assigned to the prestigious Serious Crime Section at E Division headquarters in downtown Vancouver—known as "the Ivory Tower" to all police forces across the lower B.C. mainland.

The Serious Crime Section was created in 1975 as part of a larger RCMP reorganization. The investigators were considered support staff by detachment detectives and got involved only when asked. Maile and the others were dedicated investigators, but pretty green; a fast pace and constant movement meant they often learned as they went. Such challenging on-the-job training provided more gore than glory as Maile and others stood over yet another mangled body and tried to fathom what kind of person could inflict such carnage on another.

Then along came Robert Clifford Olson.

Maile first heard of Olson in early January 1981 from Jim Hunter, an old troop mate and good friend from their days at Squamish detachment, who called to wish him a Happy New Year and tell him he'd just arrested Olson, a local rounder and career petty criminal, and charged him with possession of a firearm after taking potshots at some local teens. Hunter had also charged Olson with raping, sodomizing, and committing gross indecency on a 16-year-old girl he'd lured into his car with a job offer to shampoo carpets for ten bucks an hour at the popular Whistler ski resort. New Westminster city police had also charged Olson for possessing a gun after he'd shot at teens there and Richmond RCMP had charged him for sodomizing a teenage boy he'd met on the ferry. Olson was looking at some long prison time. *If* he was convicted.

Maile was happy for his old friend, but didn't see how any of this related to him until Hunter described Olson's car: a green Grenada with a small rear opera window. The description matched the car Maile was seeking in connection with the baffling murder of 17-year-old Mary Ellen Jamieson. The popular star volleyball player, known as Marnie around Sechelt, had been found strangled with a belt the previous August. A swatch of green paint found on a nearby rock suggested to Maile that her killer had hit it with his car. If he could connect a car to the rock through the paint, he'd have a good lead on a prime suspect and a chance at placing him at the scene. It was all circumstantial, but it was evidence. If Hunter could find the car, it would be a "Happy New Year" Maile would always remember, on the tail of a Christmas he'd never forget.

Richmond detectives had called Maile at home late Christmas Day to sweep a crime scene with his metal detector. A man walking his dog had discovered the decomposing body of a young girl partially buried in a shallow grave. No one had a clue who she was, or how or when she got there. They hoped Maile could unearth something, anything, to help identify the victim, and ideally link her to her killer. The "stranger" murders Mather had warned were coming had arrived.

Maile found nothing but rusted bedsprings. The girl was eventually identified as Christine Weller, a 12-year-old tomboy last seen riding off on a borrowed bike in Surrey on November 19, 1980.

The identification was the only break in a case fraught with complications. First, the girl hadn't been reported missing until six days later. Then, when police asked the owner what day he'd lent the girl his bike, he gave the wrong date, off by two days. Although Olson was among the known local criminals who were interviewed, he had a legitimate, verifiable alibi for that day—the *wrong* day! It was just another learning experience, another complication in a case about to explode on Maile and investigators across the lower mainland. There was no shortage of suspects; in fact, there were dozens of people to question and watch, but there was also no evidence to link anyone to this killing or Jamieson's. It was like chasing a ghost, a Houdini. It didn't help that what few clues they found were misleading.

Olson was just one among many early suspects. Even those convinced he was involved in at least some of the disappearances and murders had no evidence linking him to them. Without evidence, Maile couldn't afford to exclude anyone on their list of known career criminals, sex offenders and pedophiles. Olson stayed on the list, but the criminal histories of others made them stronger suspects.

Robert Clifford Olson was a habitual criminal and major pain in the ass to the police. At least six times, and possibly as many as thirteen, he had been arrested or imprisoned only to escape under the noses of the cops and guards in B.C., Saskatchewan, and distant Nova Scotia. A glib, fast-talking "rounder," he evolved from a youthful hustler terrorizing his neighbourhood to a prison informant—he was stabbed seven times in prison for ratting out drug traffickers operating within the walls—to a "skinner" who raped young cons half his age. Olson was the con who could con a con. For example, he convinced child-killer Gary Marcoux, while the two served time in nearby cells in protective custody, to write down how he had tortured and murdered a young girl, then passed the notes and a map to the Mounties, "voluntarily" testifying against the killer in court, "no strings attached."

Olson was brazen beyond foolhardy. Touring the B.C. Pen after it was mothballed as a museum, and pointing out his old cell to a friend, he was recognized by a guard who called the cops who arrested him on the spot on an outstanding Canada-wide warrant. Only Clifford, the story went, could get busted inside a defunct penitentiary.

Prison was nothing new to Olson. He had spent his adult life confronting, and often embarrassing, the justice system. Since his first nine-month sentence for break-and-enter in July 1957, his criminal record had been a litany of petty crime escalating to violence. In January 1981, when Maile first heard of him, Olson had 83 convictions and varied sentences for break-and-enter, theft, break-enter-theft, possession of stolen property, forgery, fraud, false pretenses, obstructing justice, parole violation, escape from lawful custody, impaired driving, possession of a firearm, and armed robbery.

Olson was released from prison under mandatory supervision for the last time on June 7, 1980. Exactly two months later, Marnie Jamieson was murdered near Sechelt. Maile was called in when her body was found nine days later.

Only after Hunter laid the first sex-crimes charges against Olson were previous incidents uncovered: allegedly fondling little girls in B.C. and Nova Scotia and sodomizing male teens in Alberta and nearby Richmond. But Olson led a charmed life. The most serious charges weren't pursued or were stayed. Sydney police had arrested

Olson in Nova Scotia but he had escaped and was never brought back, presumably because he was serving time in prison elsewhere for another offence and no one considered him worth the price of a plane ticket or the court's time.

Whatever the reason, Olson's escalating violence was a matter of public record after Hunter laid his charges. Back in custody, he posed no threat to anyone. Having "surreptitiously borrowed" his green car—not Olson's as it turned out—Maile awaited the forensic results to see if it could be tied to the Jamieson murder.

There were lots of bad guys on the loose who required more immediate attention, but Maile never lost sight of the Jamieson case. When the forensic results came back negative, Maile decided to "profile" Olson, which, back then, meant checking his criminal record, finances, and credit card records.

On February 18, 1981, Maile sent out a Canadian Police Information Centre (CPIC) bulletin asking all RCMP detachments and local city forces to forward any information they had on Olson. The three replies he got weren't much help. Then, with Olson still incarcerated at Oakalla Prison Farm, Don Celle, District Crown Counsel for the jurisdictions of Squamish, North and West Vancouver, instructed the Squamish prosecutor to stay the sex charges against Olson. Hunter got the news on April Fool's Day. He and his boss, Staff-Sergeant Fred Zaharia, immediately requested and were granted a meeting with Celle at his office in North Van, temporarily housed in a trailer during court-house construction.

Celle, who had prosecuted his first case in North Vancouver in 1974, agreed to proceed with the weapons charges but saw little hope for convicting Olson on the testimony of his alleged victim.

He had reviewed the victim's statement and found several inconsistencies that he felt would not withstand a determined cross-examination by Olson's lawyer, Bob Shantz. In his view, he simply didn't have a believable witness and, following established Crown policy, then and now, refused to prosecute a case without "substantial likelihood of a conviction." His opening exchange with Hunter initiated an emotional confrontation that quickly disintegrated into a heated shouting match between the lawyer and the cops.

"The problem we've got here is a lying bitch," Celle recalled his "throwaway opening line" 20 years later, insisting that all he meant was that he felt the girl was headstrong, wouldn't cooperate, and wouldn't be around to testify. Zaharia and Hunter, interviewed separately, both vividly recalled that Celle said, "She's a liar and a tramp."

Quite simply, the cops believed their witness; Celle did not. Whereas both Mounties saw a credible witness who would be believed by a judge or jury, Celle saw no reasonable prospect of a conviction, his basis, he claimed, for ordering the sex charges stayed. Twenty years later, Hunter continued to view Celle's refusal to meet their witness as "arrogance." Both Mounties believed that Celle stayed the charges because of the girl's history; a teen runaway who had lived on the streets. She had recanted or amended certain details in her initial statements to the police in a second interview with Hunter, but the Mounties distinguished between "lying" and an embarrassed teenager "withholding evidence."

Initially, the girl claimed that Olson had raped her in the car on the way from the Vancouver area to Squamish, and again on the way back. After Olson admitted having consensual sex with her in a hotel room, the girl confirmed that location, but denied strongly that the sex had been consensual. Considering her age, Hunter saw the sole issue to be "consent" and felt strongly that it should have been an issue to be decided by a judge, not a Crown Attorney.

In her second statement to Hunter, the girl admitted withholding the fact of the hotel sex, claiming she had feared the police would not have believed her claim that she had been raped if she said she had taken a hotel room with him. She told Hunter that Olson had originally told her they were going to the cleaning job he had promised her at a Whistler resort. When driving became hazardous due to fog, Olson suggested they stop at a hotel. She said she had agreed to this because he had promised to get them separate rooms and, at least in part, because she was afraid of him after watching him shoot at another driver he felt had cut him off in New Westminster. Any hope of flight disappeared when he booked them into the same room. After he had assaulted her in the room, she pleaded with him to take her home. They left the hotel in the middle of the night.

On the ride home, Olson again drew his gun, threatening several Squamish teens after a confrontation in a restaurant. The teens chased Olson when he left with the girl, breaking off their pursuit only when he aimed his gun at them out his car window. A short time later, between Squamish and Delta, the girl said Olson pulled off onto the side of the road and assaulted her again. Terrified that he still had the gun she had seen him use three times that night to threaten or shoot at others, her only thought was how to escape. She didn't want sex; she wanted to live and get away as soon as possible. Her opportunity came soon after the last assault, when she had convinced Olson to stop at a garage a short way down the road. She went into the bathroom, snuck out when Olson wasn't looking, and waited for him to drive off. Incredibly, she then hitched a ride home with another stranger. He was never located by the Mounties, nor was the garage when Hunter later drove her back through the area, as she couldn't remember exactly where Olson had stopped that night.

Now, meeting with Celle, Hunter was convinced the girl had been scared by Olson's gun and that they'd stopped at the hotel that night because of the bad weather. Months later, after Olson was arrested for the series of teen and child murders, her story was corroborated by others who came forward to relate identical experiences; that Olson had lured them with talk of high-paying cleaning jobs. But on the day Hunter and Zaharia and Celle met for the first time—the District Crown was based in North Vancouver, and the trio had never met prior to their first heated meeting—the issue, according to Celle, was the victim's credibility and availability. Hunter and Zaharia insist it was also about her character.

The Criminal Code of Canada, one of the oldest and arguably among the worst-written legal documents in the world for lack of clarity, allowed for Olson to be charged with "sexual intercourse with a female between the ages of 14 and 16, who is of previously chaste character." Celle recalls that charge had been sworn by Hunter on the same information disputed that day. While all agree that the girl's alleged past—Hunter argues that "living on the streets" somehow became an allegation that she had been a "child prostitute"—was debated, they remain poles apart in what impact it had on the ensuing events and decisions.

Hunter, having quickly recognized Olson as an accomplished liar, was convinced a teenager would never have a chance to escape his lies or his clutches and remained convinced she'd be a good witness. His investigation had determined that the girl had moved home, was living happily with her mother and had cleaned up her act. Refusing to simply roll over, he asked Celle to interview her before staying the sex charges. He was convinced Olson was a violent dangerous threat and could not imagine just turning him loose without at least trying to put him away. Celle, unconvinced they could even find the girl, refused.

Celle maintains his belief that the Mounties could not produce the girl, based on information he says he received with her file from the Squamish Crown Attorney expressing concern that she could not be located and was unlikely to appear in court to testify and requesting his opinion on how best to proceed with the case. Both Hunter and Zaharia deny vehemently that any concern about finding her was ever mentioned, or that it was even an issue, in the meeting that day. Both insist they could have produced her if Celle had agreed to interview her. Why else, they ask, would they argue with Celle, virtually beg him to meet with her, if they could not then produce her?

As a bad meeting grew worse, voices rose, tempers flared. Zaharia, by now clearly the "good cop" in an escalating confrontation of wills, diplomatically supported Hunter, suggested to Celle that it might be a good idea to hear all the facts from the girl herself rather than judging what kind of witness Olson's surviving victim— the last to escape him—would make. Celle refused. By now, both cops suspected that his reluctance to prosecute Olson for the sex charges stemmed from what seemed to Hunter to be his perception of her sexual past; a variation on the old theme that prostitutes can't be raped. Celle denies that was ever a factor, commenting publicly for the first time for this book: "I had no thought whatsoever that she was a hooker or a whore or a tramp or whatever has been said that I said."

The meeting grew more heated. Furious to the point of "losing it," admitting he was ready to throw a punch at Celle, Hunter stood up and moved toward the District Crown Counsel. Zaharia rose immediately in his path and ushered him outside. Alone with Celle, the staff sergeant then urged him to reconsider, imploring him to at least talk to the girl. Celle was inflexible.

Lost in the heated debate was Hunter's emerging suspicion that Olson might be tied to the Christine Weller murder. Having confirmed the outstanding arrest warrant on CPIC for sex charges against Olson issued in Nova Scotia, he was intrigued to hear Richmond investigator Bill McBratney's suspicion that Olson may have murdered Christine Weller. Like a few others who considered Olson a good, even a prime, suspect, McBratney had no evidence to support his suspicions or disprove Olson's seeming rock-solid alibi for the date of Weller's murder. Only later would the police realize they had pegged her murder to the wrong date, for which Olson did have an alibi, but that night the two Mounties interviewed Olson— Hunter for sex and weapons charges; McBratney, still accumulating evidence to lay the buggery charge in Richmond. The latter's suspicions were enough to prompt Hunter, when he forwarded clothing and other exhibits from his case to the RCMP crime lab, to ask them to also check them against any evidence on the Weller murder.

None of that was a factor that day in Celle's trailer. He had made his decision, leaving the cops free to ask E Division headquarters to go over his head and appeal his ruling to the Regional Crown Attorney. If, in hindsight, it was Olson's lucky day, it was not his last.

Both Mounties knew they were bucking the odds, that there was little hope for almost any Crown to reverse himself once he had decided on a course of action. They asked Division to go over Celle's head or give them permission to do it. Zaharia submitted a formal report, detailing their reasons for seeking to overturn Celle's decision, asked them to bring their "full powers" to appeal his decision, then phoned the head of the Criminal Investigation Branch to outline his concerns. In the end, while both may have questioned how aggressively their concerns were pursued, both agreed that Division must have at least made an effort, citing the ensuing formal letter of complaint from Vancouver Regional Crown Counsel Alan

Filmer, protesting their actions and treatment of Celle. The letter was "filed"—Hunter says he never knew it had been written until 20 years later—but the die was cast. On April 8, 1981, Squamish Crown Attorney Bruce McNair stayed the sex charges against Olson as instructed by Celle.

No one could have foreseen the consequences.

The sex charges that Celle had ordered stayed were one of four individual or sets of charges in three jurisdictions that Olson faced— sodomy of a young male laid by Richmond, and weapons charges in Squamish and New Westminster, all laid by Squamish detachment. On April 2, 1981, the day after Celle had met with Zaharia and Hunter, Olson's incredible luck held as the Richmond buggery and indecent assault charges were stayed, reportedly on instructions from South Fraser Regional Crown Counsel Al Hoem, whether, as some say, at the request of the victim or his parents, or, according to others, due to a procedural problem with the photo lineup used to identify Olson.

The Squamish weapons charges proceeded as scheduled on April 8. The alleged victim of the stayed sex charges showed up to testify against Olson—the sole witness who could identify him as the shooter, not just testify to events. If Celle had been wrong to believe she would not show up to testify, his fear that she could not withstand Bob Shantz's withering cross-examination proved accurate. She vanished after the first day. When she did not return as the trial resumed on May 22, a bench warrant was issued for her arrest, but the damage had been done.

Despite the other weapons charges, apparent escalating violence and long criminal record, Olson was released on bail at the hearing on April 8. Hunter, for one, wasn't surprised, aware that judges often granted bail when the most serious of a series of charges was stayed by the Crown. Sadly, the stay and Olson's ensuing release effectively escalated what had been a personal and professional disagreement between the cops and the Crown, one of many such debates across Canada in any given year, into a lethal systemic failure. The suspected rapist and killer walked free, just in time to celebrate the birth of his illegitimate son.

Exactly one week later, he killed his second victim.

While it is speculation to wonder what might have changed had Celle taken the time to interview Hunter's witness, had the girl told the truth the first time or had E Division brass appealed more aggressively to overturn the District Crown's decision—a decision supported then and again in a 1994 review based on Crown and police files—the facts are indisputable:

> FACT: On the dates Olson was charged and released, Christine Weller was his only victim in the Lower Mainland.
>
> FACT: Hunter did his job; he took Olson off the street and alerted Maile and others he thought might have an interest in him.
>
> FACT: The District Crown Counsel exercised his lawful authority to stay the sex charges against Olson.
>
> FACT: The Regional Crown Counsel supported his decision then and again in 1994.
>
> FACT: A rapist and killer walked free.
>
> FACT: One week later, Olson killed the first of his next 10 young victims:

Name	Age	Deceased	Location
1) Colleen Daignault	13	April 15	Surrey
2) Daryn Johnsrude	16	April 21	Coquitlam
3) Ada Court	13	June 21	Coquitlam
4) Simon Partington	9	July 2	Surrey
5) Judy Kozma	14	July 9	New Westminster
6) Raymond King	15	July 23	New Westminster
7) Sigrun Arnd	18	July 24	Coquitlam
8) Terri Lynn Carson	15	July 27	Surrey
9) Louise Chartrand	17	July 30	Maple Ridge
10) Sandra Wolfsteiner	16	May 19	Langley

Although Wolfsteiner was an early victim, killed four days after Olson married Joan Berryman, the mother of his month-old son, on May 15, 1981, the Olson investigators never knew she was missing until Olson volunteered her name months later. But in the spring and early summer of 1981, they had nothing to connect Olson to any missing or murdered teen. Several suspected him but no one could prove anything. To charge him and lose, assuming the Crown would prosecute, meant double jeopardy—no second chance to prosecute him if he was acquitted.

No one had ever dealt with a killer who crossed gender lines, an indiscriminate predator who murdered boys and girls with equal abandon. Logic, and experience, suggested more than one killer. To link these murders meant finding a type of killer most cops didn't believe existed. It just seemed too gigantic a leap, until Hunter had found James Gordon Henry, a transient killer with a serious record for violence, on trial for his life in the 1960s, living and working under the name Brown.

Hunter had taped the deathbed statement of a young, mentally challenged girl who had been lured, raped, stabbed eight times in the heart, seven in the throat, and left for dead. She had crawled through the bush, across a highway and lived long enough after being found to describe her killer. A tip from a Vancouver City street cop who heard about the girl led Hunter to Henry, whose past offences included picking up a man in a gay bar in Ontario, sodomizing him, slashing his throat and leaving him for dead. But the man had refused to die; his testimony had put Henry in jail for attempted murder. The earlier capital murder charge, which back then carried a death sentence, also involved a male victim. That charge was reduced to manslaughter. When he was released, Henry had headed west, raping a male teen in Winnipeg before reaching British Columbia where he viciously stabbed the young girl.

Realizing just how difficult their case would be to prosecute, Hunter and Zaharia went directly to the Regional Crown office, where they found a champion in prosecutor Jim Jardine, of the new Career Criminal Prosecution unit. Jardine predicted they would get a conviction and was as good as his word, successfully arguing the admissibility of the similar-fact evidence that became the legal standard across Canada. The transient killer was sentenced to 25 years. His ensuing appeal to the Supreme Court of Canada, arguing several issues including the inadmissibility of similar-fact evidence, was rejected by a unanimous 9–0 ruling, very rare solidarity in a murder appeal.

When Hunter arrested Henry, assisted by, among others, his old partner and good friend Fred Maile, from the Divisional Serious Crime Section, the teen abductions stopped for a month, leading to cautious optimism for some that the horror in the Lower Mainland was over. Then, unknown to the cops at the time, Olson came home from an extended trip and more teens began disappearing faster than ever. With Henry in custody, it couldn't be him, not that he was ever a prime suspect as Olson was becoming to some investigators. He was named on several lists, but no one had any evidence to link him to any of the crimes. Each detachment was investigating their own missing or murdered teen and had their own prime suspect. Richmond was convinced they had Weller's killer in custody and were ready to subject him to a polygraph test. They had little interest in Olson. Although Maile couldn't tie him to Marnie Jamieson, he couldn't shake off the sex-crime allegations and charges laid against him by Hunter and others. True, the decision to stay those charges had been supported right up the line to the Regional Crown, but what if they were wrong? If Olson was a sex offender or pedophile, would he escalate to murder? No one made such connections back in the early 1980s. Now married, a doting father to his new son, was Olson a monster who could kiss his child, then walk out the door and murder other children? If so, they had to stop him. Quickly. But how? They needed evidence. Tragically, that meant another disappearance, another young victim. No one wanted that but no one was sure how to prevent it. The odds were grim. The stakes were rising. The pressure, and the number of missing kids, was overwhelming.

Teens across Canada vanished by the tens of thousands every year. Most had merely left home, ending up on the streets of Vancouver and the Lower Mainland where the year-round climate was more conducive to living on the streets than in Canada's colder provinces. But this made them vulnerable to predators. As the police became more convinced they were facing a serious problem, one never encountered before in Canada, the pressure mounted from parents, the press, police brass, and politicians. Everyone knew a bold step was required to prevent pressure from turning to panic. The police had to be seen to be taking charge.

Inspector Larry Proke, of Serious Crimes, named Maile lead investigator. It was an honour Maile wasn't sure he wanted. As the corporal in charge, he now had responsibility but no authority, making him a visible target if things went from bad to worse. He had limited options: stand still under the sewage discharge pipe this case had become, prepare for the crap to start flowing downhill, or lead on, pray he was on the right path, and hope others would follow. He pushed ahead—at least a moving target was harder to hit.

Putting Maile in charge gave the investigation focus, but there was still no evidence. The real break came when a meeting of investigators from all jurisdictions with missing or murdered teens was scheduled for July 13, then changed to July 15 to allow Maile to attend. Everything changed after that.

The July 15 meeting was the first public indication that the police were more concerned than usual about the missing and murdered teens. Media attention was relentless thereafter, and parents of some of the victims, discouraged by what they viewed as plodding efforts to find the killer, began taking matters into their own hands and going public with their concerns that the police weren't doing enough. At the same time, the routinely scheduled major transfer of senior officers threatened to derail the investigation further until new arrivals were briefed and brought up to speed. Maile, as lead investigator, had high hopes that surveillance might provide the missing links, but it wasn't shaping up well.

After the meeting, Burnaby had approached the Special O unit to request surveillance assistance on Olson. It was their specialty, but for whatever reason—some hinted at too much paperwork—they resorted to "spook" cars from the Coordinated Law Enforcement Unit (CLEU), a pioneering multiforce concept blending operations with intelligence under one roof to target drug traffickers, money launderers, and organized crime. The CLEU cars following Olson kept losing him. Special O was approached again, and surveillance resumed only after several attempts at getting the wording of the guidelines "just right." Olson had remained active in the interim.

The problem confronting Maile was how best to balance his need for evidence against Olson and the urgency of protecting potential victims. No one was going to sit back and watch Olson kill a child, and that raised the real risk that the police would have to move in before they had the evidence they needed. It became a deadly game of chicken-and-egg. When Olson picked up two female hitchhikers on August 12 and took them drinking at a remote beach, the cops riding with the surveillance team crept in close to hear the conversation. Then, convinced the girls were in peril, the order was given to move in. Olson bolted but was stopped and arrested at gunpoint. The charge? Impaired driving.

The only evidence found was a name in his notebook—Kozma. Olson dismissed the name as that of some kid who'd asked him for a job. Forced by circumstances to tip their hand, which Olson knew was empty, they had their man but no evidence to keep him. Their only satisfaction that night was in saving two young girls from joining his list of victims. The girls didn't see it that way. They were pissed at the cops for ruining their party. Olson had seemed like a nice guy to them.

Sitting across the table from Olson in the interrogation room, Maile listened, at first patiently, then with increasing frustration, as Olson talked in circles, often prefacing his remarks with "What if." Their conversation was relayed by a hidden microphone to at least two detectives who monitored the interrogation. The strategy was to keep Olson talking. Experience showed that if given free rein, suspects could hang themselves; they might abruptly clam up, but too late. On those rare occasions when Olson said or even hinted at something concrete, the unseen detectives promptly dispatched investigators to confirm or refute what he had said.

The real break came when Olson denied ever having met Kozma, whose name police had found in his address book. Maile, wearied of being loped by the liar across the table, produced a statement they had taken from an associate of Olson's who was there when he picked up the girl. Maile then proceeded to shred Olson's fabrications lie by lie. Olson, visibly upset, demanded he be brought a poster of missing children he'd passed downstairs. When it was set on the table in front of him, he began violently jabbing the young faces: "That one! That one! That one! . . ." He didn't stop until he had pointed out eight faces. Maile pointed to another face, a child missing from Hope. "No." He asked about Marnie Jamieson, the popular young volleyball star in Sechelt he'd tried to link to Olson after Hunter's phone call in early January. "No. They were all local."

The case had finally been cracked. In one breath, Olson had indicated he'd killed at least eight missing children. Like Chase, the Vampire Killer, he'd struck close to home, but was much more organized in selecting his victims of opportunity.

At best, Maile still only had a weak case for a single murder charge. He still needed a confession to link the cases to each other and then to Olson, who could presumably recant his outburst to Maile at trial. Olson wanted a deal. Reverting to the third person, he wondered if there was a reward for anyone who could produce the bodies of the missing teens. Maile said he'd have to ask. No matter how much the prospect revolted him, he knew it might be the only way to get Olson to confess and put off the streets indefinitely as a Dangerous Sexual Offender.

Maile relayed the proposal to his superiors, and it filtered up to the commissioner's office at national headquarters where it was promptly rejected. That was expected, but Maile still felt as if a rug had been pulled out from under him. With nothing to offer Olson, he had no bargaining power, no hope of getting a confession, little hope of convicting him for the one murder charge they planned to lay.

In a chance encounter with a senior Crown Attorney, Maile outlined his predicament. The lawyer told him to wait, and went to his boss' office. The idea went on up the chain until it landed on Attorney General Alan Williams' desk. He promptly approved a deal to pay $10,000 to Olson's wife in trust for each body he produced. Olson would be paid nothing.

Maile learned of the approval "out of the blue" while driving with fellow Serious Crimes detectives Ed Drozda and Rick Rautio to Colony Farm to interrogate Olson. They were instructed to take him to the Sun Building in downtown Vancouver to sign the agreement. It was airtight, leaving the Crown no chance to grab back the money after the bodies were recovered.

Showman to the end, evidently having a good time, smoking cigars and smiling, Olson led the cops, gagging on his smoke, biting back their bile at their grim task, across his killing grounds, strutting brazenly from grave to grave across the Lower Mainland. By the end of his murderous spree, Olson had become insatiable, his attacks occurring only days apart. The police recovered the remains of 10 young victims.

There was no celebration, no elation among the investigators who had finally closed the most horrific killing spree in Canadian history. For Maile, who had played such a vital role in ending the terror, more heartache lay ahead. This man who did so much to end the horror was about to become the most maligned Mountie in the storied history of the Force.

It is not unusual for a criminal to seem to "bond" with a cop who has captured him. Moreover, Maile was forced to spend hours one on one with his prisoner. Olson was a glib talker but suffered from poor writing skills and a questionable vocabulary, so it was more efficient for Maile to write down what Olson dictated. (It was the only time the killer seemed embarrassed about anything.)

But you cannot rub shoulders with monsters without having demons rub off. The hatred and abuse heaped on Olson as he strutted brazenly from grave to grave was deflected onto Maile, who walked every step at the predator's side. Sadly, the Mountie who got Olson to confess despite the almost total absence of evidence was reviled and despised by other cops who accused him of being "too cosy" with the killer. Several phoned him at home late at night uttering anonymous threats and obscenities; others scrawled their invective in notes and letters. Maile's only reward, apart from a sense of satisfaction at stopping a murderous predator, was to be taken out to supper with other investigators by the Crown counsel who oversaw Olson's guilty plea.

Maile may have been Olson's final victim, but they grow 'em tough and resilient in Beaverlodge, Alberta. Maile did what had to be done to get a monster off the streets—no more, no less. It was the best anyone could have done under the circumstances, and better than most could have done. If appearing "cosy" with a monster was the only way to put him away and return nearly a dozen missing children to their grief-stricken families, he'd do it. The cowardly late-night callers had done nothing to help solve the case, provided no evidence that could have spared Maile the charade. Hunter credits Maile with being the driving force behind the investigation and laments the fact that he was never properly recognized. High praise from a man who also had taken Olson in, was maligned by the lawyers who freed the killer, then had watched the Attorney General's office, which governs the Crown Attorneys, pay $100,000 to put the same killer back behind bars. That wasn't Hunter's fault and certainly not Maile's. The only formal review of the case confirmed that.

Rebuffing demands for a public inquiry into the Olson investigation and the wildly unpopular deal, Attorney General Williams requested an internal case review—Serious Crimes routinely "autopsied" its cases to learn what they had done right and what wrong and to correct any mistakes or oversights. This report would be written by Mounties outside the Olson investigation. Intelligence Staff Sergeant Mert Mohr, a 27-year veteran who had spent half his career in coveted postings to the high Arctic, was one of the five Mounties assigned to the task. They had no mandate to find fault or point fingers, just to recount what had happened.

Their chronological report, submitted about a month later, was promptly rejected. Not what the minister wanted. Make it read more like a "pocketbook." Mohr was approached and agreed to rewrite the report on the sole condition he could do it alone. No one had a problem with that. He was handed the original report on a Thursday afternoon and given a month to rewrite it.

He submitted his "pocketbook" the following Tuesday morning. Five numbered copies were made; none were ever made public. Days later, Mohr retired. He wishes now he'd kept a copy of what some consider to be the first Olson book.

The 128-page report laid no blame and pointed no fingers, concluding that, in the absence of evidence at the time of Olson's arrest, there had been no choice but to make the deal: it was a textbook example of "reasonable men making reasonable decisions with the information they had available." It seemed complete vindication for Maile for setting up the only deal Olson would accept, the only deal that would close the case and jail the killer indefinitely. The huge backlash from the press and public for paying "blood money" was countered quietly by others who considered the money well spent; the investigation had consumed millions of dollars, whereas this final drop in the bucket took the killer off the streets, likely forever, and returned the remains of the missing children to their grieving families.

It was the larger irony that troubled some: that the lawyers and bureaucrats who had freed Olson after the police arrested him back in January—when there was one victim—had willingly paid handsomely to put him back behind bars, this time with less evidence, no witness, and after 11 victims.

Before retiring, Mohr had checked CPIC for the total number of missing kids in Canada that year. There were over 1000 just in British Columbia, and tens of thousands more across the country. Even if you factored those who had likely returned home and whose parents had simply never thought to inform police—whether dozens or hundreds, no one could say—it was still an alarming number of missing, abducted, and runaway children and teens.

Next, Mohr queried all correctional institutes across the province for names of known dangerous sexual offenders and pedophiles released in the two-month period Olson roamed free. *One hundred and eighty!* And that was just in British Columbia. How many more were released across the country, or came west for sunny skies, warm weather, young victims?

On January 11, 1982, Olson pleaded guilty to 11 murders, adding Sandra Wolfsteiner, 16, who had not been reported missing to police during the investigation.

• • •

Olson had shattered our complacency, put a face on the monster. That same year, Bob Ressler, the FBI pioneering profiler, coined its name: serial killer. Olson was Canada's first; he would not be the last.

Once again, the Mounties had gotten their man. But at what cost?

Olson's rampage devoured staff, budgets, and careers, generated mountains of paperwork, and collapsed in a public relations fiasco. Everyone from constable to commissioner knew there had to be a better way. When the Attorney General announced after Olson's trial that this horror would never again happen in British Columbia, the police weren't sure what he based that on. They were a little wiser and no less dedicated, but the nagging doubt wouldn't go away that if it started all over the next day, next week, or next year, were they any better equipped? If they were ever to beat someone like Olson at his own game—a deadly game of cat-and-mouse in which the bad guy set the agenda and all the rules, rewriting them at his whim—there had to be a better system of gathering and sharing intelligence, linking crimes on computer databases, and simply talking to each other like they finally did on July 15, 1981. This wasn't Hollywood. Victory was never assured; some days it was not even imagined.

The Mounties, and hopefully the whole country, would learn from Olson's terror. Mather was right; it had happened here. And if it happened in British Columbia, it was sure to happen elsewhere. Perhaps it was already happening. What if Olson was just the tip of the iceberg, not an isolated horror but a sign of things to come? A sign of the times?

In 1982, months after Olson pleaded guilty and went back to prison for life, Sergeant Mike Eastham, the colourful recruiter who first got Maile thinking about joining the Mounties, called a meeting in Kamloops in the southern B.C. interior, a historic railroad hub located at the junction of two large rivers. The three major highways that intersect there had been strewn for nearly a decade with the bodies of young women, many of them hitchhikers, who had been abducted, raped, and murdered. Fed up with the carnage, Eastham hosted a Highway Murders Summit for investigators from British Columbia and Alberta to exchange information on their rape and murder victims who bore marks of vicious assault or mutilation. He expected 10, maybe 15 cases. He got 40! Teens, young women, transvestites mangled, chewed, their nipples excised, twigs and sticks and other indescribable foreign objects protruding from their vagina or anus. *Forty!* No one was too sure what it meant or what to do about such carnage. But one thing was certain: Olson hadn't killed them all.

The evidence was chillingly clear: more than one monster had been stalking British Columbia at the same time as Olson. If any one of them was ever caught, it was for something else. No one was ever charged with the Highway Murders. Nor was anyone charged with killing Marnie Jamieson in Sechelt; Maile never forgot her.

At the low point of those dark days, when it was impossible to prove Olson was the killer or exclude anyone else, Maile, besieged on all sides, feeling despair deepen as pressure mounted with each missing and murdered child on a growing list, sought out MacKay, a friend he trusted, an investigator he respected. He was afraid he was losing perspective, worried he might drag the investigation down the wrong path, doubting his instincts, unsure where else to turn. North Vancouver had escaped the terror; MacKay had no stake in the case, had nothing to lose by telling the truth, and was enough of a friend to tell Maile if he was wrong. Scanning the list of suspects and their criminal records, MacKay tapped a name. "Him. Never heard of him but I'd take a real close look at this guy."

Maile looked past MacKay's pointing finger at the name: Clifford Olson.

Maile grinned, relieved: "We are."

That was MacKay's sole involvement in the Olson investigation. His destiny lay with a low-level con named Spankie and his gang, a chance encounter that would change his life and revolutionize policing across Canada and around the world.

3

Spankie and the Capital Gang

Locking Olson safely behind bars failed to quell public outrage over the deal that was widely perceived as buying justice with "blood money." Refusing demands for a public inquiry may have seemed at the time a sincere effort to spare the families of the victims prolonged suffering. In hindsight, however, it seems safe to speculate there was at least an element of political butt-covering; the last thing the British Columbia government, specifically the Ministry of the Attorney General and its Crown Attorney's office, wanted to admit publicly was that the police had locked Olson up eight months earlier and the courts had set him free. Be that as it may, the refusal left many festering questions. Aside from unwarranted potshots by the press and the public at the police, unfair but totally understandable given the lack of disclosure by the politicians in the aftermath of the investigation, a far simpler question lingered: How had Olson claimed so many victims in such a short time?

The young people who had the tragic misfortune to cross Olson's path were victims of opportunity, quite simply in the wrong place at the wrong time. If it hadn't been them, it would have been others very much like them, shifting the tragedy and grief to other families but doing nothing to stop the reign of terror. Unlike psychotics who cannot stop themselves, psychopaths like Olson choose not to. In both cases, the horror ends only when they are captured or die. They roam free because they are clever and cunning and sometimes plain lucky.

While Olson may have abducted some of his victims, it seemed clear that others went with him willingly. Why? Because he offered high-paying jobs to teenagers, the psychological equivalent of passing candy to a baby. No parenting skill, the most earnest advice to "beware of strangers," can withstand such allure. But an even simpler answer was provided by the two girls who cursed the police for crashing their private little beach party, and probably saving their lives by arresting Olson: he seemed like a nice guy!

The image of the killer staring out from newspaper front pages, magazine covers, and nightly newscasts—defiant, unshaven, collar open, hair tousled, hands manacled—seared our souls, but those details belied the larger picture: monsters don't always look like monsters.

It was a lesson Ron MacKay had learned early.

In the summer of 1960, between leaving Royal Roads and joining the Mounties, MacKay was working in Vancouver when he spied a familiar face in a newspaper photo. The caption confirmed it was Chuck Heathman, the hired hand who had worked on the family farm a decade ago. MacKay had been only eight or nine, but he recalled vividly the time Chuck had hitched up a horse and put its collar on upside down. It had raised doubt that he really had all the experience he'd claimed to get the job, but MacKay's father was a trusting man, always looking to find the good in people. Anybody could make a mistake. It had seemed harmless, actually humorous, at the time. In fact, MacKay could recall nothing scary about Charles Merle Heathman back then. He was good to the kids, worked hard, tried hard. Everyone seemed to get along fine.

But Chuck was a different man when he got to drinking. One Saturday night, off on a bender in the nearby town of Wapella, he broke into a house and robbed it, hiding his loot in the MacKay barn loft. No one suspected anything until the Mounties showed up a few days later to chat with Chuck. He confessed and retrieved his booty from the barn. The police arrested him and drove off. About six months later, Chuck was back looking for a job. MacKay's father, known to most as "L.R." for Laughlin Ronald, still looking for that elusive good in people, ever quick to forgive and give a man a second chance, hired him back. All went well. Chuck was still good to the kids. Learned how to collar a horse. Seemed a better man. Then a neighbouring farmer complained he'd been robbed and

Chuck disappeared. MacKay never saw or heard of him again until he picked up the newspaper and recognized his picture.

According to the article, Chuck had landed in a real jackpot this time—then apparently dug himself out. Charged with raping and murdering a paperboy, he had been found not guilty. The verdict meant he could not be tried for the crime again (it would be double jeopardy), and Chuck apparently couldn't stop himself from bragging to the reporter that he had raped and killed the boy, and that the stupid cops had let him get away with murder. The "stupid cops" also apparently read the story and promptly charged Chuck with a related offence. He was convicted.

It was an eye-opener for MacKay. He'd never suspected Chuck could commit such a heinous crime. He had looked so normal, seemed like a nice guy, and now this. It was a valuable early education for the aspiring Mountie: evil comes in many guises. It was also an early lesson that some bad guys are very stupid and just don't know when to shut up. MacKay would thrive on them as a cop.

A classic example occurred on September 15, 1980, two months before Olson began killing. In a call at home at 1:15 that morning, MacKay got a tip that two gunmen who had shot a man while robbing a bank were holed up in Room 643 at the Delta River Inn, packing to head for Toronto that night on the redeye flight. MacKay called constables Mike Woods and Kirby Kinnon and told them to meet him at the upscale hotel, then raced to the scene without stopping at the office to get his gun.

In fact, only one cop brought a gun. They also had only one set of handcuffs among them, an inauspicious start to apprehending two armed robbers who had already shot one man (admittedly an accidental ricochet) in the bank job. Huddled in the hotel lobby, the trio debated how best to get someone inside the sixth-floor room to open the door after 1:30 a.m., grab back the stolen money, and arrest the two suspects—all without getting shot. This would take some planning.

One option was to just go up and knock on their door—they had no authority to kick it in—pretending to be delivering a pizza. Upon sober reflection, that plan seemed fraught with peril, particularly if the men inside the room had not ordered pizza. MacKay, as the senior rank at the scene, ruled it out and suggested a plan that seemed far less risky and far more likely to get one or both of the armed gunmen out into the open. Enlisting the aid of the hotel desk clerk, all four rode the elevator to the sixth floor. The clerk waited for the Mounties to get into position, out of sight but with a clear view of the door, then called the room on the house phone. He identified himself to the man who answered, then explained there were two police officers from North Vancouver in the lobby with him who would like to come up and chat with him. He said he was just calling ahead to make sure it was all right to send them up so late at night. The man in the room said that was fine. Send them up. Seconds later, the door burst open, a man flew out of the room and "rabbitted" down the hall . . . and literally into the outstretched arms of the law.

Handcuffing their prisoner, who seemed pretty young to be robbing banks at gunpoint, they escorted him back into the room. It seemed empty. With only one gun among them, and the possibility of an armed robber lurking somewhere nearby, they moved carefully around the room. Woods found the second suspect in the tub hiding behind the shower curtain. He was unarmed. He too looked young.

Woods led him out, arrested him, then literally held onto him until Constable Mark Tatz of Richmond detachment arrived with a set of plastic cuffs. Both suspects were 17, kids really, prompting the question: Why were they out robbing banks?

One of the teens said he was from Montreal where it was the crime of choice, adding that old habits die hard. His macho facade cracked when MacKay found the stolen loot in a wall vent; and it shattered when MacKay, looking for the gun used in the robbery, stepped up on a chair and felt blindly along the top of the window valance. He felt a "sticky thing" and recoiled, knowing at once it wasn't a money bag or a gun. Surprise and curiosity turned to dismay and disgust as he produced a battered rubber sex toy.

To be exact, it was a vulcanized vagina, torn and adorned with clippings of nudes. Its battered condition suggested it had been used regularly, roughly . . . and recently. MacKay was not amused.

His young suspect looked more pained than he likely would have had MacKay found the gun. With all due respect to Rick Mather and the FBI, it didn't take a profiler to see the exposed behavioural buttons on this young lad, and MacKay began pushing them. The teen's discomfiture grew visibly every time MacKay demanded to know which sick young pup had been using the "device." The young suspect vehemently denied it was him, then, desperate to change the topic, confessed to robbing the bank in North Vancouver. When MacKay persisted in asking who owned the sex toy, the youth also admitted to robbing a fried-chicken outlet.

The Mounties got their man, two boys actually, recovered the stolen money, and solved a seemingly unrelated robbery. A good night's work by any standard. It was all part of the thrill of working the streets and major crimes. MacKay loved his job. Could never imagine leaving it.

But he hadn't counted on meeting Spankie or his gang.

On the evening of November 17, 1983, Constable Brian Sargent, a young fraud cop working for MacKay at North Vancouver detachment, arrested 24-year-old Michael Timothy Spankie, running with a 17-year-old girlfriend, for tallying nearly a million dollars on stolen credit cards. Aware that he probably had two days of free spending before the cards were reported stolen and an alert issued, Spankie had moved quickly. He thought nothing of treating his friends to an $800 meal at a fancy restaurant, tipping the *maître d'* another $150 for a good table, superior service, and his silence if the cops came looking. It wasn't that Spankie wasn't appreciative. He'd always murmur a polite "thank you" to the name on the card whenever he paid for a meal, gas, lodging, or anything else that struck his fancy, then vanish out the door.

Most of the frauds had been committed in Richmond, but it was Sargent, in neighbouring North Vancouver, who tracked Spankie down and smoked him out. That hadn't made Sargent very popular in Richmond, but MacKay valued his accomplishment.

As the son of an Ontario civil servant with the Ministry of Natural Resources, Sargent had been all over Ontario, living in some of the most remote parts of the province. He studied history and political science at the University of Western Ontario in London. At age 22, he followed his girlfriend's lead and applied to join the Mounties, thinking they sounded more exciting than the Ontario Provincial Police. The rest of Canada couldn't be any worse than some of the "shit postings" his father had moved them to. At least with the Mounties he'd find new shit postings to other parts of the country. He was accepted; his girlfriend backed out and left to become a teacher. Before they could issue him a patrol car, Sargent rushed to get his driver's licence. He was sure it would come in handy.

Sargent showed early he had the right stuff for working the streets. Or maybe he just led a charmed life. Dispatched to an assault, he arrived alone, outnumbered, and the smallest person at the scene where three huge toughs in their late teens had beaten a B.C. Transit bus driver almost senseless. Ignoring his predicament, Sargent started to arrest the trio for assault. They quickly warned him to stop right there or they'd have to hurt him too. Fortunately, he was a reader, and now tore a page out of a bestselling book of that era, Joseph Wambaugh's *The New Centurions*, in which a big-city American cop leans into his patrol car and requests an ambulance, describing those standing around him as the victims. When they demand to know what the cop is doing, he just says they're coming with him—in his car or in the ambulance. They get in the car. Sargent now pulled the same ploy. And they got in his car, under arrest for assault.

By comparison, Spankie didn't seem much of a threat. There was no way for Sargent to know that his life had just changed forever. Aware there was also a warrant out on him for armed robbery, Spankie started talking fast. He had just gotten out of jail and had no desire to go back. He told Sargent he could help solve the Gilbert Dutra murder if the cops would drop the fraud charges and make the bank warrant disappear. This went way beyond credit-card fraud so Sargent hauled Spankie back to the detachment and had him repeat his story to MacKay at 9:00 that evening.

MacKay was familiar with the details of the murder. Dutra and his girlfriend had been shot over an unpaid drug debt, driven to a gravel pit, and dumped. He was dead, but his girlfriend had gasped when she was tossed out of the car by the two contract killers. They had driven a tire iron through her chest and left her for dead. But she was one very tough, or very lucky, lady. She had refused to die. She had also recognized Ian McAskill as one of her assailants and identified him to police.

McAskill was in jail, but Spankie said he knew the other killer, Roch Pelletier. Spankie claimed he had helped Pelletier, well known to police, clean his car after the double shooting in the back seat. But, he added, Pelletier had since sold his car, without the legal paperwork of course. There was no paper trail. If MacKay could find the car, he would likely find evidence to link Pelletier to the shootings.

MacKay suggested that it would help a great deal if Spankie met with Pelletier while wearing a "wire"—a concealed microphone. Spankie, anxious to please, willing to do anything to avoid jail, quickly agreed.

Spankie just kept talking. The meeting took an intriguing turn when, having offered to help solve one murder, Spankie gave MacKay a chance to prevent another. He claimed he'd been given a contract to murder a guy he knew only as "Ralph" by Conrad William "Connie" Gunn, a major drug dealer recently released from prison on lifetime parole. Gunn was a local legend who once held a Vancouver cop hostage at gunpoint—one incident among many that gave him the clout to sit on any Organized Crime board of directors. Gunn, quite simply, was a big fish in a big pond.

Spankie described "Ralph" and MacKay recognized who he was—a local rounder who, according to Spankie, had stuck his nose where Gunn felt it didn't belong. Spankie produced a .38-calibre gun he claimed came from Gunn who said it was "cool." It was, in fact, quite "hot." MacKay had it tested; ballistics matched it to an execution in Coquitlam where the victim, like Dutra and his girl-friend, was shot in his car—"capped behind the ear." Then he and the car were dumped into the ocean—the "saltchuck" in the Vancouver vernacular. This unexpected bonus forced MacKay to act quickly: he urged his boss to have Spankie's fraud and robbery charges "disappeared" if he helped them find the evidence they needed against Pelletier and Gunn.

The immediate priority was to find Pelletier's car without him knowing they were on to him for the double shooting in the Dutra murder. Spankie agreed to visit his crime associate wearing a wire. He didn't get much information, and the car was found largely by dedicated police work by MacKay, Serious Crimes, and Surrey GIS. They found blood traces that linked the car to the victims and arrested Pelletier as he boarded a bus for Quebec. With that one safely behind bars—threatening to find the rat who turned him in—MacKay turned his focus on Gunn, getting approval in principle from Mountie headquarters in Ottawa to hide Spankie in the Witness Protection program with a new identity in another province if he testified in court.

Spankie was warming to his work and kept talking. He alerted MacKay to a 30-pound cocaine shipment heading for Vancouver Island. Spankie knew the importer and offered to provide the date and location it would arrive. It was the icing on the cake—a rare opportunity to nab an importer several levels higher than the street-level dealers normally busted by the drug squads.

On the pretext that he had fired all his ammunition practising, Spankie met with Gunn on December 20, 1983 to ask for more bullets for his hit on "Ralph." Once again, he was wired, in the hope that Gunn would confirm the contract and name the intended victim.

But as the tape rolled, disaster loomed. The recorder had been accidently set at the wrong speed, and the four-hour tape had run out after two. Listening to the inane chatter, MacKay despaired of getting the evidence he needed for an arrest warrant that he could execute whenever he deemed best. Then, miraculously, Gunn corrected Spankie, in the dying seconds, on the final eight feet of tape, that his target was "Cliff" not "Ralph" and advised him:

"Shoot him in the head. He's a tough motherfucker."

Bingo!

Christmas had come early. With a warrant in hand, MacKay put the tape safely on ice and prepared to intercept the drug shipment to the island. Having persuaded Spankie to testify against both Gunn and Pelletier at trial, MacKay began paying his informant to gather information from the coke importer, resorting once more to the tried-and-true taped conversations. He had to chuckle when Spankie, paying cash and demanding receipts, bitched about how much it cost to gas up his car. He had no idea of the price of gas, having always used someone else's stolen credit card!

With the heat off and the fraud and robbery charges looked after, paying his way with the first money he'd earned in years, life seemed rosy for Spankie. Wearing a wire as always, he had met with the importer and convinced him he had a buyer from Quebec for his cocaine. He thrived in the role of middleman, advising the importer his "moneyman" was coming to town the next day from Quebec. The importer quickly agreed to meet him, and Spankie assured him he'd see to all the arrangements. Behind the scenes, MacKay and Staff Sergeant Bob Hawke, the NCO in charge of the drug squad at the Victoria detachment, had arranged to bring in an undercover Mountie narc from Montreal to make the deal and bait the trap. All seemed well.

Then Spankie went for a spin that spun him toward the abyss.

On January 18, 1984, Spankie was stopped for driving without a licence by a young traffic cop. Faced with a ticket he didn't want, Spankie did what he always did in a jam: talked. Fast! Claiming to be working undercover for the Mounties, he insisted he had helped solve a double shooting, and was going to help prevent a murder and take down a major cocaine shipment. The cop was skeptical. Everyone he stopped had a story, although he must have found this to be one of the more creative dodges to avoid a ticket. Spankie persisted: "Call MacKay," he said. "He'd confirm everything."

Still dubious, the traffic cop switched his radio frequency to call in on what he believed was a secure police frequency. When the call was forwarded to the hotel where he was camped out with Hawke, MacKay confirmed Spankie's claim but Hawke warned him the damage was done. He knew a criminal entrepreneur on the island who made his living monitoring police calls with his bank of scanners and selling the information to criminals happy to pay well to be kept current on police activities and plans. If the traffic cop had transmitted his request on anything but the scrambled radios he and MacKay were using, the information had been recorded and was already on the market. The obvious buyer was the drug importer.

Hawke's fears were borne out within the hour, when Spankie met with the importer. Listening to the covert transmission over Spankie's wire of the icy greeting he got from a drug dealer who had seemed his best friend a short time ago, Hawke knew the jig was up. MacKay bitterly called off the drug sting and kissed 30 pounds of cocaine goodbye.

Then he immediately alerted Vancouver Serious Crimes to execute the arrest warrant on Gunn before he got wind of what Spankie was up to. Gunn was promptly jailed over the vocal protests of his parole officer, who argued that the man was only *suspected* of awarding murder contracts, that all they had were allegations.

MacKay also had Spankie, but if his witness was going to stay alive to testify, he had to be hidden. Lodging him in a safe hotel under 24-hour police guard, MacKay asked national headquarters to expedite Spankie into Witness Protection as previously approved. But Ottawa is a town of schedules and committees and meetings, and the committee to approve Spankie's relocation was not sched-uled to meet for another week. MacKay argued that it had to be now; that next week could be too late. If Spankie died, the case died with him. They'd already lost the drug bust and there would be bad people looking for Spankie. Protest proved futile. MacKay sighed, arranged to keep moving Spankie to different hotels for the next week, and uttered a silent prayer that he would never have to deal with bureaucrats up close. It was safer on the streets. Maybe saner. At least MacKay understood those wackos.

Spankie was eventually whisked out of province and out of sight, given a new name and anonymity, then brought back to testify at the Dutra murder trial several months later. Pelletier finally knew who had put him in jail, but revenge would have to wait while he sparred with his former accomplice, McAskill, each blaming the other for that double shooting. McAskill drew deep gasps from the crowded courtroom as he accused Pelletier of not only impaling the woman with a tire iron, but stabbing her as well, then drawing the knife slowly across his tongue to lick off her blood. The woman also caused a stir on the stand when asked, during cross-examination, what she had carried in her purse the night of the alleged shootings. She thought a moment, then answered she had the usual things a girl carries around with her, rattling off: "Lipstick . . . brush . . . mirror . . . kleenex . . . hypodermic syringe . . . .32-calibre revolver."

Pelletier and McAskill were both convicted for Dutra's murder and the attempted murder of his girlfriend. McAskill was later murdered in prison but Pelletier proved more elusive. He escaped custody, was recaptured, and escaped again, and is believed still at large.

MacKay resumed catching bad guys and Spankie resumed hiding from them for a year, then returned to testify against Gunn. Police intelligence reported that a $100,000 murder contract was out on Spankie but could not prove who had awarded it. Despite all precautions, frequent moves, constant police protection, driving his informant to and from court in the trunk of his car, MacKay worried the net was tightening.

His instincts were confirmed the night he stopped at a red light at the major intersection of Hastings and Cassiar, returning home from Spankie's secret hotel location. Through his open window, MacKay heard a familiar North Vancouver radio transmission blare out of a white Chev Monte Carlo idling beside him. It was a police broadcast, but, glancing over, he realized at once the men weren't cops. He turned down his own police radio quickly lest it give him away, sitting totally silent, staring straight ahead. Fearing the worst, he skirted the east end of Vancouver, continuing along Highway 1 over Second Narrows Bridge leading to North Vancouver en route to West Van, the ferry at Horseshoe Bay, Squamish, and the popular ski resort at Whistler. Both cars crossed the bridge. There was no chase, no sense of urgency, no immediate peril. Perhaps they had not recognized him, and weren't following hoping he'd lead them to Spankie. Maybe he was just getting paranoid.

MacKay knew the roads in the area well and pulled ahead to lose them in the maze of the Capilano Highlands. Backing into a darkened side street, he turned off his headlights and radioed in, identifying himself and reporting a fictitious location up the road. Happily, no one asked over the air why he was calling in for no apparent reason. Several minutes passed, then the white Chev blazed by toward the location he'd called in. He wasn't paranoid. It was getting dangerous. One small step from deadly.

Testifying the next day in court, MacKay gazed down from the stand at a reputed "gun for hire" sitting in the courtroom. The "Albanian Shooter" peered out from behind a newspaper, stared, then ducked back behind the paper. Likely just a bluff to turn up the heat on Spankie's guardian. Or not. He hadn't been in court when Spankie testified, looking smart in one of the new ties MacKay bought for him. Nor was it calming when he and Sargent were approached in court by Gunn's lawyer, Ken Young, a very prominent Vancouver lawyer noted for his devastating cross-examinations. Young had noted that the "Albanian Shooter" had come to court packing a gun, and said he wanted no part of anyone getting shot, particularly not him.

Having an assassin upset at you was a real concern, no matter which side of the law you were on. This gunman and his brother had been charged with beating a bouncer half to death, then coming back and beating and shooting him again, then returning yet again and attacking the man as he lay helpless in hospital awaiting surgery. If he had a contract to kill someone in that courtroom, that person should take the threat very seriously. Any doubt as to the identity of his target, or targets, grew thinner that same week when Sargent's neighbours got a headless Strawberry Alarm Clock doll in a box delivered from Sears. It seemed there'd been some mistake; the doll was supposed to have been delivered to Sargent. The stakes were rising; the clock was ticking.

Late that night after testifying in court, while visiting with Spankie and his security team, MacKay got a call from his boss, Staff Sergeant Tom Hill, alerting him that the "Shooter" had cancelled a scheduled drug deal, calling the undercover Mountie who was posing as a buyer to say he had to beg off because he'd just been given a contract to murder two guys and had to go to court to get a look at them. There was no evidence that the contracts existed, and no proof who had ordered them or who were targeted. But common sense and cold logic, and the "Shooter's" coincidental appearance in court the day MacKay was on the stand, left little doubt he and Sargent were the targets. Both were advised to stay alert.

Sargent arrived home first. As his wife cooked supper, he reached around her, shut off the stove, told her to get the kids and follow him. They were going to a hotel for the night. She asked only what to pack. Nothing. There'd be others coming to do that. He didn't elaborate. She quit asking. They continued moving to a new hotel every day after that.

By the time MacKay got home, his family was asleep. He didn't disturb them, but lay awake all night, his handgun within easy reach, doing what he could to protect his young family as they slept. Lulled by the sounds of the slumbering house, alert to every sound, every sigh, he broke the news to his wife the next morning. The boys didn't need to know yet and went to school as usual. Then MacKay headed to the office to see if anyone had a plan.

There were limited options. Lacking sufficient evidence to arrest the hit man, unable to prove who had put out the contracts or who the targets were, there wasn't much they could do. It was all too vague. While the targets seemed obvious, and the natural instinct was to relocate the two Mounties and their families, the reality was that MacKay had to stick around until the end of the trial. He moved his family in with his wife's family on Vancouver Island but later moved them to a hotel so the kids could go back to school. If the gunmen were pros, it was unlikely they'd go after them.

A couple of weeks later, with the trial winding down, MacKay went to see his commanding officer to ask him what he planned to do. At one point, discussing their options while driving over a bridge, their boss, Superintendent Roy Byrne, worried that he likely shouldn't be seen driving around with them if they were marked men. It could be dangerous. MacKay and Sargent, unsure if he was joking, were not amused.

Byrne, from Security Services Branch, was well known for wearing white belts and shoes. He had no investigative background, but did know how to run a prohibitively expensive project and stay within budget. Quite simply, he broke one investigation into three, treating a three-part project as three separate entities—Dutra, Gunn, and the drug bust that never happened. But no matter how you cut it, they consumed the entire special operations budget for the year, and exceeded it by the end. That upset Chief Superintendent Jack White, who exclaimed "This is all one project! Spankie! Spankie! Spankie!" Hastily scribbling something akin to "Don't give me this bullshit!" he tore the top page off a stickum pad, handed it to MacKay, and ordered him to "Take this back to that jackass and stick it on his forehead." The "jackass" was, of course, a superintendent—not the type of order a sergeant, no matter how good his record as an investigator, got every day from a senior ranking officer.

But if White wondered where Byrne's head was at, no one doubted that his heart was in the right place when it came to rewarding his troops for a job well done, a fight well fought. It was very rare—in fact, no one could recall another incident—when a murder contract had been thwarted by nabbing the man who issued it rather than the killer who took it. Byrne believed it was an unprecedented coup and recommended that MacKay and Sargent be awarded a highly coveted Commissioner's Commendation for making the Gunn case—the murder contractor—and building a case around one witness. Especially when that one witness was Michael Timothy Spankie. Byrne's recommendation went out in October 1984 and disappeared into someone's In basket.

MacKay eventually served notice that he felt it was time to get him and his family the hell out of North Vancouver and E Division. He and Sargent met with Assistant Commissioner D. K. Wilson (second in command of E Division, later promoted to Deputy Commissioner en route to a new career in Australia as the equivalent of RCMP Commissioner), who agreed it was likely wise to move on. He asked them where they'd like to go. While MacKay didn't want to leave British Columbia, he said he'd settle for another western province where he could continue investigating major crimes, and requested a posting to Calgary. Wilson nixed that, fearing it was too close and that MacKay would be too visible working high-profile crimes if the bad guys continued looking for him. He suggested it would be better to try to hide them in a more distant posting. MacKay asked for anywhere but Ontario or Quebec where it was the provincial police who investigated major crimes, relegating Mountie investigators like him to the sidelines. Wilson understood, but thought Ontario was the logical choice. Sargent had no problem going to London or even Toronto, but was aghast when Wilson suggested Ottawa.

"Why the hell would anybody want to go to Ottawa?" Sargent demanded.

Wilson, who'd spent 11 years at national headquarters, was nonplussed: "It didn't do my career any harm."

So MacKay and Sargent packed their bags and their families for Ottawa. Things moved quickly now, and MacKay began cutting ties not only to his work but to their community. He had no choice but to abruptly resign as chairman of the Seycove Community School Association where both sons had attended school. Ottawa beckoned. A new life. A new start. And the most bureaucratic posting in Canada. His lack of French would hurt him for the first time since leaving the military college at Royal Roads.

The posting hit like a death sentence. Worse, a *living* death sentence. But it was, he had to agree, an ideal hiding place in the vast, nameless, faceless, at times mindless bureaucracy where they would rather put an informant in peril and jeopardize a major murder case than move a committee meeting up a week.

Two weeks later, MacKay and his family moved out. Admiring their recently installed cupboards didn't make trooping out the front door of their home for the last time any easier, nor did watching the workmen carry in the new bay window he'd finally ordered. MacKay's only comfort was that Gunn was convicted on two counts of counselling murder and sentenced to two more life sentences on top of his lifetime parole.

The last he heard of him, the career criminal was living comfortably in a stately home in North Vancouver whence the Mountie from Moosomin had taken it on the lam.

MacKay arrived in Ottawa in October 1984, unannounced, unwelcome, and feeling a tad unloved. National headquarters, a morgue for investigators, had no policy or guidelines for protecting one of their own. No one had a clue what to do with this unilingual anglophone from the Wild West. Nor did anyone seem to particularly care. Left to his own devices, MacKay tried to settle into the last place on Earth he wanted to be, convinced that the people there were no better equipped to look after him than they had been to look after Spankie. At least there was a program for informants; there was nothing comparable to witness relocation for officers.

For the first time, perhaps because of all the time he suddenly had on his hands, or because his refusal to uproot his family had been eclipsed by his forced relocation, MacKay began to consider writing the exam for promotion to commissioned officer.

His total lack of French haunted him in Ottawa. The only position open to him was to run the print shop. He applied, but the more he thought about it, the less it appealed to him. He was applying for all the wrong reasons. It wasn't a job he wanted, perhaps not a job he'd do well. It wasn't that the job was beneath him, not at all; but there was likely someone out there who'd applied who really wanted it, and would be sure to do a good job. MacKay was an investigator and wanted to get back into operations, not support services. He withdrew his application.

Then, unsure what else to do, he went home to spend time with his family, leaving his phone number and asking someone to call when they knew what they wanted him to do.

Things improved gradually over the next six months. In early 1985, MacKay was assigned counterterrorism duties, specializing in

Armenians and white supremacists. That October, he and Sargent were formally honoured for their unique success with Gunn. Byrne's recommendation for them to be awarded a Commissioner's Commendation had resurfaced a year after it had been submitted. It had been decided by the powers that be that a letter of commendation from their commanding officer would suffice. Even if MacKay was disappointed, he must have been cheered at least slightly by the irony that the presenter was Assistant Commissioner Tom Venner, who as a young detective had chased Gunn in Alberta when he was active there many years ago.

In August 1986, MacKay was promoted to staff sergeant and put in charge of Threat Assessment for the Calgary and Seoul Olympics, the Francophonie Summit in Quebec, Toronto's G7 Economic Summit, and the Commonwealth leaders meeting in Vancouver. He passed his exam and oral board for inspector in 1988, then flew out that same afternoon to investigate an alleged threat against the Prime Minister involving a hit man then in a federal prison in South Carolina. Although the alleged contract on the "President" of Canada proved to be merely a flaw in the transcript of a U.S. civil trial, the investigation had expanded into Texas and Florida before those in high places were convinced it was all a big mistake.

In October 1988, he and Inspector Brian Watt were transferred to Special Projects to review the Air India bombing investigation, the most deadly aviation disaster in Canadian history and the type of assignment that could become a career. Work on the Air India review was interrupted twice as they were reassigned to investigate a shooting at the Canadian Embassy in Peru. They concluded it was neither a terrorist act nor a political coup and soldiered on, happy to be working cases again. Fate, having dealt him a joker like Spankie, was now about to deal him an ace assignment.

In 1989, the FBI Behavioral Science Unit opened its Criminal Investigative Analyst course to foreign police forces through its Police Fellowship training. The RCMP was invited to be the first to send a candidate, ideally a college graduate with major-crime experience, to be trained as Canada's first "profiler" at its Academy in Quantico, Virginia. Deputy Commissioner Henry Jensen, who had

personally recruited MacKay and Watt to review the Air India investigation, added the further proviso that the candidate should be a
commissioned officer. Several qualified candidates were asked in
Ottawa and beyond; all declined. MacKay, however, had qualified
earlier for promotion to inspector and, given his extensive investigative experience, the academic qualifications were waived by the FBI.
Most importantly, he was interested.

MacKay marvelled at the privilege of rank, watching the Mountie
bureaucracy that had frustrated his efforts to protect Spankie turn
into a well-oiled machine for Jensen. In amazingly short time, he
was fast-tracked and promoted to inspector on May 18, 1989. Four
months later, nearly a decade after dismissing FBI profiling as irrelevant to Canadian law enforcement, he left for Quantico to become
Canada's first.

History had repeated itself. Just as the Mounties had not been
MacKay's first choice growing up, he was not theirs to become the
first Canadian, in fact the first non-American, profiler. He had won
that honour by default. No matter. The spark was lit. The revolution
had begun. Policing around the world was about to change forever.

4

Quantico

MacKay arrived in Quantico on September 28, 1989, with mulish cynicism and a "show me" attitude. Set in the rugged beauty of a marine corps base in Virginia, 40 miles south of Washington, D.C., the FBI Academy had grown from a single barracks graduating its first 100 agents in 1935 to a 385-acre site in May 1972, its graduates increasing tenfold.

Invisible among the trappings dedicated to developing physical and mental agility—oval running track, dormitory residences, research labs, classrooms, prestigious library, auditorium, gymnasium, weight room, and indoor swimming pool—was the windowless concrete tomb in the bowels of the Forensic Science Research and Training Center, opened in 1981, that FBI profilers called home. Profiling, little more than a curiosity to most police investigators back then, was called in as a final act of desperation to crack only the most bizarre and complex cases. Its practitioners were not yet lionized by Hollywood, the fawning press, or adoring public—there was little recognition, sparse glory, rare thanks. If they should help solve a case, the profilers would insist to all who would listen that it was the investigators who had closed it, and the investigators would not argue.

MacKay and his classmates would be toiling in the claustrophobic confines alongside the cellar-dwelling profilers, 60 feet underground, cut off from sun and sky, as they pored over the dark, grim images of their work—crime-scene photos bearing witness to the most depraved violence one person can inflict on another.

Steve Amico, a classmate from the U.S. Secret Service who had arrived a couple of days earlier and knew his way around, welcomed

MacKay at the front desk and escorted him to their shared office to meet his four other classmates: Detective Jim McCormick, New Jersey State Police; Special Agent Mike Prodan, California Justice Department Bureau of Investigation; Sergeant Sievers, Illinois State Police; and Gus Gary, an agent with the Bureau of Alcohol, Tobacco, and Firearms (ATF) that traced its roots to Eliot Ness and his Untouchables. Amico and Gary lived close by and went home at the end of every day; MacKay and the others were billeted in single rooms on the 12th floor of the Jefferson Building.

They would become, depending on how you did the math, at least fourth-generation profilers dating to the previous century.

The first generation are generally considered to be fiction writers: crime novelist Sir Arthur Conan Doyle, who created Sherlock Holmes, and Edgar Allan Poe, who penned horror mysteries complicated by unusual characters and suspects ranging from ravens to orangutans. The first true-crime profiler was probably Dr. Thomas Bond, surgeon and lecturer in forensic medicine. He included behavioural observations with the medical facts of his autopsy report on prostitute Mary Kelly, believed to be Jack the Ripper's last victim, which was sent to Robert Anderson, Head of the London Metropolitan Police Criminal Investigation Department, on November 10, 1888. The murders abruptly stopped, and Jack was never identified or arrested, becoming one of the most enduring legends in the history of crime.

The first modern profiler was another doctor, psychiatrist James A. Brussel, whose psychological insights helped lead police to arrest George Metesky, the "Mad Bomber" of New York City in 1956. By analyzing letters sent to newspapers after bombs were set off in theatres and train stations during the 1940s and '50s, Dr. Brussel suggested the police look for an Eastern European man in his forties, probably living with his mother or maiden aunts in Connecticut. They should expect to find him "wearing a double-breasted suit, buttoned." When police arrested Metesky in the Waterbury, Connecticut, home he shared with two maiden sisters, he was dressed casually. Asking to change for his journey, he was allowed the privacy of his bedroom, emerging in a double-breasted suit—buttoned!

Howard Teten, a 20-year FBI veteran, and his partner Pat Mullany, a former Christian Brother, were the first laymen to intrude into the exclusive behavioural domain of doctors with the creation of the Behavioral Science Unit (BSU) in the early 1970s. Described as a "Mutt and Jeff" pairing, at times more Abbott and Costello, they profiled violent crimes, often given only minimal information, with unnerving accuracy. Through their successes (Teten once advised a cop, correctly, to knock on doors in the neighbourhood of a vicious murder until he found a pimply-faced teenager who would confess before being asked a single question about the murder) the BSU proved a legitimate challenge to the inalienable right of the specialists; the "alienists" of the previous century who diagnosed the mentally ill deemed "alienated" from their "normal faculties."

If the FBI intrusion was considered medical heresy by the profession, it withstood the test. The knowledge grew with every prison interview begun after Ressler joined the BSU in 1974. The Chase Vampire case, Ted Bundy, and the Atlanta Child Murders, among a host of other high-profile and lesser-known serial rampages, all confirmed that investigative insights were ideally suited to a field that was more logic and observation than magic, a blend of art and science.

The list of visionaries grew to include John Douglas, Richard Ault, Roy Hazelwood, and others who carved out their own unique domain. Profiler training was limited to FBI agents who spread the word to others via their popular road shows. The doors were opened to outsiders in 1983 when then-director William Webster mandated the Police Fellowship program to be run within the National Center for the Analysis of Violent Crime (NCAVC) when it was officially opened the following year. In 1984, Detective Sam Bowerman, of the Baltimore County Police, was the first graduate of the 10-month pilot course. Four Fellows were trained in 1985, six in 1986, four in 1987, and five in 1988. All 20 Fellows, and five of the six selected for training in 1989, were American. MacKay was the sole exception; a conscious step by the Bureau to spread the word internationally.

The early months at Quantico were an intense primer—heavy reading, research, and academic study in a host of topics—to prepare for the practical training that would follow. In class most days from 8:00 a.m. to 5:00 p.m., MacKay and his classmates listened and learned and applied their lessons to make the leap from "solving" crimes to "understanding" them. Go beyond the clues and crime scene to see the big picture, they were told. Study the picture to understand the artist. Beyond the Academy, they benefited from the experience and expertise of prominent lecturers at University of Virginia, the Armed Forces Institute of Pathology, and a week with the NYPD Crime Scene Unit based in the Bronx. Their schedule was as flexible as it was ambitious, to accommodate disruptions as their instructors were often summoned to the field to profile an ongoing case; the class rolled with the punches, understanding, as investigators, such unpredictable "operational priorities." There was lots to keep them busy: complete assignments (such as "Read 36 books"); review; discuss; debate; study alone; work together. And if they finished that, there were always more administrative forms to complete—no job was ever finished before the paperwork was done.

The primary class texts were hot off the presses: *Sexual Homicide: Patterns and Motives*, co-authored by Robert Ressler, Ann Burgess, and John Douglas; and *Practical Aspects of Rape Investigation* by Roy Hazelwood and Burgess. As the titles suggest, they were not "light" reading by any definition and just the jumping-off point for the study of an endless litany of serial rape and homicide, predator typologies, sexually-exploited children, abnormal and deviant psychology, forensic pathology, blood-spatter and statement analyses, introductory and forensic psychology, crime-lab techniques, crime-scene reconstruction, threat assessment, media relations, and, of course, writing a profile report.

The FBI and behavioural academe had come a long way from the days of the Sacramento Vampire. Richard Trenton Chase, released from a hospital psychiatric ward over the protests of the nurses who worried that he was pulling the heads off of birds and drinking their blood, had been fairly easy to profile. The separate analyses prepared by Ressler and Vorpagel had borne startling similarities.

Chase was a classic "disorganized" killer, who heard voices and selected his victims by rattling doors to see if they were open. He lived nearby and made no effort to cover his trail. A tip to police from an old schoolmate had played a big part in his arrest, as tips often do, but the profiles could not be discounted.

The FBI became quite adept at profiling disorganized killers and rapists, and these accounted for the bulk of the cases that MacKay and his classmates reviewed in 1989 and 1990. But the case of Edmond Kemper taught them there were far more dangerous predators on the loose—the "organized" predators, who planned their attacks and covered their tracks carefully.

Edmond Emil Kemper was perhaps the first such killer interviewed in prison by Ressler. A giant of a man at six foot nine, weighing 300 pounds, he was initially rebuffed by police in Santa Cruz, California, when he called from a pay phone in Pueblo, Colorado, to turn himself in for murdering several college coeds, his mother, and her friend. Kemper frequently visited after-hours police haunts and was well known to the cops he had called. They dismissed him as a drunken prankster until he provided information over the phone that only the "Coed Killer" could have known. All those nights drinking and laughing with the cops at their police club had disclosed every step they were going to take to trap the serial killer—they were unaware they were talking to him. Similarly, Kemper had talked his way through several police stops with dead or dying young women propped in the car beside him or dumped in his trunk. His rampage of terror had single-handedly catapulted Santa Cruz to the unsought notoriety of eclipsing Detroit as the murder capital of America in 1972.

In addition to providing the evidence to convict himself of the heinous murders—he would routinely decapitate his victims and keep the heads as trophies—Kemper was early proof of the critical role that deviant fantasy played in motivating serial predators. As a child, ostracized for his size, he would make his sister tie him to a chair, have her pretend to throw a switch, then fall over twitching in his morbid game of "execution." From ripping heads off Barbie dolls as a child to decapitating his victims, including his mother, in adulthood, Kemper was consumed by competing fantasies. Neighbourhood pets would disappear and resurface in pieces. Growing up, he read pornography and detective magazines; applied to be a state trooper after being released from a mental hospital where he'd been sentenced as a teenager for shooting his grandparents because, as he later explained to police: "Just wondered how it would feel to shoot grandma." His fantasies persisted years later when he stalked beautiful young college coeds and hitchhikers, torn between wanting to chat, to date them, and "wondering how her head would look on a stick."

Largely but not exclusively on the basis of the FBI interviews with killers like Kemper, the authors of *Sexual Homicide: Patterns and Motives* had charted the primary differences between organized and disorganized predators as shown in Table 4.1.

Table 4.1
PRIMARY DIFFERENCES BETWEEN
ORGANIZED AND DISORGANIZED KILLERS

Organized	Disorganized
Average or better intelligence	Below-average intelligence
Socially/sexually competent	Socially/sexually incompetent/ inadequate
Skilled work	Unskilled work
High birth-order status (oldest/older child)	Low birth-order status (younger child)
Father's work stable	Father's work unstable
Inconsistent childhood discipline	Harsh childhood discipline (possible abuse)
Controlled mood during crime	Anxious mood during crime
Uses alcohol with crime	Minimal use of alcohol
Precipitating situational stress (sets him off)	Minimal situational stress
Lives with a partner	Lives alone
Mobile—car in good condition	Lives/works near crime scene
Follows crime in news media	Minimal interest in media accounts

| May change jobs or leave town post-crime | Significant post-crime behaviour change (increased use of drugs, alcohol, abuse, finds religion, etc.) |

These, the broadest distinctions, were further subdivided for serial rapists initially as *compensatory, exploitive, displaced,* and *sadistic.* The categories would evolve into simpler terms over time:

- *Power reassurance.* A "peeping tom" familiar with the area where he strikes. Uses stealth to attack women in their homes, entering by a bedroom window or balcony patio door. The most common type of rapist, a loner with low self-esteem, a night owl and underachiever who mistakes a smile for a come-on. Fantasizes that the sex is consensual and tries to involve his victim with hugs and kisses. Typically polite, but may use any force necessary to complete his assault, then often apologizes afterward. A "gentleman" rapist to media headline writers, presumably male.
- *Power-assertive.* Masks his deviance with exaggerated bravado. Believes "real men" take what they want. A good mixer who believes women owe him sex when he buys them drinks, that a wife's duty is to provide sex on demand—slaps her around if she doesn't. Confident, assertive, controlling.
- *Anger-retaliatory.* Hates women; rapes to punish them. A lone wolf, often drinks heavily and becomes more angry with each drink. Blitz sneak attacks. Prefers seclusion and rarely enters homes. Explodes when a "last straw" real or imagined slight ignites accumulated stress. Excessively violent.
- *Anger excitation/sexual sadistic.* The deadliest rapist and most likely to murder his victims, after prolonged abuse. Meticulous planner but victim is often one of opportunity in the wrong place at the wrong time. Feeds off the terror of his victims as they endure his extreme physical, psychological, and sexual abuse/torture. A "collector" who often lures his victims with a trap, alone or with a partner he dominates, often a wife or girlfriend he has isolated from her friends and family to become the centre of her world and the one who must be obeyed.

Such grim insight was an eye-opener for MacKay and his class-mates. They recognized each "type" of crime because they had investigated most or all of them at some point during their careers. Now they knew not only why the differences, but the type of person most likely to commit them. The categories were not inviolate. Traits could overlap. Not every predator would always meet every indicator, but profiling was high-stakes gambling, playing the odds, the art of the safe bet, not some unyielding scientific absolute. It helped steer you toward the dark side, away from the light, through myriad shades of grey, not to identify the predator but to predict the type capable of, and most likely to commit, specific barbaric crimes.

These new insights came at a price. Even the most hardened major-crimes investigators reach a point where daily exposure to the carnage and violence people can inflict on each other becomes fatiguing, mentally unhealthy. To avoid becoming what they hunt, they find relief in gallows humour. Under the watchful eye of Special Agent Ed Sultzbach, doubling as instructor and class "den mother," any diversion was welcome. MacKay unwittingly did his part to lighten the mood.

As British Prime Minister Winston Churchill once observed, the Americans and the British are a common race separated by a common language. It held true for Canadians too. While reviewing a murder case in which the bodies of two victims were burned on a couch, MacKay drew blank stares and muffled laughter by calling it a chesterfield. To the Americans, "Chesterfield" was a cigarette brand. The case suddenly became a clear illustration of how smoking could be harmful to your health. It was a welcome relief, broke the tension, and when he realized the mixed metaphor, MacKay laughed along with them. The group bonded a little tighter. And MacKay became an urban, or urbane, legend thanks to Special Agent Al Brantley, who never wearied of recounting the tale to his classes over the years.

Even Hollywood had a walk-on role. Actor Scott Glenn joined the class for several days to research his role for an upcoming movie called *The Silence of the Lambs* adapted from a Thomas Harris novel. Glenn was playing FBI profiler Jack Crawford, based loosely on profiler John Douglas. The plot seemed a tad far-fetched—no trainee would ever be assigned to profile a high-profile killer like Hannibal Lecter—but a mad psychiatrist who ate his patients? The class was learning almost anything was possible when it came to deviant criminal and sexual behaviour. The movie was a Hollywood blockbuster, swept the 1991 Academy Awards, and made Douglas a celebrity when Best Actress Jodie Foster shouted her thanks to him from the Oscar podium. Profiling turned suddenly sexy, the pitch line for endless books, movies, and television series.

As Christmas neared, MacKay pored over dozens of cases that had been investigated exactly as he would have investigated them in the past. They remained unsolved. But by applying his new profiling skills, though he still had no idea who did them, he had a clearer grasp of what type of person to look for. He was learning to understand how they had probably acted before, during, and after the crime. He could see beyond the actual rape or murder and recognize the fantasy that compelled the predator to act out of rage, power reassurance, or sexual sadism. He could predict with reasonable accuracy the predator's age, education, ethnicity, social skills or lack of them, employment history, parental relationships, marital status, and prior criminal history.

It was an epiphany. The FBI had indeed "shown" him, met his sole condition, overcome his skepticism. MacKay was a convert. Much easier than being a prophet to unbelievers, as he would learn soon enough back in Canada.

Before breaking for the holidays, MacKay and his classmates were invited to the Canadian Embassy Christmas soirée in Washington, D.C. It gave him a chance to advise his superiors on the value of what he was learning and enjoy a reunion with his old friend Bob Ross, Liaison Officer for the Canadian Security Intelligence Service (CSIS LO). Each had ushered the other's wedding and had last met when MacKay was in town while working in Threat Assessment. It was all pleasant diversion as he prepared for the pace to escalate in the new year.

The final phase of the Quantico training was even more gruelling than the first; the instructors set a torrid pace. But MacKay and his classmates never faltered, pushing themselves as hard as ever, or harder, to learn and apply everything they could. It was a promising development. If six strangers from competing jurisdictions could ally and bond so easily, there was hope for success back in the outside world. MacKay, as a Canadian, was probably a stabilizing factor, viewed as neutral and nonthreatening by the Americans who knew the Mountie carried no hidden political agenda, had no axe to grind. He was a breath of fresh air, as creative as he was pragmatic and honest. Who else, they may have wondered, would try to solve a crime with a smoking sofa instead of a smoking gun?

With the help of his classmates and the enthusiastic support of his FBI and outside instructors, MacKay had mastered the application of "signature" crime-scene evidence and victimology to distinguish between organized and disorganized predators, as opposed to former general observations that were not specific indicators of the type of personality who raped or killed a certain way, such as where the body was dumped, how it was arranged, what injuries or degradations were inflicted, and whether the damage was pre- or post-mortem. Most importantly, he learned and never forgot the core truth that the investigators in the field would still solve the crimes and arrest the suspects. Profiling and crime linkage were tools to lighten dark paths, warm a cold trail or refocus a dead-end investigation rather than to solve crimes directly. The priority was to catch the bad guys and get them off the streets by any and all means. Then, MacKay reasoned, there was glory enough for all.

In the fall of 1989, MacKay was asked to accompany two of his instructors, FBI profilers Gregg McCrary and Roy Hazelwood, to address the Metropolitan Toronto Police's fledgling Sexual Assault Squad (SAS). The SAS, the first in North America, had evolved from the Scarborough Rapist Task Force, created in 1987, the year after Alison Parrott was murdered, to solve a series of brutal assaults on the eastern fringe of Toronto. Sadly, despite their best efforts and a profile prepared by McCrary the previous November that suggested the cops were chasing a sexual sadist, they were no closer to solving either case. The violence was escalating in Scarborough. There was a 12th victim by about the time MacKay, McCrary, and Hazelwood were visiting Toronto, and the toll showed no signs of letting up. The rapist would never stop himself, and everyone realized that if McCrary was right it was only a matter of time until he killed a victim. Judging from the first seven attacks (see Figure 4.2), it seemed inevitable.

Figure 4.2
F B I Profile of Scarborough Rapist
N O V E M B E R 17, 1988

Metropolitan Toronto Police, Toronto, Ontario, Canada, May 4, 1987, May 14, 1987, July 27, 1987, December 16, 1987, December 23, 1987, April 18, 1988, May 30, 1988. N CAVC—Serial Sexual Assaults (Criminal Investigative Analysis) Foreign Police Co-operation (F.P.C.)

The following criminal investigative analysis was prepared by Special Agent Gregg O. McCrary, in consultation with Supervisory Special Agent James A. Wright and other members of the National Centre for the Analysis of Violent Crimes (N CAVC). The analysis is based upon a review of the materials submitted by our agency, and the conclusions are the result of knowledge drawn from the personal investigative experience, educational background and research conducted by these crime analysts as by other N CAVC members. It is not a substitute for a thorough well-planned investigation and should not be considered all inclusive. This analysis is based upon probabilities, noting however that no two criminal acts or criminal personalities are exactly alike and, therefore, the offender at times may not fit the analysis in every category. This analysis contains information of a confidential and sensitive nature, and is provided for your investigative assistance. It should not be disseminated except to other criminal justice agencies with a legitimate investigative or prosecutorial interest in this matter.

VICTIMOLOGY

Analysis of the victims in an effort to determine their risk factor is of significance. The susceptibility of these women becoming victims of a sexual assault was examined in conjunction with their individual lifestyles, background, and overall social and physical environments. We found nothing in any of these women's backgrounds or lifestyles that would elevate their risk of becoming victims of a violent crime and/or sexual assault. We consider all of these victims to be low-risk victims.

There are observable similarities in that the victims are white females 15–21 years of age, with six out of seven living in the Scarborough area and three of those living in extremely close proximity to one another. The significance of this will be discussed in greater detail in the crime analysis section of this report.

The fact that four of the victims either traveled from or through the downtown area immediately prior to the attack is noted, but is not felt to be of significance in this analysis. If the offender was selecting his victims from a downtown location and surveilling them to their residential area for the attack, we would expect to see a far more random geographical pattern to the attacks than there is. With the exception of the Mississauga attack, all are clustered in the Scarborough area.

Another notable similarity among the victims is their small physical stature, ranging from 5'1" and 95 pounds to 5'3" and 135 pounds. This will be discussed in more detail in the crime analysis section also.

HOSPITAL AND LABORATORY EXAMINATIONS

The result of the medical and laboratory examinations of each of the victims is complete and specific details are readily retrievable from those reports; therefore, no attempt will be made to summarize the findings.

All reports are consistent with and tend to corroborate the individual victim's specific allegation regarding each attack.

CRIME ANALYSIS

A meaningful behavioural analysis of a series of sexually motivated attacks is best accomplished by examining the assailant's verbal, sexual, and physical behaviour during the commission of the attacks. In conjunction with these considerations, the following aspects are being set forth as significant.

The process by which an offender targets and/or selects his victims is of obvious importance. We feel your offender uses bus stops for staking out points. He surveils streets rather than homes and does so at night. Some victims were victims of opportunity while others appear to have been previously targeted to a degree. We believe the offender has seen victims or potential victims in passing, but had no urge to attack and at other times has seen victims, had the urge to attack, but the moment was inopportune.

The successful attacks occurred when the urge, opportunity and victims coincided. The victims are being targeted by the offender in the areas in which the attacks are occurring. He is following them short distances before attacking them.

The six victims in Scarborough were all approached from behind, while the victim in Mississauga was approached from the front. He gained control over all the victims by the immediate application of injurious physical force. He maintained control of the victims through the use of physical force and verbal threats of bodily harm and or death, all of which were often accomplished while brandishing a knife in a threatening and intimidating manner.

All victims were attacked outdoors, while walking alone, near their residence during the hours of darkness.

Typically, this type of offender starts his attacks in an area with which he is familiar. This familiarity is usually the result of the offender living or working in that area and gives him a sense of security and comfort as he knows the neighbourhood well, can plan escape routes etc. The behaviour exhibited by your offender is consistent with this premise.

We believe your offender resides in the Scarborough area, specifically within walking distance of the first, second and fifth attacks. Because he lives in his attack area it is of utmost importance to him that the victims not see him. This is one of the reasons he prefers to approach the victims from the rear. Upon contact he forces them face down into the ground and/or demands they keep their eyes closed to ensure they do not see him.

The victim in Mississauga was approached in a slightly different manner. After following her for a distance on foot, he approached her under the guise of asking directions. This approach allowed the victim to see his face, but was short in duration as the offender did not finish his first sentence before physically assaulting this victim and forcing her face down to the ground. It is our opinion that the offender was less concerned about being seen by his victim as he does not spend a great deal of time in the Mississauga area and believes that it is unlikely he would be recognized or seen there again.

Another reason your offender approaches his victims from behind is that he harbours some inadequacies. These inadequacies are further evident in his verbal behaviour as he scripts many of his victims to say, "Tell me you hate your boyfriend and you love me." "Tell me you love me, tell me it feels good" and other ego-gratifying statements.

Another indication of his inadequacies is evident in his victim selection. He selected victims that appeared non-threatening to him. As noted in the victimology section, the victims are physically small and could offer no real resistance to the attack. Each victim was walking alone at the time of the attack and was virtually defenseless.

Anger, however, is the primary behaviour exhibited by your offender. His intent is to punish and degrade the victims as he is angry at all women. This is evident in the blitz style approach and the majority of his verbal behaviour as well as the type and sequence of sexual acts forced upon the victims in conjunction with the punishing physical force used against them.

The typically profane verbal behaviour combined with scripting the victims to describe themselves as a bitch, a cunt, a slut etc., evidences his anger and his need to punish and degrade his victims. This anger is also apparent in your offender's sexual behaviour. By forcing the victims to perform oral sex on him after he has repeatedly vaginally and anally assaulted them he is punishing, degrading and humiliating them. The type and sequence of sexual assault is consistently observable in the series of attacks.

His anger is unmistakable when observing the excessive physical force he uses against the victims. What is of concern is the escalation in violence observable in this series of attacks. He is using far more physical force against the victims than is necessary to control them. In addition to this, the offender has stuffed articles of clothing into the mouths of victims and in the case of the sixth victim, not only broke her collar bone, but poured dirt on her and rubbed it into her hair and onto her body. This is a symbolic gesture which expresses the assailant's opinion of women.

We do not believe the offender would attack a victim with a premeditated idea of murdering her. However, we would opine, based upon our research and experience, that if confronted by a victim who vigorously resists his attack, your offender is the type who would likely become so enraged he could lose control and thereby become capable of unintentionally murdering the victim.

This type of behaviour is observable in your offender to a lesser degree in these attacks. In analyzing the interaction between the individual victims and the offender it can be seen that the victims feel overpowered by him and are generally compliant and submissive. Still, when the victims either misunderstand a command or delay, even momentarily responding to a demand, the offender immediately becomes enraged and escalates the amount of violence directed at the victim.

The offender's escalation in violence is observable also as the first three attacks could been seen as attempted rapes where no penile penetration occurred, while the rest of the attacks were successful rapes from the offender's view point as he achieved penile penetration. This expansion of the sexual nature of the assaults was accompanied by an escalation in the verbal and physical violence directed at the victims.

Also observable in the offender is the development of sadistic tendencies. He asked the seventh victim, should I kill you, thereby making her beg for her life. The sadist achieves gratification by the victim's response to his attempts to dominate and control her either physically or psychologically; by posing a question that made the victim beg for her life he is deriving pleasure.

He has shown adaptive behaviour, indicating he is becoming comfortable in committing the assaults and feels unthreatened and in control. This is exemplified in the sixth attack. While he was accosting the victim and attempting to gain control over her, a car pulls out of a driveway a few inches away and drives by them. He does not panic, but forces the victim into some bushes near a house and continues to assault her.

OFFENDER CHARACTERISTICS AND TRAITS

Your offender is a white male, 18 to 25 years of age. It should be cautioned that age is a difficult category to profile since an individual's behaviour is influenced by emotional and mental maturity, and not chronological age. No suspect should be eliminated based on age alone. The behaviour exhibited throughout these assaults suggests a youthful offender rather than an older more mature one.

As noted above, we believe your offender lives in the Scarborough area. He is familiar with Scarborough, especially the initial assault sites, and, therefore, in all probability lives in the immediate vicinity of those first assaults.

The offender's anger towards women will be known by those individuals who are close to him. He will speak disparagingly of women in general conversation with associates.

He had a major problem with women immediately before the onset of these attacks. His anger would have been apparent not only for the particular woman involved but those close to him.

He is sexually experienced but his past relationships with women have been stormy and have ended badly. In all probability he has battered women he has been involved with in the past. He places the blame for all his failures on women.

If he has a criminal record, it will be one of assaultive behaviour. The arrests will likely be for assault, disturbing the peace, resisting arrest, domestic disturbance, etc.

His aggressive behaviour would have surfaced during adolescence. His education background will be at the high school level with a record of discipline problems. He may have received counseling for his inability to get along with others, his aggressiveness, and/or substance abuse.

He is bright, but an underachiever in a formal academic setting.

He is nocturnal and spends a good deal of time on foot in the target assault area.

We believe your offender is single.

The offender has an explosive temper and can easily become enraged. This rage transfers over into the rest of his life.

He blames everyone else for his problems.

His work record will be sporadic and spotty as he cannot hold a job due to his inability to handle authority.

He is financially supported by his mother or other dominant female in his life.

He is a lone wolf type of person. He can deal with people on a superficial level but prefers to be alone.

The personal property of the victims which your offender took from the assault scenes is being kept by him. These effects are viewed as trophies by the offender and allow him to relive the assaults. He will keep these items in an area which is under his personal control which he feels is secure, but yet allows him ready access to them.

The nature of these attacks will continue to be episodic and sporadic. In all probability, they will continue to occur outdoors as he is familiar with the area and this familiarity gives him a sense of freedom and mobility which would be denied if he were to attack indoors. Each attack is precipitated by a stressor in the offender's life. This stressor could be either one in fact or in his mind.

The offender recognizes his inadequacies and attempts to mask them, but very often overcompensates. These inadequacies are not known by casual acquaintances, but are well known by those closest to him.

POST-OFFENSE BEHAVIOUR

Your offender harbours no guilt or remorse for these crimes. He believes his anger is justified and, therefore, so are the resultant attacks. His only concern is being identified and apprehended.

Any further questions regarding this analysis or discussion regarding investigative strategy and interview techniques should be directed to SA Gregg O. McCrary or SSA James A. Wright, F.B.I. Academy, Behavioral Science Unit.

On June 27, 1990, MacKay graduated as the first non-American profiler among only 32 members admitted to the exclusive International Criminal Investigative Analysis Fellowship (ICIAF), and as valedictorian of what John Douglas called "the best class ever." High praise indeed. MacKay, to show his gratitude for what he'd learned and to take advantage of reviewing more unsolved crimes than he'd ever seen in Canada, promptly volunteered with New Jersey State Police classmate Jim McCormick to stay an extra month to help clear the huge backlog of cases. He also contributed more than a half-dozen Canadian cases to the Crime Classification Manual being prepared by the FBI profilers to systematically classify homicides, sexual assaults and arsons.

A daunting challenge awaited, one made even more intimidating by the fact that MacKay was the sole profiler in all of Canada. He was alone but not without allies. Before leaving, he cemented a strong friendship with Supervisory Special Agent James Wright, asking him to be his FBI contact when he needed a second opinion, someone to confirm or question his first profiles. MacKay felt a special rapport with Wright, considered him his mentor and advisor, and knew he'd assess his work honestly. Aside from some good-natured ribbing over Canadian spelling, Wright invariably approved and agreed with the early profiles he received.

In July, MacKay packed his bags, gently stowed his replica Eliot Ness credentials from ATF classmate Gus Gary, and headed home to the reception historically accorded all prophets in their own land: rejection, ridicule, and outright obstruction. It wasn't a total surprise. Pragmatic as always, MacKay reasoned that if it was easy, everyone would do it. He had been trained by the best, and had made valuable new professional contacts who had become his friends over the past 11 months. The cautious enthusiasm he felt as he headed home to Ottawa was tempered by what he knew lay ahead. The next time he entered a room crowded with hard-nosed, skeptical investigators, arms crossed, legs splayed, defiant "show me" eyes, he'd be the guy on the other side of the dais. MacKay would show them if he got half a chance. He'd been shown—converted. He would spread the word. His phone would ring. It was only a matter of time before someone needed his unique skills. Those calls, as Robert Keppel, chief criminal investigator for the Washington State Attorney General's Office, warned, would never be for help with routine cases:

> When what are apparently signature murder cases . . . cross [jurisdictions] or overwhelm a local police force; when serial cases in another [jurisdiction] require an outside pair of eyes to bring them into focus; when the brutality of a homicide makes even the most veteran detectives shudder—that's when the phone rings. . . .

MacKay was ready, but if he thought Quantico had prepared him for anything, he was wrong. When his phone rang the second day back on the job, the call caught him completely off-guard.

5

First Strikes

MacKay returned to work on July 24, 1990, anxious to promote what he'd learned at Quantico and to offer his profiling skills across Canada. He got his first call the next day, but it was not what he expected. Paul Allan was calling from the Metropolitan Toronto Police to congratulate MacKay on his graduation, to welcome him back, and to ask for a meeting to discuss how best to adapt his new profiling skills to the Major Crime File (MCF), a computer database that was designed to link serial crimes and that Allan said had been around for years.

MacKay had never heard of it, but then he'd been out of the country for almost a year. When had Metro brought its system online? he wondered. The surprises continued. The MCF belonged to the Mounties; Allan was the Metro coordinator. It turned out that the Ontario Provincial Police was also online via coordinator Pat McVicar. MacKay pressed for details.

The MCF, a direct consequence of the Olson case in British Columbia a decade earlier, had been developed to address the stinging complaint that the police had no handle on the number of missing children or what was happening elsewhere in the province. In the early 1980s, the police had admittedly toiled with archaic systems. In Vancouver, Maile had relied on the memory of "the elderly woman upstairs" to locate archived reports and dated documents; Eastham, in Kamloops, had used a shoebox crammed with loose slips of paper as his Rolodex. If anything good had come of the Olson horror, it was that Mountie brass and the politicians had had to face the fact that they were not providing investigators with the necessary tools to do their jobs. Traditional methods just didn't work, at least not quickly enough, for new threats like Olson.

Now, solutions were being devised and were available. Once again, the FBI had led the pack and the Mounties had followed their lead.

While studying at Quantico to be a profiler, MacKay became aware of, though had only passing contact with, the FBI's vaunted Violent Criminal Apprehension Program, known far and wide by its acronym VICAP. The computer database housed details of bizarre and particularly violent homicides submitted by police across America and could link similar crimes no matter where or when they occurred. It was another valuable investigative tool, a determined effort to track mobile serial killers and help investigators in different jurisdictions know that they may not be the only ones chasing a specific predator. While the Atlanta Child Killer, the Sacramento Vampire, and others had hunted their victims close to home, Ted Bundy had cruised across America, stalking athletic, beautiful young women who parted their long hair in the middle. He was stopped often, even taken into custody on occasion, but escaped every time. As the toll rose on his cross-country spree, the police had no way of knowing others were chasing the same killer. Had they been able to link his crimes, they might have seen a pattern or at least the direction in which he was heading. That may have allowed police to capture him sooner and spared the last few victims. The key was to link the crimes.

If that seemed a novel idea, it certainly wasn't entirely new. In 1958, Detective Pierce Brooks, a 10-year veteran with the Los Angeles police, had a cop's gut instinct about two of the many murders he was investigating. He was sure both killers had killed before and set out to try to link them to other local or distant homicides. His only resource was the public library, where he spent countless hours—on duty and off, days, nights, and weekends—scouring newspapers for murder accounts and details of persons with a similar MO (*modus operandi*, mode of operation). Weeks stretched to months, but Brooks was a man on a mission and, after a year of dogged persistence, he read an account of a similar crime in another jurisdiction. Contacting investigators there, he requested a copy of their killer's fingerprints. They matched. His killer now had a name and face: Glatman.

Harvey Murray Glatman has been described as the first "signature" killer, able to change his MO but not his sadistic fantasy. For

Glatman, it was all about control, roped victims, and "trophy" photos. A rare sexual sadist, he lured his victims with offers of easy money to pose nude for his camera, just as Alison Parrott was lured to her death a quarter-century later. Though grossly unattractive, he had no trouble talking his way into a woman's apartment or talking her into his car on the pretense he wanted pictures for his personal collection or for a crime magazine spread. The ruse worked well on the aspiring starlets flooding into postwar Hollywood who found taking their clothes off for strangers easier than waiting tables to pay the bills. It was an open secret among modelling agencies and pure capitalism in action: the photographer got his pictures, the model got paid, and her agency got its cut. Everyone went home happy—until Glatman came on the scene, leaving a trail of hyena-ravaged skeletal remains in the remote California desert. He believed his victims were unlikely to tell friends or family they were heading out to take off their clothes for a stranger, and counted on the fact that they would not be missed, or at least not reported missing, until long after he was done with and had disposed of them.

He hadn't reckoned on Brooks' brilliance or persistence, however; in 1959 he went to the gas chamber.

After witnessing Glatman's execution, Brooks pushed for a national computerized database to link crimes for the rest of his career, promoting the value of a system that could identify and link similar crimes no matter where or when they were committed across America. He took his dream with him when he left the LAPD as a captain to serve as a police chief in Oregon and Colorado, finally knocking on the door of the FBI. A quarter-century after California politicians had refused to spend—they said "waste"—the money to equip cops with computers, U.S. Senate hearings heard his message. It was cold logic bolstered by the violent excesses of the 1960s and 1970s, all capped by the 1981 Attorney General's Report on Violence in America, which found most Americans lived in terror. With the land of the free and home of the brave seen to be disintegrating into a land of the spree and home of the depraved, the FBI, already tasked as a lead agency in antiterrorism and drug interdiction, was assigned the job of creating the national database long envisioned by Brooks.

Finally, in 1985, Brooks sat down at a desk, flipped a switch, and watched his dream come online: VICAP. Costs for the first two years were estimated at about $3 million—not much more than was spent just tracking Olson in British Columbia, without knowing for a very long time it was Olson they were chasing or where he'd struck.

A natural adjunct to profiling, VICAP was the result of Brooks' sustained arguments that it was not enough to know the type of criminal police were chasing; that no matter how valuable an investigative tool profiling was, its true potential would never be realized until there was a system to also link those apprehended for, or even suspected of, other crimes. Just as the FBI had penetrated criminal minds to better understand how they worked, VICAP plotted a turnpike of connecting dots to show where a killer had been and where he was going: a breathtaking breakthrough that, sadly, was widely ignored, as many major police forces refused to take the time or make the effort to submit their cases.

VICAP, like profiling, became part of the FBI National Center for the Analysis of Violent Crime (NCAVC). While these valuable investigative tools could overlap, they served distinctly separate functions—the same, but different, as wags observed. VICAP had strict criteria and accepted only clearly defined types of cases:

1. Solved or unsolved homicides or attempts, especially those that involve an abduction, are apparently random, motiveless, or sexually oriented, or are known or suspected to be part of a series.
2. Missing persons, when the circumstances indicate a strong possibility of foul play and the victim is still missing.
3. Unidentified dead bodies when the manner of death is known or suspected to be homicide.

The FBI also asked investigators to submit cases with an arrested or identified offender to VICAP for comparison with others across the country. Should a serial killer be identified by "signature" or MO, VICAP could help coordinate multi-agency investigations and task forces, a vital response to a mobile predator who was crossing county and state lines. Once in the system, the case would be continually compared to others in the database to try to link it to behaviourally similar crime scenes.

That behavioural link was vexing to investigators steeped in traditional investigative techniques. Cops over the centuries had grappled with "means, motive, and opportunity" to finger prime suspects. FBI research into the behavioural aspects of the criminal mind—the basis of all MacKay's presentations—threw a monkey wrench into that time-honoured equation. Police could normally winnow thousands of suspects who had the means and opportunity to commit a violent crime to a more manageable list by also determining who had the motive to rape or murder.

According to MacKay, however, the key was to understand whether they had *wanted* to attack their victims or were *driven* to it. It was a vital distinction, separating MO from "signature"—at times muddied by "ritual." The three concepts could overlap and were easily confused. For investigators steeped in gathering hard facts and evidence that could be presented in court, worrying about such behavioural aspects that would be inadmissible must have sounded like an unconscionable waste of time and effort. MacKay sympathized, understood their frustration perfectly, and would have felt exactly the same way before his training at Quantico. For the benefit of the investigators in his audiences, he tried to keep it simple.

Investigators are most familiar with a criminal's MO—what he does to commit his crime. It is learned behaviour that will change with experience over time, as all deviants from cat burglars to serial killers will retain what works and abandon what does not. The clues they leave at the crime scene become the evidence against them in court.

In contrast, the subtleties of profiling were maddening. There were no absolutes. The common mistake most people make in trying to understand "signature" is to think of it as a unique calling card, when in fact it is actually distilled from many factors, including but not limited to MO, victimology, victim selection, timing and time of day, and even weather patterns. For example, some predators were seasonal, others struck only when it was hot, overcast, raining, a full moon, whatever. All those factors and more had to be considered to identify criminal signature, the behavioural core unique to a specific predator.

A further complication was the common confusion between *signature* and *ritual*, the fantasy-driven behaviour that is the primary component of signature. Even though there were no absolutes when dealing with the deviant criminal mind—even if there was an overlap between signature and ritual—ritual would most likely remain excessive, going beyond what was necessary (MO) to commit the crime. A good example is the "overkill" of victims who are clubbed or stabbed dozens of times when any one of the blows or thrusts would have been fatal. It's possible to see similar ritualistic behaviour in crimes committed by different people, but the core of the signature would not change, would remain unique to an individual and allow the profiler to identify the personality type most capable of, and most likely to commit, a specific crime. What he did, how he did it, and what he said while doing it all become of vital importance to help point the investigators to the "type" of predator most able and most likely to attack that specific way.

The trick, MacKay would explain, was to see the big picture, impossible without analyzing the seemingly unlimited combined factors of ritual and MO to identify signature. The first two may change; the last will not.

Shoving a moth down the throat of a young victim in *The Silence of the Lambs* is ritual, and a component of signature. MO, on the other hand, is learned behaviour. Each crime, from break-in to butchery, teaches the criminal what works, what does not. Experience teaches him the best way to gain and maintain control over a victim, or break into a home or business, and escape undetected. Unlike signature, MO often changes over time and space. The danger in confusing the two is that a serial rapist or killer might easily deceive police into thinking they were chasing different predators because of apparent changes in his MO. That was exactly what

Olson had confessed to Maile a decade earlier: that he had killed his victims in different ways to throw police off his trail.

In a perfect world, the differences between signature and MO would be as clear as day and night, but MacKay cautioned his audiences that for every rule there is an exception. If his violent fantasies became more complex as a predator matured, his ritual and therefore even his signature could reflect that change, though his core fantasy would remain the same. The trick was to spot and understand the core behavioural signature. If a man rapes out of anger at age 18, MacKay explained, his assaults will still reflect his rage at 40.

It was like chasing a shape-shifter. Just when you thought you got it—poof!—it changed. But the core behavioural signature would remain constant over time and space, and profiling could spot that. It wasn't evidence, wasn't admissible in court, but it would point the investigators in the logical direction to find their man and the evidence to charge and convict him.

Conceding that both signature and MO were valuable indicators, MacKay hammered home how profiling could keep an investigation focused in the right direction and away from tantalizing wrong paths and blind alleys that would predictably beckon, particularly when one or more predators had claimed multiple victims. The cops in the field would still get the glory of the arrest. Profiling would simply help them get it faster, more efficiently, and at a far lower toll in human misery and dollars.

The profiler, he added, could also apply his experience and special training to determine whether crime-scene behaviour had been influenced by the environment of a particular crime or unanticipated complications had affected the deeds and decisions during the crime. For example, while a disorganized predator would attack his victims of opportunity when and where he found them, an organized sexual sadist would stalk his hunting ground, not always a specific victim, and take him or her to a spot where he felt safe enough to take his time inflicting his tortures.

When time is of the essence, as it always is with serial crimes, it just makes sense to ask for help from someone who can unravel the compelling core fantasies and crime-scene signatures sooner. At that stage, MacKay was the only game in town—in fact, in Canada.

The next step would be to link the predator to other crimes he may have committed in different places and earlier times. That's where VICAP helped and where the MCF failed. VICAP's three-fold role was to help police and sheriff departments work together: cooperate, communicate, coordinate. Otherwise, the serial killer had every advantage, moving undetected in the shadows, aided by public terror and police confusion complicated by an overwhelming number of suspects or none at all. The predator just had to keep moving on. The reality was that investigators' concern stopped at the edge of their particular jurisdiction. Once unknown subjects ("UNSUBS" in the FBI lexicon) crossed into the next county or state, they were someone else's problem. There were always enough other homicides and serious crimes to investigate without worrying about the one that got away. VICAP was a solution to that problem, a chance to catch the killer and close all the cases no matter who caught him or when.

The concept, and the specially trained analysts, were brilliant. VICAP offered an efficient and cost-efficient solution to the escalating violence that seemed to be consuming America. But its Achilles' heel quickly surfaced. Like any computer system ever devised, the value of its output was determined by the quality of the information put in. "Garbage in, garbage out" is the standard catchphrase. It was an immediate problem that has yet to be adequately addressed more than a quarter-century later.

Americans assert their rights and powers far more stridently than Canadians. Americans fought a revolution to gain their independence and waged civil war, at least in part, to extend freedom. The FBI, including profilers and VICAP, must wait to be invited to participate in outside cases. The federal government has no power under the Constitution to make city police, state troopers, and county sheriffs and their deputies request a profiler or submit their cases to VICAP. As a result, due to horrific non-compliance, there are gaps in the VICAP database large enough for a serial killer to drive a windowless white van through. Investigator arrogance and petty politics have thus put millions of Americans in harm's way, and their fate is sealed by their local elected officials, not the FBI.

Some states have created their own version of VICAP; other systems can capture sexual assaults and, with analysis, determine if they are linked serial rapes that can lead to serial murder. But fragmentation remains the problem. There is simply no state or national database in America that captures both sexual assaults and homicides on the same database that can then be compared nationwide.

MacKay was stunned to learn the Mounties had created their own version of VICAP, the MCF, devised by Superintendent Henny Lind of the Informatics Branch based at national headquarters in Ottawa. Lind had reviewed VICAP at Quantico and seen that this was something the Force needed and could create. God bless Lind for seizing the initiative, a major response to Olson, MacKay thought, but he was troubled. During the decade he had spent investigating major crimes, in his years at RCMP national headquarters, in his 11 months at Quantico, he had never heard a soul breathe a word about the MCF. He wasn't surprised that Paul Allan was finding "investigator resistance" in Toronto, but wondered if it wasn't more investigator ignorance. Was the MCF being ignored by police across Canada because they refused to do the necessary paperwork or because they didn't know it existed? He couldn't believe he was the only one in the dark and it didn't make a whole lot of sense to have a cutting-edge high-tech system if no one knew about it. MacKay agreed to meet with the Metro and OPP coordinators in the near future but faced more pressing priorities.

On his visit to the Metro Sexual Assault Squad in Toronto with FBI profilers Hazelwood and McCrary the previous fall, he had been invited downtown to OPP headquarters, a stone's throw from Lake Ontario. The FBI had invited the provincial police to select a candidate for the next profiler class and asked MacKay to represent them in the selection process. He agreed when the OPP selected Sergeant Kate Cavanagh, a seasoned investigator in several fields. MacKay met her for the first time on August 1, sharing his insights and experiences over lunch to help prepare her for Quantico en route to becoming the second Canadian profiler and first woman profiler in Canada. That afternoon, MacKay called Keith Davidson in Vancouver to discuss his interest in becoming the profiling coordinator for E Division. His former sex-crimes investigator jumped at the offer. Later that same day, searching for a catchy title for the new section he hoped to create within Special Services, MacKay doodled VCAS— "Violent Crime Analysis Section"—and submitted it to his boss in a memo the next day, outlining the profiling services he could provide and urging the creation of VCAS within the branch.

Basing VCAS at national headquarters would centralize operations—and control—but MacKay knew from his own experience in the field that investigators were loath to deal with Ottawa, believing their requests for help or equipment disappeared into a black hole. They would be happier dealing with a local coordinator, a familiar, friendly face who could prioritize and process their requests for profiling assistance. The ideal, and easiest, solution was to adapt the FBI/Pennsylvania State Police model and create a series of regional or divisional coordinators across the country to help allay cynical investigator resistance. Even so, VCAS and profiling promised to be a tough sell. A week later, MacKay submitted a second memo, suggesting he tour all regions of Canada and introduce VCAS and profiling to all Mountie divisions, detachments, and outside police forces. He knew from his own "show me" days that the personal touch was imperative for success.

Then his phone rang.

On August 10, 1990, after MacKay had spent about two weeks on the job as Canada's first profiler, Windsor police placed the historic first call for help. Windsor, nestled along the shores of the St. Clair River across from Detroit—for years the murder capital of America—was now gripped in its own terror. A serial rapist had attacked seven sleeping women in their own homes. Advising his caller what to send him—victim statements, maps, weather reports, crime-scene photos, medical reports, crime stats—he was equally clear on what not to include. At no time is a request for profiling assistance ever to include a suspect name or description to avoid tainting the process and polluting the analysis.

Determined to make the first profile for a Canadian police force by a Canadian profiler a success, MacKay succeeded in a most unexpected way, proving you don't always have to arrest a suspect to stop him.

The serial rapist was entering homes through bedroom windows, and from the details provided by the police, MacKay profiled a "power reassurance" or "gentleman rapist" who would fantasize that the forced sex was actually consensual. He would try to involve his victims in his attacks, kissing and hugging them, inflicting "normal" and oral sex he thought would please them. He probably lived nearby or frequently visited the area where the attacks occurred. MacKay advised the police to look for someone shy and polite. He'd come across as a nice guy to cover his low self-esteem. Probably a loner, maybe a night owl, possibly an underachiever. He wouldn't look or sound dangerous.

The police were amazed. MacKay's profile fit one of their suspects to a T. They hadn't seriously considered him because he'd seemed like a decent guy, not the type at all who'd skulk through bedroom windows at night and assault sleeping women. MacKay advised the Windsor investigators to confront the suspect "forcefully" with their suspicions. If he was the rapist, he'd fold, possibly confess. He had learned at Quantico that, though all rapists suffer some personality inadequacy, this particular breed is also considered the wimp of rapists, the most likely to flee or negotiate to avoid confrontation or resistance.

Concerned they still had no evidence to charge the man with the rapes, but anxious to end this reign of terror, the cops were willing to try anything. They confronted the man, told him they knew it was him, that they were on to him and, by God, they'd get him and put him away.

The rapes stopped.

The end of the attacks could have been coincidental; perhaps the rapist had moved on, been arrested for something else, or even died.

But experienced major-crime investigators aren't big fans of coincidence. No one doubted that MacKay's profile had helped put a rapist out of business, proving the value of profiling in its first test, a shining example of street justice.

If it galled the seven victims that no one was ever charged with their rapes, felt denied their day in court, hopefully they also enjoyed some sense of closure. It had been their courage to come forward and describe the crime in detail, reliving their torment by recalling to police what their attacker did and said before, during, and after their ordeals, that had helped MacKay profile their assailant. They had played a vital role in helping police put an end to the attacks and ensure no other women suffered what they had. By helping deter him from further attacks, they had refused to be victims. They had fought back, turned the tables, and stopped him.

MacKay never received any public credit for his role in stopping the Windsor rapes. That was fine. He was the first to admit that he existed to help the investigators in the field. They were the ones who would make the arrests, lay the charges. Still, he had helped end a crime spree. It was an impressive debut, but if Vorpagel was right, he had merely won a battle. The war went on.

His first profiling notch in his Sam Browne, MacKay resumed studying the MCF. He contacted Davidson in Vancouver on August 23, less than two weeks after profiling the Windsor rapes, to discuss what to do with a system that no one seemed to know about and which, after several years' operation, had yet to link a single crime to another. What had seemed an ambitious effort to prevent, or at least limit, the horror of another Olson also seemed, at first blush, a well-intentioned failure. Agreeing to study the MCF further, Davidson rose to the challenge beyond all expectations.

With Davidson solidly on board in Vancouver, MacKay pushed ahead in Ottawa. On September 6, he obtained two copies of the MCF user's guide from CPIC, and was unnerved to find they were each about the size of a city telephone book. No investigator would have had time to read them, let alone try to understand them.

That same day, he took advantage of a meeting with Dutch Inspector Carlo Schippers, en route to Quantico for training with OPP profiler Kate Cavanagh, to discuss the need and interest European police might have for a VICAP-type system to track mobile predators as national borders began disappearing in the new Economic Union. There was a need, and there was interest.

MacKay began to envision a system that would have worldwide appeal. He wasn't convinced the MCF, or even VICAP, was the solution. If he had any hope of improving either system, he needed help. A mentor. Staff. Budget. Mandate. Prying them loose from bean-counting bureaucrats and egocentric senior brass threatened to become a war of attrition that he seemed ill suited to wage.

But his FBI tutoring was about to pay an unexpected dividend. To everyone's great surprise, MacKay proved to be an astute political animal, as adept at winning bureaucratic battles as he was proficient at profiling bad guys. Everyone, he had learned, had behavioural buttons to be pushed, including the cops to whom he preached VCAS and profiling.

In mid-September, MacKay accompanied Cavanagh, soon to be heading to Quantico, to analyze a ghastly homicide in Orillia in the picturesque heart of Muskoka cottage country due north of Toronto. The next day, he addressed the Metro Police Sexual Assault Squad, which was still no closer to catching the elusive Scarborough Rapist since he had first visited with FBI agents McCrary and Hazelwood while studying at the FBI Academy. After lunch with Metro MCF coordinator Paul Allan, he spent the afternoon extolling the virtues of his new skills to 45 Peel Regional officers responsible for public safety west of Toronto. The next day, he met with Pat McVicar to see how the OPP were using the MCF, then went back to help Metro Homicide profile a case in Toronto before returning to Ottawa.

Then his phone rang again.

Three elderly women had been brutally murdered in Vancouver. MacKay was asked to review the grisly homicides, two seemed to be the work of a single killer. If MacKay could link all three behaviourally, it meant British Columbia had another serial killer on the prowl—distinguished from a spree killer by the presence of a cooling-off period between murders as defined by the FBI. Two of the women had been killed outside their homes and had sustained severe vaginal trauma; one had been kicked viciously, the other had a broken broom handle inserted up to her collarbone. The third victim appeared to have been killed by someone else. She had been murdered inside her home and suffered no visible vaginal trauma. In fact, she had been violated with plastic candlesticks shoved so deeply inside they were discovered only at her autopsy.

The police had questioned a man whose wallet and ball cap were found in her apartment. He had insisted they were stolen, he'd simply forgotten to report it. However, a hair found on the ball cap tied him to the third victim and he was convicted of her murder.

MacKay had linked the other crimes behaviourally. But the prosecutor was happy with one conviction, and the case was never revisited. No one was ever charged with the other murders. More alarmingly, the man was convicted of a single murder, eliminating the evidence MacKay had seen in the third victim that his violence was escalating. The changed MO had not changed the ritual. His belief that the man was responsible for all three murders and a growing threat, but the single conviction negated all that.

It was history repeating itself. Just as the Crown's office had been satisfied to prosecute Olson on the gun charges and stay the sex charges, once again they had lost any hope of identifying a possible serial killer early. Presenting evidence from all three of these latest crimes could have had the killer designated a Dangerous Sexual Offender and taken off the streets indefinitely. A single conviction guarantees eventual parole, and virtually every study of serial killers predicts that prison is no more than a holding pattern; most, likely all such killers, will resume killing soon after release. That was the real advantage of VICAP or the MCF or any other crime-linkage system. It allowed police to link crimes to a single predator, and overwhelm the court with compelling evidence that the man was an ongoing threat to public safety. Bur it had to work. And it had to be used.

Blind Lady Justice was not the problem; it was the lack of effort, and of understanding that these vile serial predators were the extreme depth of career criminals. Their victims weren't banks or invaded homes that could make good their losses through insurance; these were vulnerable young lives—women, teens, and children— snuffed out in their prime. But until the prosecutors and the politicians and even many in the senior ranks of the police realized that an abomination like Olson was not a fluke of nature, not an isolated case, the investigators in the field would continue to lock up predators one by one and resume chasing them when they were paroled after serving a fraction of their sentence. It made absolutely no sense, but it was easier and cheaper in the short term to ignore the larger threat. Those in charge wanted a bandage, not a cure.

The Major Crime File (MCF) was a classic example of that.

MacKay knew instinctively the MCF had to be fixed, likely scrapped and replaced. Mastering the bureaucratic game to get approval to make VCAS his one-man shop was a coup, achieved with lightning speed by one so new to the game. Tailoring his memos to give his superiors what they wanted without losing what he needed, he got his first break in September when Assistant Commissioner Denis Farrell issued a memo to all Criminal Investigation Branch (CIB) officers announcing the creation of VCAS and asking their help to select regional coordinators in all RCMP divisions across Canada, except Ontario and Quebec, which would be coordinated through Metro Toronto Police, the OPP, and their provincial equivalent to the east, Sûreté du Québec (SQ). Those accepted for Criminal Investigative Analysis (despite the ominous acronym, CIA was merely the formal name for psychological profiling) would be specially trained to meet what was expected to be a growing need. To gauge just how great that need would get, to plot the future by studying the past, MacKay requested sexual assault and homicide data from Statistics Canada.

On November 6, MacKay advised the CPIC Advisory Committee that VCAS would be evaluating the MCF and headed west on his first two-week promotional tour a week later. He had an ambitious agenda with presentations scheduled in Vancouver, Prince George, Kelowna, Nanaimo, and Prince Rupert. At each stop, the first day had MacKay explaining to major-crime investigators what he'd learned at Quantico and how VCAS could help them do their jobs better and faster and generally make their lives easier. The ensuing days were allotted a review of specific cases that the investigators were urged to submit for review to see if MacKay could help. He suffered no delusions, knew exactly what to expect from each audience of potential clients: polite greetings, fixed smiles, folded arms, and unblinking "show me" eyes.

He'd been there himself many times before, patiently listening to the latest brainwave of the newest commissioned officer to show up proclaiming "I'm from headquarters. I'm here to help." Now MacKay was that dreaded apparition across the table.

There were also meetings scheduled with senior Mountie brass, notably Assistant Commissioner Palmer and Chief Superintendent Cummins, to seek their support in selecting coordinators and defining their jobs. MacKay had laid out the duties and selection criteria for VCAS coordinators in a memo in advance of his meetings, sent out over a high-level signature. The nod went eventually to Corporal Keith Davidson.

Unlike E Division colleagues MacKay, Maile, and Sargent, Davidson had known at a fairly early age he wanted to be a Mountie. Raised an "air force brat," he joined the Force in 1975, prompted largely by his older sister's husband, a plainclothes investigator whose stories made the job sound exciting. Determined to work in the field after a stint in uniform with the world-famous Musical Ride, he became a constable investigating sex crimes and missing persons in North Vancouver when MacKay had been the sergeant in charge of Major Crimes. Davidson was good at his job, but the time came, as it often does for those who witness heartache and tragedy up close, that he'd had his fill. Transferred to manage the radio dispatch centre, he discovered, to his surprise, that he was quite analytical.

In 1987, eight years after the RCMP had become the first police force in the world to log its fingerprint files into a computer database, desktop computers were still relatively new and only then being distributed to field investigators, years after every secretary at national headquarters had one. As radio dispatch manager, Davidson was named computer coordinator, responsible for overseeing the installation and implementation of the new system. Boasting zero high-tech skill or knowledge, he began taking computer courses.

The new Reviewer Analyst System, designed to identify similar crime patterns and link cases, was a delayed and partial response to the earlier criticism that the Mounties had no handle on the missing children in the Olson case or what was happening elsewhere in British Columbia. The MCF had been approved but remained operational in name only. MacKay's profiling skills were the cutting edge of what could propel the Mounties into the front ranks of behavioural analysis, but while there were improvements in staff and budget, and a clearer mandate, Davidson found that they still lacked the tools to do their job the way it could be done. State-of-the-art hardware was crippled by archaic software that had been the standard for the 1980s but lagged hopelessly behind the advancements and needs of the 1990s.

What Davidson sought was a new "relational" database, wherein each "field" of information could be specific and consistent. There was simply no consistency in how investigators completed reports: Was the "red" car of one report also the "rust" car of another? Could "concrete" be linked to "cement," and were the words even spelled right? There had to be a way to distinguish between the name "Green," the colour of a suspect car, or the lawn where the body was dumped. Such seemingly minor discrepancies quickly accumulated, making a computer search impractical, requiring an analyst to read each and every document, then try to forge links between similar cases. That might work in a tiny jurisdiction like Prince Edward Island, but certainly not in a vast expanse like British Columbia and definitely not across Canada where cases thought to number in the hundreds would actually number over a hundred thousand! It was nightmarishly frustrating and unproductive. Worse, it was a waste of time, and time lost investigating serial crimes just added to the toll of victims.

When Davidson got involved in 1989, he was initially assigned to

Missing Persons, then transferred to Major Crimes. He realized at once there had to be a better way to input, track, and recall information. Using software for reading blocks of text, he taught himself data processing by trial and error. When MacKay contacted him a year later upon his return from Quantico, his job satisfaction had become a passionate mission. Far more than building a better mousetrap, it was a quest to find or create a Holy Grail that could link crimes, save lives, and get the vilest predators off the streets forever.

Davidson saw the potential immediately, recognized the rare opportunity to make the world a better place, and champed keenly at the bit for a piece of the action. When he got his chance, he exceeded all expectations and drove policing boldly into a new frontier with a prototype system that, in its debut, helped solve in minutes a brutal crime that had stymied traditional investigative techniques for months.

But until that day, nearly two years away, the body count continued to rise across Canada.

Back in Ottawa, MacKay impressed upon his superiors that for him to accomplish what he'd been trained to do, he needed help and needed it now. In particular, he needed a noncommissioned officer with experience investigating serious crimes to research the systems and options and then oversee the transfer of the MCF to VCAS from CPIC. He had hoped to be reunited with Mike Woods, a familiar, trusted, and proven investigator who had helped in the arrest of the young bank robbers in British Columbia, but Woods had just finished French-language training and his boss, Joop Plomp, was not about to surrender such a treasured asset.

Discouraged, but far from derailed, MacKay presented his Christmas wish list to Special Services Branch on December 21, requesting that the position of Sergeant in charge of Major Crime File be created. To elevate VCAS and profiling beyond token curiosity and lip service, to review, repair, or more likely replace the MCF as a way to link serial crimes, he didn't need a lot of people, but he needed good people, hand-picked by him. With the approval of his superiors, he cast his nets upon the bureaucratic waters at national headquarters.

It was lean fishing.

6

Prophets and Allies

As 1991 dawned, MacKay's need for help was evident to anyone aware of his gruelling 16-hour days spent lecturing and consulting on cases. On his first road show west to promote VCAS and profiling, he concluded every presentation by asking the investigators in the room for cases they would like him to review. It was the moment of truth, his gauge of what impact he had made. There was almost always a case or two, but sometimes six or ten, requiring another day just to wade through them to see if profiling could help focus them. He'd made a small dent in investigator resistance but knew he had to keep pounding home his message if he hoped to breach the formidable Blue Wall separating the police from "polite society," and sometimes from each other. It was an invisible but palpable barrier and no one outside of policing circles—not lawyers, politicians, reporters, and certainly not John Q. Public—ever fully grasped just how territorial police forces can be, or how zealously each unit within each force guards its turf.

MacKay had known exactly what he faced before setting out. His reception was never worse than he had expected, and often better than he'd dared hope. A year earlier, he too would have been the cynical cop in the audience, his "show me" skepticism demanding proof that the help being offered truly would make a difference, would simplify his life, help him catch bad guys. He'd have wanted to see how it applied to his real life, not just hear how wonderful it was. Now, he seized each and every opportunity not only to spread the word, but to allay cops' fears that he had any intention of encroaching on their turf. Profilers, he would explain, were not out to steal the power or the glory from the investigators in the field.

There was glory enough for all. All could bask in the shared satisfaction of closing a case, catching a bad guy, getting him off the streets, if only for a while. If they could link a predator to other cases, it would be a giant step toward getting that predator designated as a Dangerous Offender who could be jailed indefinitely. It just made sense to use any tool available that would not only help solve vicious and bizarre cases but help prevent others by catching a serial predator faster.

In room after room of homicide and sex-crimes investigators, MacKay stressed patiently that neither he nor profiling nor a computer would ever identify their suspect or "solve" their cases. They would just point them toward the "type" of people most capable and most likely to commit such heinous and bizarre crimes. He could help steer them in the right direction in those baffling cases plagued with countless suspects or none at all. It was a tool, not a solution. In that regard, it was no different than a polygraph. The result of the lie-detector test was inadmissible, but cops never hesitated to use it to turn up the heat on suspects—or to eliminate them.

All listened, and a few quickly believed—more from frustration to the point they'd try anything to warm a cold trail or close a case than from any sense of conversion—but many complained that if it wasn't evidence, couldn't be used in court, what use was it? This complaint was chronic, recurring at each stop. Police were trained in gathering evidence. They wanted facts. MacKay patiently persisted, explaining again and again that profiling could help lead them to the evidence and facts they could use in court. The younger cops, it seemed, grasped the difference more readily.

Despite remaining a voice in the wilderness, MacKay made early inroads. His track record as a major-crimes investigator stood him in good stead with his audience. His personal appearances allowed him to field questions and address concerns immediately, eye-to-eye with men and women who often plied their trade nose-to-nose. If many remained unconvinced, there was enough favourable word-of-mouth to legitimize his efforts.

There seemed no doubt that being closeted in a room with the investigators he was trying to help was the best way to proceed, but it was also time-consuming. So in a preemptive strike for national exposure, he wrote a short article that appeared in the first edition of the RCMP *Gazette* for that year—a succinct overview of VCAS and profiling. He'd kept it deliberately short in the hope harried and overworked investigators and senior police brass would actually take the time to read it.

The article was informative and a model of political bridge-building. Beyond briefly listing his investigative background and what he'd learned at Quantico to introduce himself, MacKay gave prominent attention to Kate Cavanagh, the OPP "Fellow" then attending the FBI Academy.

Convinced there was strength in numbers, no matter how small the numbers, MacKay was determined to forge alliances wherever and whenever he could. Mounties had no investigative powers beyond drug enforcement and those granted by a handful of other federal laws in central Canada, and could play no role in major rape or homicide cases unless invited in by a provincial or municipal police force in Ontario and Quebec. The OPP was a vital ally and the article, accompanied by photos of MacKay and Cavanagh, served as early notice that MacKay was willing to share, even surrender, the spotlight for the greater good. It stressed that profiling was a "Canadian" police initiative to be shared jointly by the Mounties and the OPP with all police investigators. There would be no turf wars over it. Everyone would benefit if they simply asked for help. All that mattered was that cops across Canada, no matter what their jurisdiction, understand that profiling could help, it was available here, and it should be used.

MacKay's approach, before the OPP had their own qualified profiler, was politically astute, but it went far beyond posturing. It was logical and, in his mind, simply the right thing to do. To let profiling, and whatever alternative system he planned to create to replace the MCF, slam onto the rocky shoals of police jurisdictions would be a sin. Nothing would be accomplished, and innocents would suffer and die needlessly. He was determined not to let that happen.

On March 12, his efforts received a tremendous boost with a high-level overture from J. L. G. Favreau, RCMP Deputy Commissioner of Operations, who forwarded MacKay's criteria for regional and departmental VCAS coordinators to the Deputy Attorney General of Ontario and every Ontario police force with 500 or more members, and invited them to send candidates to attend the first VCAS training session at the Canadian Police College. Favreau left no doubt he fully supported the initiative to share the full range of VCAS services with anyone who would benefit. The ability to profile sexual homicides, serial rapes and murders, arson, and bombings, and conduct threat and indirect personality assessments, would not remain an exclusive Mountie domain.

Fresh from Quantico, eager to spread the word of his new profiling skills across Canada, MacKay was confronted by the difficult, potentially insurmountable problem of police jurisdiction in the two most populated provinces, Ontario and Quebec. Each had its own provincial forces to investigate major crimes and incredibly large and powerful municipal forces in two of Canada's largest cities, Toronto and Montreal. Turf wars, no matter how often or zealously denied publicly, were common, sometimes calamitous.

Quebec posed a particular problem for MacKay. Political tensions were simmering over the Meech Lake Accord, but his concern was far more basic than any heated debate for the future of Canada. Complicating his being an outsider and a "Horseman" was a lack of French. Unlike politicians from across Canada who could speak it— but not well—he had no comprehension of the language.

Then Quebec came calling.

Lieutenant Claude Tremblay and Sergeant Gerry Séguin were polygraphists with Sûreté du Québec, the provincial police commonly known as the SQ, QPP, or QPF. Both men were keen to find new ways to nab more bad guys faster and wondered how MacKay's new profiling skills could be applied to complicated or cold cases in their province. Tremblay called to arrange a meeting. It would give them a chance to check each other out and, if all were happy with what they saw and heard across the table, how best to proceed.

Tremblay and Séguin drove to Ottawa on January 9 and, over lunch and a few beers, all were convinced there was a future for profiling, and for MacKay, in Quebec, and were satisfied that they had much in common and no hidden agendas. The Quebec cops warmed to MacKay's vision for regional coordinators across Canada, proof to them that he was bright and willing to share, not cornering all power in Ottawa but empowering others to liaise between him and the grunts beating the bushes in the fields. The Mountie freely admitted that the duo was a godsend to open the door to a province that was vital to have onboard. He also confessed up front his total inability to speak French, promptly proving it by mispronouncing Séguin's name for the rest of the meeting. Séguin let it slide—for a year—anxious to address more pressing issues.

The first task was to get MacKay some exposure in Quebec. Tremblay and Séguin used their influence to have him invited to speak to an investigative seminar hosted by L'Institut de police du Québec, or IPQ, which was akin to the Ontario Police College in Aylmer and has since been renamed the National Police Academy. The audience would comprise police chiefs, senior managers, and veteran investigators from across the province. Séguin was himself speaking at the seminar about his newly acquired specialty, "statement analysis," and arranged simultaneous translation for MacKay's presentation for the benefit of Quebec cops and officials who were as strong in English as MacKay was in French.

All went well with Tremblay assisting, translating questions for MacKay and applying what the Mountie had already shared about profiling with him and Séguin. The "polite" reception warmed a tad when MacKay tossed the translators a poser, describing one predator as being "crazy as a shithouse rat." Translation stopped in midsentence while the translators passionately debated *le mot juste*, the right word, to translate his colourful idiom, but every cop in the room got the gist. MacKay had cleared a crucial hurdle.

● ● ●

Two weeks after his Quebec coup, MacKay took his profiling message down the road to the Ottawa-Carleton Regional Police. As always, the presentation lasted a full day, and at the end he asked if the investigators in the room had any cases they would like him to review. They asked him to take a look at the baffling case of murdered teenage prostitute Melinda Sheppit.

Nothing about Sheppit, 16, fit the normal pattern for working girls. She wasn't a street kid selling herself to support a drug habit, nor a runaway fleeing family abuse. She had issues with her mother, but lived happily with her father and seemed to be doing well at St. Patrick's high school where she was a full-time student. A neophyte, she had learned the trade with an Oshawa escort agency on the eastern fringe of Ontario's Golden Triangle, the most densely populated area in all Canada, and had been strolling the sidewalks of Ottawa's trendy downtown Byward Market for only three weeks. The teen was last seen getting into a car just after midnight on September 30, 1990. At about 11:00 that same Sunday morning, as church bells tolled in the distance to summon the faithful to worship, her half-naked body was found at the rear of an outdoor parking lot a block and a half northeast of where she'd been picked up.

An autopsy confirmed the girl had been strangled and had been in the early stages of pregnancy. There were no signs of violence or a struggle; it was a "soft" kill in profiling parlance, the "gentlest" homicide the attending pathologist had ever seen. This only served to make the victim seem more fragile and struck an uncharacteristically personal chord with the baffled cops tasked to find her killer. It made no sense. Who would want to kill a kid like this?

The only clue seemed to be a missing mock snakeskin stiletto shoe that MacKay suggested her killer had likely taken as a trophy to remind him of the murder and help him relive it.

A review of the crime-scene photos, autopsy reports, and investigators' notes until well past midnight produced scant insight. MacKay's profile indicated a white male age 25 to 35, an introverted night owl who probably lived with his parents and lacked self-confidence. If that seemed vague, it nevertheless helped the cops prioritize the calls, tips, and leads flooding in. As with Olson a decade earlier, without the evidence to single out a main suspect, they couldn't exclude anyone and interviewed literally hundreds of known sex offenders, violent criminals, and deviants.

MacKay analyzed statements and provided ongoing advice on investigation and interrogation strategies on the case, at one point suggesting new tactics on the fly while monitoring, via closed-circuit TV, the detectives grilling a suspect on another case who was also on the list of Melinda's possible killers. Anything to help the cops find and push the right behavioural buttons for a confession.

But the case remained unsolved. In desperation, the cops called in Dr. Peter Collins, believed by many to be the sole forensic psychiatrist with a Master's degree in criminology in Canada. Collins had ridden on patrols with Ottawa police as a young student, and was well known, popular, and respected for his keen psychological insights to criminal behaviour. It never occurred to the Ottawa-Carleton police to tell MacKay they were bringing in someone else, and Collins had no idea anyone else had already profiled on the case until he was told that his findings were exactly what "the Mountie" had told them.

Collins had hung around police long enough to know he'd just unwittingly crossed an invisible line: he'd been used to confirm or refute an earlier analysis. Professional ethics and common sense made him urge the cops to tell MacKay they'd brought him in to consult on the case.

Just exactly who called whom first remains a topic of lively debate years later, but however they connected, it led to what some consider the most significant encounter since Stanley found Livingston.

Dr. Peter Collins is a wisecracking, fast-talking, compact dynamo who shoots from the quip. His unique expertise in diagnosing mental illness with a special focus on sexual deviance and violent behaviour, is overshadowed on a first meeting by a sense of familiarity. Though a consummate professional, Collins projects a composite television character—the son "Martin Crane" of *Frasier* never had, a psychiatrist happy to work with cops. To the cops he toils alongside most closely, he's "George," the Jason Alexander character on *Seinfeld*. In his younger, bearded days, he was a ringer for the UFO-haunted, shark-clubbing, pre-*Opus* Richard Dreyfuss. Cops liked him easily, respected him because, above all, he was a gifted psychiatrist with the common touch, and the common sense required to cope with life on the streets.

Collins, the only mental-health professional in Canada to work full-time with police investigations, has taken the road less travelled. When he "caught" his first murder in September 1977, he was hooked. Fascinated with law enforcement, he concentrated on policing in graduate school. Collins completed his degree at the University of Ottawa and worked as a criminologist for the territorial government in the Yukon, spending time with the local Mounties. He returned to Ontario, staying in contact with the local police, attending crime scenes and honing his interest in forensics while attending McMaster Medical School in Hamilton. His youngest brother, Evan, also studying medicine at McMaster, suggested Collins should combine his criminology credentials with medicine. It made sense; he was interested in forensic pathology, essentially "autopsy medicine" which applied the law to science. But his interest in things behavioural, largely a byproduct of the fascinating characters he'd met patrolling the streets in Ottawa, led him to the established field of forensic psychiatry. His work was almost always in an operational capacity—where the action was.

At five-foot-six-and-three-quarters, Collins was always the shortest man among the Ottawa cops he worked with, who had to be at least five-foot-ten. Nor did the bearded college kid look the part. But he measured up in his own way, his stellar work with both the Metro Toronto Police Sexual Assault and the Homicide squad leading to his first long-term, paying contract after several years consulting for free. As a consulting psychiatrist, Collins endeared himself to the cops by never pretending to be one of them. By refusing to intrude, he was welcome inside the Blue Wall and ended up working more cases with more police forces than he'd ever have been able to do in uniform.

The cops respected Collins and were comfortable with him because they knew him. So it was no surprise that they asked him to review the Sheppit case independently of MacKay's profile. The Mountie had experience and a proven track record, but he was still the new kid on the block.

The agreement of their profiles boosted MacKay's credibility with the local cops and was the cornerstone of what would become an enduring professional alliance and personal friendship. MacKay, for all his achievements, arrests, successes, and brilliant ideas was, at the end of the day, a cop. Collins was a doctor. More to the point, he was a specialist, working at the prestigious Clarke Institute of Psychiatry at the University of Toronto. That meant a lot at trial. If the streets belong to the police, the hallowed halls are the domain of lawyers. Whether they are in court to defend, prosecute, or judge, they all went to the same schools. All inhabit a privileged world, their *Bleak House* perception of the mean streets tempered by the police huddled behind their Blue Wall. Nothing illustrates more clearly the low regard they can have for police than the Crown staying the sex charges against Olson over the protests of the arresting officers and their plea to at least interview their witness; a decision that was supported up the chain of command without hesitation, back then and to this day.

Such travesties were played out routinely in courts across Canada. They were always blamed on lack of evidence or an unreliable witness, when what the lawyers really meant was the case was too hard, would take too long, cost too much, clog the courts. Without saying it in so many words, it was always the cops' fault. Far too many legal professionals too often dismissed the cops as the Great Unwashed, little removed from the rabble they brought to justice. While the poets among the police might have viewed themselves as the "handmaidens" of justice, to the professionals and politicians they were like the nurses of the legal profession—considered vital to the system, but tragically underappreciated and desperately overworked.

Doctors were different. Like the lawyers, doctors were professionals, had schooled for years, were recognized by the courts as experts, had degrees mounted on their walls, were cultured and refined.

Cops, in the view of many professionals, were often crude louts who collected hats and shoulder flashes, spoke with vile tongues in uncivil tones, drank beer out of the bottle and belched. Collins navigated both worlds with ease—neither he nor MacKay fit their stereotype—and when the two agreed to collaborate, it posed a formidable challenge to the systemic arrogance of the legal system.

Collins was Toronto-born and raised, reared by Jewish parents with strikingly different backgrounds. His mother had survived internment in the notorious Mogilev concentration camp on the Bug River in the Ukraine, which was liberated early in World War II by advancing Soviet troops. His father served with the Canadian Army Show, the entertainment troupe that also featured young comics Johnny Wayne and Frank Shuster. He was the eldest of four children—one brother and his sister are doctors, his other brother is an artist and teacher in France.

His early interest in pathology and human behaviour led him to the streets with Ottawa police in 1977–78. As the investigators got to know him, they began calling him to attend crime scenes. It was, he would always claim, an excellent education by outstanding teachers. It didn't hurt that his mentor was Tom Flanagan, then head of Criminal Investigations and future chief of police. For six months, Collins worked with the newly formed Night Patrol Unit and an "old clothes" squad that would investigate anything and everything. Working from early evening until 4:00 a.m., he'd go home, nap, read *The Globe and Mail*, attend classes, then go back on patrol.

Collins was intrigued with MacKay's efforts. He immediately grasped the significant difference between the art of the Mountie's profiling efforts and his own medically scientific approach to analyzing the criminal mind; most importantly, he understood that profilers had to have a police investigative background. It wasn't medicine and it wasn't magic; it was narrowing possibilities to probabilities, blending investigative experience with behavioural indications at a crime scene. Without a police background, any self-styled "professional" profiler would have as much chance of dissecting a crime scene as a cop would have picking up a scalpel and pronouncing himself a brain surgeon. Consequently, Collins never claimed to be a profiler, has consistently denied any suggestion that he is one, and stresses that to anyone who asks and will listen to the answer.

The novel alliance between MacKay and Collins was not predestined. The genesis of what would become a small behavioural elite in Canadian policing began with the murder of that 16-year-old girl in Ottawa. While nothing could undo it, some good did come from tragedy; Melinda Sheppit left the world a little better, a little safer, than she had found it. Her still-unsolved murder was the catalyst for bringing together two disparate worlds that had clashed in British Columbia over Olson a decade earlier with tragic consequences. With MacKay and Collins working both sides of their respective Walls, it is less likely to happen again. There are women and children alive today because of their accidental meeting.

There were other, more immediate, consequences. The Sheppit case underscored MacKay's need for help. If 1991 was to be the breakthrough year for profiling in Canada, that goal would require his full attention and total effort. Trying to be all things to all investigators, and everywhere at once, was a recipe for disaster. There were only so many hours in the day and MacKay was already working most of them. His plan to base VCAS coordinators across the country would help ease his profiling duties, as they could prioritize cases.

But the MCF lingered in the background and that problem had to be addressed with all haste. By now, MacKay was persuaded—by the few investigators he'd met who had ever used or even heard of it—that the MCF was a well-intentioned failure, easier to replace than repair. But his focus was on profiling; he desperately needed someone to devote their full energies to devising a better mousetrap for linking serial crimes.

Unlike the MCF, he didn't want rocket science. The MCF, designed by information technology specialists, may have been an IT marvel, but it bore no relation to the needs and pressures facing cops in the field. In public studies, cops routinely listed "paperwork" as their top job-related stressor, more feared than taking a bullet in the line of duty. Anyone walking onto their turf with yet more forms to fill out had better be able to prove it would truly help their investigations. The MCF simply offered no evidence of that, and if it came to be associated in cops' minds with profiling, as seemed inevitable, the MCF could seriously undermine MacKay's efforts.

As if he didn't have enough on his plate, the world didn't stop to accommodate MacKay's agenda. In late January, geopolitics reassigned him to protect MP John Crosbie for the nine days of Operation Desert Storm. He squeezed in his presentation to Ottawa Police, and profiled the Sheppit murder, on his day off on January 23, 1991. Thankfully, military victory was quick, perhaps because the American-led allies stopped and declared victory without the bother of eliminating Saddam Hussein, and MacKay was soon free to return to helping Canadians truly at risk—women, children and teens.

His immediate problem and priority was his support staff or, more precisely, lack of it. No revolutionary ever changed the world without the help of others, including the "grunts" who bought the glory with their toil and sweat. MacKay presented his case to Assistant Commissioners Favreau and J. D. "Denis" Farrell, who had chaired his promotion board to qualify him for Quantico. He explained what he had (which wasn't much) and what he needed (which was a lot) to make it work. In short, he needed authority to scrap the MCF and replace it with something better, and for that he needed them to create a position in VCAS and let him recruit someone to help. Naturally, he was told to put it down on paper. With his third draft in fewer days he won immediate approval to recruit a warm body of his choosing.

That would prove harder than getting the approval. Among the legion of uniformed officers at RCMP national headquarters, damned few had ever investigated many major crimes. Frustrated with candidates referred to him by Staffing Branch, few of whom had ever seen a murder scene, MacKay short-circuited the system. He tapped into his network of trusted colleagues with informal queries and obtained career printouts for candidates with a strong background in major-crime investigations. The result was an incredibly short list.

MacKay had already decided to create a new Canadian crime-linkage system by adapting the best aspects of the FBI's VICAP and other existing U.S. systems. Each stop on his first road show west to promote VCAS and profiling had convinced him that the MCF could not, should not, be salvaged. The vast majority of investigators he met had never even heard of it, and the handful who had all complained of excessive paperwork that they felt wasted valuable time better used to interview suspects and collect evidence in more traditional ways. The well-intentioned experiment had become a complicated, cumbersome, time-consuming albatross around their necks. Worse, none of the 800 cases entered into the MCF by 1990 had ever been linked. It had to go.

MacKay, who had introduced Keith Davidson to VICAP specialist Ken Hanfland the previous August at the Canadian Police College and urged them to collaborate, met with them in Vancouver again that November to discuss the MCF and bounce ideas about what any replacement system should have. Hanfland's insights were invaluable. As a Major Crime Specialist with VICAP after it had been launched by the FBI, he now worked for crime-signature pioneer Robert Keppel at Washington State's HITS program (Homicide Investigative Tracking System) to link serial murders. VICAP was undermined by the fact that only 20 of the 50 American States had historically contributed cases, virtually assuring that many serial predators fell through the cracks, free to roam and rape and kill with impunity.

MacKay had learned at Quantico how serial rape often escalated to murder, particularly when it involved one of the handful of sexual sadists stalking the land at any given time. Davidson grasped that concept easily; in his experience as a sex-crimes investigator, sexual homicides were the extreme and inevitable conclusion of progressively more violent sexual assaults.

Sexual sadists were the rarest and most horrific serial predators. They posed a threat and inflicted suffering beyond all proportion to their relatively small number, which was probably never more than 2 to 5 percent of all sexual predators. But the costs of finding and stopping them easily and quickly soared into the millions of dollars because they were the best liars, were the coolest under pressure due to feeling no shred of guilt or remorse, and never attacked unless they believed they could get away with it.

Police in Toronto were learning that for themselves from the horrific details accrued from interviews with the victims of the Scarborough Rapist and facts culled from their hospital charts. They had vainly swept the shadows for that sadistic bogeyman and found nothing. Eerily, his attacks had stopped abruptly the previous May, after his 12th victim. The girl, 19, had been mere steps from home. If Metro police relaxed, unsure why the rapes had suddenly ended but thankful that they had, MacKay could have advised them not to celebrate too quickly. The options were limited: he had died, had been arrested for another crime, or had simply moved on to new hunting grounds. Only a great deal of time, or another victim, would reveal which. MacKay had reviewed Gregg McCrary's FBI early profile based on the first eight attacks and agreed with him: the Scarborough Rapist, if not stopped, would eventually begin killing his victims. It was a clear illustration of the need for a system that could make the connection between serial rapes and later serial murders.

In Vancouver, Davidson warmed to his task and picked Hanfland's brain for any insights he could incorporate into the new system they envisioned. With a little imagination, and a lot of research and hard work, they knew they could produce a system that would prove itself, overcome investigator resistance, and convince the most cynical investigators to take the time and make the effort to complete the forms they would devise.

The forms were critical to success. Any computer database is only as good as the information submitted to it. Nowhere was the concept of "garbage in, garbage out" more true or more threatening to success. There was no margin for error if they ever hoped to get the support they needed, first from Mountie brass, then from detachments across the country, and ultimately from city and provincial forces across Canada.

Any new system also had to be a demonstrable success to politicians at all three levels of government if they were to avoid Washington, D.C.'s grievous oversight that had crippled VICAP. To realize its full potential, the Canadian system required mandatory compliance. Anything less would allow serial rapists and killers to fall through the cracks as they too often did in America. If the politicians would legislate mandatory compliance, make it the law for investigators across the land to complete and submit their forms for all suspected serial cases—or particularly violent, bizarre, or suspicious cases—he was sure he could deliver a system that would eclipse the MCF, surpass VICAP, and be the envy of the world.

Davidson was keen to start, and MacKay tapped his American contacts to get him invited to attend the Minnesota State Sex Crimes Analysis System conference in mid-February. Any misgivings Davidson may have had about leaving balmy British Columbia in midwinter for the arctic cold of middle America was quickly eclipsed by the warm welcome he received. He returned brimming with ideas and bearing armfuls of manuals.

Ottawa posed a steeper learning curve.

On his first day back in Ottawa after his second promotional road show to Halifax, Truro, N.S., Fredericton, and Charlottetown in April, then to Quebec to meet with Montreal Urban Community Police and the Sûreté at the beginning of May, MacKay met with Corporal Greg Johnson on May 3, 1991. The interview went well and he asked Johnson to join him in VCAS to review and replace the MCF. When he learned what was involved, the seasoned investigator initially begged off, admitting he was a "techno-dolt" when it came to computers, that any button more complicated than *On/Off* was beyond his skills.

MacKay disagreed, believing, in fine Mountie tradition, that he'd got his man. He wanted a proven investigator, not a techie. That, in his opinion, had been a major failing of the MCF; it was designed for IT technicians, not the grunt cops who needed to use it. David-

son, who did know his way around computers, was already applying what he'd learned in Minnesota to designing a working prototype in Vancouver, but if Johnson could help devise a system at
national headquarters that he understood, it followed that anyone
could understand it. Luckily, he took it as a compliment, and Johnson agreed to help create a system that would appeal to the investigators in the field, get them talking to each other.

The first obstacle was his boss, Chief Superintendent Mike
Thivierge, who was unhappy to learn MacKay was stealing his best
man. Ordering Johnson not to sign anything, he vowed to carve
MacKay a new orifice. But MacKay prevailed, convincing the senior
ranking officer to surrender Johnson "for the greater good." It took
Thivierge less than a week to find a replacement and Johnson
assumed his new duties on May 8. It became his full-time job the
next month.

Johnson, another expatriate from E Division, was a proven investigator and had led a homicide probe while working at the RCMP
detachment in Surrey near MacKay's old haunts in North Vancouver. He had moved from his birthplace of London, Ontario to
Cooksville at age seven, then to Paris, France, at nine, finally landing
at Waterloo, Ontario, at thirteen. He always considered this last his
hometown.

Johnson grew up wanting to be a "narc," working undercover to
nab drug traffickers and importers. At age 19, he applied for the
Mounties, seeking what he perceived would be life in the fast lane,
but came up short—literally. By *1/16th of an inch* to be precise,
according to the RCMP doctor who told him he didn't measure up
to the Force's standards. Johnson asked him to measure again. And
again. The doctor was inflexible: Johnson didn't meet the minimum
height requirement for federal policing. Short people could,
however, work surveillance as "special" constables. Johnson hesitated at the offer, seeing it as a job, not a career. Finally, though
upset that anyone would quibble over a fraction of an inch, and
more than a little suspicious the Force was lying and that he'd been
"screwed," Johnson took the offer. He was 19, single, and wanted
to be a cop. Simple as that. He reported for duty on January 4, 1974.

Johnson still hoped to convert later to the regular force. That dream was dashed when his older brother, a Mountie corporal who carpooled with Staffing Inspector Ralph Culligan, told him that wasn't going to happen, because if they let Johnson transfer over, it could spark a mass exodus of "specials." Johnson promptly quit.

Finding he was tall enough to be a real cop with Peel Regional Police, he joined that force just in time to participate in the "Mississauga Rail Disaster" and mass evacuation set off by the derailment of a train transporting toxic chemicals.

Johnson had a self-deprecating sense of humour, that rare ability to laugh at himself as easily as at others. He would dramatically recount how he was awarded an Ontario Medal for Police Bravery at the Mississauga disaster for his role in the orderly mass evacuation of thousands of residents in the middle of the night without mishap or looting, then admit the award was presented to "me and a thousand other guys." He would then deadpan how he got no citation for the night he was nearly shot in the line of duty while fearlessly disarming a youth in the dark shadows outside the home of Ontario Premier Bill Davis near Brampton Park.

In that incident, Johnson's partner, Sergeant Dave Hazelton, spotting the light glinting off a gun barrel, drew a bead on the youth and screamed at him to drop his weapon. Then Hazelton, who had survived a year in Vietnam by being careful, stared in disbelief as Johnson strolled into the line of fire, sauntered up to the boy, and gently disarmed him. It was a toy gun, but Johnson hadn't known that when he stepped into Hazelton's sights. He was pleased with himself, so Johnson was shocked to hear that his partner was still yelling. But now Hazelton was screaming at *him*, threatening to shoot *him* for being "a fucking idiot."

It was the maddest Johnson had ever made anyone until that summer of 1991. Then it was "*déjà vu* all over again." One of Johnson's first tasks when he set out to review the MCF was to read the massive user's guide. Handing it back, he told Staff-Sergeant Russ Ward, the NCO in charge of Informatics and a keen MCF proponent, that it was too hard to understand. "That's because you're too fucking stupid," Ward declared before storming off. Johnson didn't argue, conceded it could be true; but he'd never met a good investigator yet who was going to take the time to even skim through that manual. At that moment, he vowed to help exterminate the MCF in any way he could.

On June 25, Davidson met with Johnson in Ottawa to review the MCF while MacKay planned how best to snatch control of the doomed system. Davidson, working on a prototype out west, arranged for Johnson, accompanied by Gerry Séguin from the Sûreté and a member of the OPP, to spend the next eight months touring America, visiting Quantico, Iowa, New York, New Jersey, Minnesota, Washington, and Pennsylvania to review existing crime-linkage systems best known by their creative acronyms: VICAP, HITS, HALT, HEAT, ATAC. He wanted to build a better mouse-trap, not reinvent the wheel.

By early summer, MacKay had added two more promotional road shows—two weeks in Winnipeg. Thompson and Brandon, Manitoba; and Regina and Saskatoon, Saskatchewan; then 11 days touring Yellowknife, Edmonton, and Calgary. The results were predictably mixed. Chief Superintendent Callen, in Winnipeg, understood at once the need for and value of a regional VCAS coordinator for Manitoba, and promptly appointed Constable Bob "Turbo" Urbanoski. As a young innovative inspector, Turbo had solved the murder of Helen Betty Osborne, a shy young Cree stabbed to death with a screwdriver, by arresting four suspects identified by the public response to his newspaper appeal for help when he was posted to The Pas—*16 years after the crime*! By contrast, Callen's F Division Chief Superintendent, Doug Egan, saw no similar need for Saskatchewan and simply attached the responsibility to an existing position already overwhelmed with work. The tours concluded with talks in St. John's, Gander, and Cornerbrook, Newfoundland in early July.

There had been one pleasant diversion amid MacKay's harried pace. On July 4, he lunched with Carlo Schippers, an investigator from the Netherlands, and his Canadian fiancée, Gladys Bourassa, the daughter of a former senior Mountie official. Schippers had recently graduated from Quantico with Cavanagh, of the OPP, and had missed MacKay, still in Quantico, when he had dropped by a year earlier. On that occasion, with time to kill, Schippers had toured CPIC and reviewed the MCF. That was where he had met his future bride—the only match ever made by the Major Crime File.

It was a brief diversion. Three days later, Davidson requested permission to host Project Eclipse in Vancouver. From October 17 to 24, investigators from the FBI, South Carolina and New York State Police, the RCMP, and the OPP, and all VCAS coordinators from Western Canada met to review 25 unsolved murders in Vancouver. For a week, some of the most brilliant police minds on the planet pored over cold cases trying to link them and profile the killers. The collaborative venture proved what could be accomplished at the international level when everyone works together. It solidified alliances on both sides of the border, gave the coordinators their first real taste of the challenges ahead, and gave everyone who participated a revived sense of purpose and ownership in their work.

By year's end, MacKay had won approval to transfer the MCF to VCAS. All eyes now turned westward where Davidson continued tinkering behind the scenes to perfect his prototype Major Crime Organizational System.

He called it MACROS.

7

MACROS Prototype

The only thing more sacred to most cops than their turf is their family. On February 21, 1992, MacKay got a phone call at work from his wife, distraught that she had just received a collect call at home from Clifford Olson. MacKay was not amused. The incident had been all the more devastating because she had answered the phone expecting to hear the voice of her son who had left for Japan a week earlier. She refused the call and hung up, but couldn't understand how the convicted serial killer had gotten their unlisted home phone number. On a hunch, MacKay phoned Quantico.

When Olson had first learned that MacKay was a qualified profiler, he had contacted him periodically at work, anxious to meet and chat. MacKay had declined, explaining that he couldn't justify the expense to meet just with him. So Olson rounded up other convicts. Still, even though MacKay continued to accept collect calls at work from him every month or two, he continued to balk at a meeting. He just saw no point in giving the killer an audience to let him "run off at the mouth." The deeper reason was that he knew Olson couldn't stand the anonymity of prison. It had been more than a decade since he had pleaded guilty to murdering 11 teens and children in the Vancouver area, and he missed the limelight. MacKay had no intention of stroking his ego or feeding him the attention he craved.

Olson had persisted, calling FBI profiler John Douglas, who, in fact, had first alerted him to MacKay's existence. Douglas and Gregg McCrary had expressed interest in interviewing Olson to MacKay at the end of January, but the meeting had never happened. Olson had kept calling Douglas regularly, and during one conversation had asked for MacKay's number. Seeing no harm, and perhaps a way to get rid of the nuisance, Douglas had given Olson what he thought was MacKay's work number but was his home phone.

Douglas promptly apologized for his error and MacKay just as promptly phoned the warden at Kingston to make sure it would never happen again. Life was complicated enough without Olson inserting himself into the mix.

Olson eventually turned his attention elsewhere, contacting virtually every major jurisdiction claiming to have bodies buried in their province, state, or city. He was always clever enough to say that he had an accomplice who was still in their jurisdiction—in other words, that they still had a serial killer in their midst.

A few fell for it. Olson got to breathe fresh air and enjoy a car ride until they figured out that he was "loping their mule," then it was back to prison to start writing and calling around again. What the heck, he had nothing but time to kill for the rest of his life.

Now MacKay's most pressing concern was once more the bad guys still on the outside. Earlier in the new year he had gotten his first call for profiling assistance from Gerry Séguin in Quebec.

On January 9, 1992, exactly a year after first meeting with Séguin and Claude Tremblay to discuss profiling, MacKay had visited Montreal, then driven on the next day to visit a homicide scene at St-Calixte. Reviewing the case on-site reminded him of two other murders that had occurred earlier in Piedmont and Ste-Adèle, Quebec.

In 1987, Louise Blanc, a woman in her thirties, was found dead in the Laurentians north of Montreal; in 1989, the body of Pauline Laplante, in her forties, was found in the same area. Both victims had been tortured before they were murdered. Their killer had then used their stolen bank cards to access their accounts, attempting 16 withdrawals before the automated teller finally "ate" the cards after his persistent efforts to try to withdraw more than the maximum

$500 allowed. It seemed clear to the investigators that their killer was unfamiliar with the intricacies of automated banking.

The cases were so old, so cold they were considered historic. The St-Calixte homicide was fresh, and pins stuck into a map showed a close proximity among all three. MacKay linked them all behaviourally.

Back then, the cops had been working the crime scene for several days before they got their first break—by dumb luck more than investigative prowess. The police had been staying at a hotel quite near where the body was found and the taped-off crime scene tended to draw a crowd. At one point, a woman bystander, staring into the distance, asked them, "What's your man on the hill doing?"

The cops had no man on the hill and, grasping that the killer was likely watching them from a safe distance, had sped to the heights on the far side of the freeway. By the time they got there, the man was long gone. Crouching on the worn patch of ground where he had evidently sat, the cops had peered past the broken and snipped branches and had a perfect view of the distant crime scene. Extending their search, they had located the shrubs that had concealed his parked vehicle.

The present victim didn't have a bank card, but MacKay recognized similar ritual within the crime scene, part of the signature of a sexual sadist. Alarmingly, he also saw a change in behaviour, an escalation in the violence. He felt that the perpetrator was the same one who had killed the two earlier victims and predicted he would kill again within a year if the police didn't stop him quickly.

There was no way to tell where else the man may have struck without a functioning crime-linkage system. Out in Vancouver, Davidson was on the brink of realizing that dream.

Davidson had returned from the Minnesota crime-linkage conference the previous year with wide-eyed enthusiasm. The state's system was just coming online, and in that flush of excitement, he had also had a chance to rub shoulders with analysts from other parts of America who had been using their own systems, each of which had its own strengths and weaknesses. For example, although

Minnesota's system seemed a carbon copy of Iowa's, the first to target rapists and sexual assaults instead of homicides, he felt he could combine the two by adapting what worked and scrapping what didn't.

Davidson fully embraced MacKay's national dream for a Canada-wide system but now saw more clearly how many problems could plague even the earliest stages of such an ambitious venture. The solution was obvious to him: a provincial prototype that could be up and running much sooner. MacKay, knowing better than to stand in the way of a Mountie on a mission, encouraged him to proceed, to work with Hanfland, who lived almost next door, then sagely stepped aside.

Hanfland and Davidson were the ideal marriage of experience and enthusiasm. The former FBI analyst had been a contemporary of Pierce Brooks, who had first envisioned a computerized linkage system while scouring newspapers at a California library trying to link Harvey Glatman's heinous murders. Hanfland had learned well from the master and, after Minnesota, Davidson, like MacKay, believed Washington State's HITS was probably the best system in America.

Davidson set out to build his new system in two phases. First he would address the issue of data entry: the content and relevance of the questions listed in what would become a 10-page booklet for investigators to complete. The second phase would determine what the information meant and make the actual crime linkages. There could be no knockout without a good setup punch.

MACROS evolved directly from the American experience with a few Canadian innovations thrown in, making it the first system designed to catch both serial sexual assaults and homicides.

If it worked, MACROS would mark a huge advance over the American systems. VICAP, the FBI national database, probably the best-known system, could only catch murders; Minnesota's and Iowa's systems concentrated on sexual assaults. Including "survivor" crimes such as rape was an important consideration on several counts. First, there were always more rapes than murders.

Second, and just as importantly, Davidson believed from his years investigating sex crimes that a sexual homicide was basically a fatal sexual assault.

His first priority was to pick the right questions for answers he'd need from investigators if he ever hoped to link their cases. Hanfland's insights proved invaluable.

To avoid the "garbage in, garbage out" scenario that would doom any computer database to failure and oblivion, Hanfland had devised a formula to determine what questions to include on the investigators' form and what to exclude. It was no simple task. Literally thousands of key facts, themes, and clues could surface during a major investigation. They had to be included in the data but the process had to be kept simple enough that the cops in the field would actually take the time and make the effort to submit their cases. They had to believe this new layer of paperwork would truly pay off, would help them find monsters in the shadows. They had to believe that if they could at least answer every question on the form they had done a thorough investigation. The criteria for a question's inclusion became known as Hanfland's Rules:

1. How available is the answer?
2. How reliable is the answer?
3. How relevant is the answer?

Each answer was scored on a scale from zero to three, making the total maximum value for a question nine. Any question that scored seven or higher was automatically retained; one that scored four or less was automatically eliminated. The majority, scoring five or six, were reconsidered and kept if, after discussion, it was determined that the answer would be reliable and relevant, even if not readily available. Similarly, any question that scored low on reliability or relevance was tossed unless a better reason could be found than that the answer was readily available. In other words, the trick was to devise a form with questions that meant something, instead of just being easy to answer.

The early stages of the project enjoyed a level of creativity uncharacteristic for traditional policing. Davidson learned as he went, improvising and improving at each step. He grasped early that the person creating the forms and the person filling them out were likely approaching the task from different perspectives and with different expectations. Analysts would be looking for "themes," most likely a totally foreign concept to the investigators answering the questions. To compensate, Davidson tried to style the questions so that they were also "diagnostic." For example, using "bondage" as a theme, diagnostic questions could relate to neatness, excessiveness, and symmetry—the "what" and "how" answers that could hopefully help link the patterns of signature and ritual to lead the investigators to identify the "who" and "why" of suspect and motive.

Then there were the questions investigators often didn't ask at the outset of a major-crime investigation. What changed if, for example, there were two predators working in the same area at the same time, working alone or in tandem? Did two men prey differently than a man and woman? It was optics. Perception. There was seldom a hard-and-fast or "right" answer. No two people generally looked at the same thing the same way once a variable was introduced.

The problem that Davidson had seen time after time at meetings was people getting hung up on the details of "how would you query that question" instead of ensuring that they had included good "screening" questions. Even then, the system, and the analysis of the submitted cases, would be only as good as the information received. It sounded so simple when Hanfland explained it, but proved surprisingly problematic for others. For that reason, it could never be assumed that everyone understood what had been explained, or grasped the distinctions between the different answer options. It wasn't that the investigators were dim, but a specific reflection of a basic fact of life: there is no "common" understanding of anything.

To overcome that, there was no option but to write a user's manual that defined everything. As a former sex-crimes investigator, Davidson was the first to admit that his attention to detail bordered on "anal" but also knew from personal experience that it was exactly that focus that could win or lose a case in court. If wrong questions were presented on the form, the answers would be meaningless. If people thought they understood, and clearly did not, it was a recipe for disaster. There were no shortcuts. He couldn't stress that point enough. Everyone had to understand that establishing "data entry conventions in advance of any data entry" simply meant, to use a simple example, when "forcing" answers into primary colours, it didn't matter whether you considered "turquoise" was green or blue. There was no right answer, but you had to pick one so everyone would know to enter and search for it. It was the only way to prevent two investigators from describing the same vehicle as both "red" and "rust." It mattered less whether you used "concrete" or "cement" than that it was spelled right.

That was the heart of data integrity. Consistency. Relevance. Of course, such concepts were tedious and boring to investigators. It was the one aspect of the job that everyone wanted to avoid. Davidson's message was clear: Avoid it at your peril because it could make the difference between the success or failure of a high profile, politically sensitive, media driven, multimillion-dollar task force. Screw it up and it would haunt you forever.

Davidson continued researching his prototype, determined to eliminate all possible margin for error. But there were some things over which he had no control.

Without a commitment from E Division command and the city police forces across the lower British Columbia mainland to use MACROS, it was destined to suffer the same fatal flaw that afflicted the American systems. Although the FBI had the only national databases, only 20 of 50 states contributed cases, leaving glaring and potentially lethal gaps throughout the "big picture."

MacKay had agonized over how to secure mandatory compliance even within the RCMP, let alone the outside police forces across Canada. He and Davidson and Johnson, who had been dispatched with Séguin and a member of the OPP to tour America and review existing systems, were horrified at the devastatingly low compliance rate. Investigators in many states and cities submitted their cases as a last resort, and too often only when the mood struck them. There was no rhyme nor reason and there seemed little doubt that hundreds, perhaps hundreds of thousands, links went undetected. The end result was to put Americans, particularly women, teens, and children, unnecessarily in harm's way. As Vorpagel always told his students, thousands of Americans died violent deaths every year. One could only speculate how many could have been prevented if the federal, state, and municipal politicians had *made* the police submit their cases for analysis and possible linkage.

The MCF was an object lesson in non-compliance. Reporting was estimated at 6 percent. That meant that an incredible 94 percent of Canadian police officers, with coordinators in place at the three largest police forces in Canada—RCMP, OPP, and Metro Toronto—didn't know it existed or didn't care, and certainly weren't inclined to use it. No system could function with those numbers against it.

The key to any replacement system was to capture the necessary data without putting any extra burden on investigators that would stop them from filling out the forms. It was a precarious but vital balancing act. Paperwork was consistently at the top or near the top of the list of police stressors and there was no way to introduce a comprehensive system without adding to that burden. MacKay knew it would require an outstanding sales job.

Touring America, Johnson was identifying the same issues. If there was no way to control compliance, to make investigators submit their forms, the problems that crippled the U.S. systems would inevitably plague any Canada-wide initiative. The lower number of crimes in Canada might lessen the problem, but having a bit of a compliance failure was like being a bit pregnant. It would grow bigger.

There was also the question of designing and applying the best technology. By 1992, Davidson benefited from advancing technology that had replaced the room-filling mainframes of Brooks' day with much cheaper, more manageable, and more powerful desktop computers. But it was still all very new, and personal computers were only then finding their way onto investigators' desks.

Davidson had done well with MACROS but it was expected to house and potentially link hundreds of cases across E Division. A national database would have to be able to house and potentially link a hundred thousand. All that would take commitment from senior levels, a budget, a staff. There was an awful lot riding on MACROS making a strong debut. Davidson's system proved up to the task.

In June 1992, a 15-year-old girl walking home from school on the last day of classes in Surrey, B.C. was hit on the head in a blitz attack, dragged into nearby bushes and brutally raped. The rapist made no attempt to conceal or disguise himself and the young victim was able to help a police artist produce a likeness that was published and broadcast by the media.

As with Olson a decade earlier, the assault generated incredible public interest and intense media scrutiny, and, again as in Olson, investigators were quickly swamped with more than 700 leads, tips, and suspects.

Nothing panned out, police had no evidence to charge anyone, and the local Mounties hit a dead end with their investigation. In September, willing to try anything, they turned to Davidson and his fledgling MACROS, which now had more than 800 cases logged on its database. Davidson asked the investigators to complete the 10-page MACROS form, cautioning that they were asking him to pick the right grain of sand out of a sandbox. They completed the form; but at least they would be able to say they had tried everything possible. Davidson keyed the data into the computer, and the room fell silent as it whirred into action.

Within a half-hour, MACROS recorded a "hit."

Then another. And another. Eyes popped. Mouths dropped.

The room buzzed with excitement. After months of dead ends and cold trails, the investigators stared numbly as MACROS linked the Surrey rape "descriptors" to unmistakably similar assaults in nearby Richmond, Burnaby, and distant Prince Rupert where a man with no prior arrests had been suspected of committing a series of minor sexual assaults on young girls. Contacting the police there, they learned that the man had moved to the Lower Mainland a few years later, but the Prince Rupert cops had his photo. The Surrey investigators requested that it be wired to them immediately and promptly arranged it with several others in a photo lineup they presented to the young victim. She pointed to him immediately. Checking further, the cops determined the man had accosted a Richmond woman with a knife in an underground parking lot in February. She had screamed. He had screamed. They had then run off in opposite directions.

Confronted by the Surrey investigators, the man confessed. Russell Dean Wishinski, 23, was charged with aggravated sexual assault in Surrey and assault with a weapon in Richmond. He pleaded guilty and was sentenced to eight years in prison.

The system worked! The stellar debut of MACROS had effects that rippled far beyond the lower B.C. mainland. The impact at RCMP headquarters in Ottawa was such that the brass was finally prepared to sink some money into MacKay's dream for a national linkage system. His first step was to send Johnson south to learn more from the Americans about what worked, what didn't, and why. Johnson was accompanied by Séguin and Sergeant Sharon Olver of the OPP.

Davidson viewed the venture as a political "dog and pony" show, duplicating to a large extent what he had already learned during and after the Minnesota conference. He was probably right, but, as always, MacKay's strategy had a practical aspect. Davidson had warned how vital it was to make sure everyone understood what was being said and done at the outset to avoid potentially devastating problems down the road. Perhaps it was as simple as once again using Johnson as the touchstone: if he understood, it was probable everyone would. If Johnson suspected that was the thinking behind the tour—well, anything for the greater good.

The MACROS database continued to grow. There were another dozen successes, but none that matched the dramatic impact of the debut on the Surrey assault, which Johnson first learned of from MacKay on his return from his American tour. Johnson was convinced that that single case had lit a candle under the foot-draggers at RCMP headquarters who seemed intent on ignoring or undermining MacKay's vision. As an expatriate, he felt that E Division's willingness to proceed alone and develop the prototype system was typical. From what he'd learned about the FBI's reluctance to decentralize VICAP, to let individual states administer regional bureaus as a way to have them "buy in," increase support, reduce interagency rivalry, and broaden reporting compliance, he was convinced they were on the right track with their plan to have the Mounties coordinate ViCLAS in every province except Ontario and Quebec, which would have to have their own provincial police coordinators.

MACROS had marked a particularly rewarding moment for MacKay as well. He believed that Davidson and MACROS had laid the groundwork for a national system that could ultimately link all serial crimes—rape, homicide, arson, bomb attacks, even bank robberies—across Canada, wherever and whenever they occurred. Before he eventually won full support from Assistant Commissioner Joop Plomp, Plomp's predecessor had seemed to favour closing MacKay down and "cutting our losses." If some in high places had believed profiling and crime-linkage were pipe dreams in those early days, MacKay believed that they dismissed his innovations because they hadn't thought of them, didn't understand them, and could find no policy in any manual to control them. When in doubt, the answer for some above him seemed to be to ignore new ideas, hope they went away, and, if they persisted, shut them down at source.

MacKay wasn't going anywhere but forward. Even before Johnson headed south or the dramatic debut of MACROS, he had already doodled the name for the new, nationwide system that existed only in his mind: the Violent Crime Linkage Analysis System.

ViCLAS.

It had a ring to it.

It also didn't hurt that it sounded like the FBI's VICAP. Nothing wrong with that. It would seem more familiar and be that much easier to market. The difference would be that, as MACROS had proved out west, ViCLAS would be able to link serial sexual assaults as well as homicides.

It was an aggressive plan. MacKay would remain the spirit and driving force behind the scenes; Johnson would be the public face of ViCLAS—the welcoming, charming "have a good day" happy face that characterized the 1990s.

MacKay now had a demonstrable success in MACROS, a clever title in ViCLAS, and the sense that he had the right plan based on his experience with the American systems, input from Hanfland, and further in-depth reviews by Davidson and Johnson. That just left the step of actually devising the system. Help came from an unexpected source.

John Ripley and Paul Leury, two bright young computer science students in their final year at Ottawa's Algonquin College, were looking for a worthwhile project for their final semester when they were recruited by Sergeant Bill Hillier of RCMP Informatics. The kids were a godsend: keen, creative, local. And they came cheap—a bureaucrat's dream. To MacKay, Johnson, and Davidson, the students' ability to digest what was important to major-crime investigators and to think "outside the box" to find creative solutions and applications, made them invaluable.

The technological side of the equation finally in capable hands, MacKay had time to promote his national system, still on the drawing boards but benefiting from MACROS' success.

The first public mention of ViCLAS was made at the University of Windsor, host to the first annual conference on serial and mass murder. It was an ideal setting, in the city where MacKay had profiled his first case—the serial rapist—a year earlier, and across the river from Detroit. The press loved it.

But the murder and mayhem just kept on coming.

On April 28, 1992, nearly a month after the Windsor conference, MacKay and Cavanagh, now graduated from Quantico, took a break from helping FBI Agent Roy Hazelwood prepare his equivocal death testimony for a trial in Guelph, Ontario to meet with OPP Sgt. Ron Gentle. Over lunch, they profiled the double Blackburn murders.

The Blackburns were an elderly Toronto couple who supposedly had been at their Orangeville cottage but whose bodies were found in the trunk of their car in the driveway of their Toronto home. MacKay and Cavanagh's profile fit a suspect known then only as "the house hermit" and identified later as David Snow who had abducted a woman in Vancouver and held her captive under a bridge for eight days, then captured another and ordered her to drive all three of them to another location. The women escaped and Snow disappeared into the bush. He resurfaced on July 12, and attacked a 50-year-old restaurant manager who hit the alarm as he assaulted her. By the time the Mounties arrested him in the restaurant parking lot, he had draped a plastic bag over the woman's head and was twisting a wire from a hanging basket around her neck. The woman was unconscious, near death.

After being convicted for the series of abductions and sexual assaults in B.C., Snow was extradited to Ontario, convicted of the Blackburn murders, and jailed indefinitely as a Dangerous Sexual Offender.

In November, Séguin called. The sexual sadist prowling north of Montreal had claimed a fourth victim. It had been nine months since MacKay had profiled the St-Calixte lust murder and predicted he would kill again within a year.

The latest victim had been found tortured and murdered at Deux-Montagnes, her bank and credit cards stolen. In view of MacKay's prediction, the SQ investigators had moved quickly. Even the skeptics were convinced now of the value of profiling.

They caught the break they needed to close the case when the killer used the stolen bank card at a corner store/garage and the security camera caught the man on tape.

Though it wasn't a clear image, the tape revealed that he was standing in line for the bank machine when a woman entered the store. He stepped aside to pick up a chocolate bar, and she stepped up to the machine and withdrew cash. She talked to the suspect and they left together. The man returned alone about five minutes later, got back in line, and withdrew $300 they would later determine was to buy marijuana.

Knowing the time of the woman's transaction, the SQ tracked her through the banking records, unsure if she was still alive. Séguin and another major-crime investigator visited her home, found her safe, and recounted what they knew about her using the bank machine at what time and what place. She confirmed it all, and yes, she knew the man she had left with. *He was her husband!*

Séguin had caught himself a major break. She had used her own card on the day her husband had killed another woman, just before he could use his victim's stolen card—he had no card of his own. When he came back inside alone and used the card, everything had been neatly recorded on the store security camera.

Serge Archambault, 36, was promptly arrested and charged with the brutal first-degree murders of victims Chantale Briere, 24, and Rolande Asselin-Beaucage, 47. After a lengthy interrogation, with Séguin phoning in for progress reports from a bar where he and MacKay awaited word, Archambault confessed to those two murders, the most recent of the four that MacKay had linked behaviourally. The killer then shocked the cops by admitting to another homicide prior to the first two known murders back in the 1980s— that of Anna Maria Cordina, Archambault's former coworker and lover, who had been reported missing to Montreal Urban Community Police by her parents.

When she and Archambault had broken up, she had called his wife to denounce him. Archambault later phoned Cordina to say he'd like to get back together. She agreed to meet him at the food-processing plant where they had both worked and he was a manager. According to Archambault, she had arrived happy, glad to be getting back together; she'd even brought a bottle of champagne. He told her that it was a nice surprise, and that he had a surprise for her too, but first they should drink the champagne. When they had drained the bottle, he told her to close her eyes, then led her by the hand to the garage, through the vacant reception area. Ordering her to keep her eyes closed, he reached into a pile of wooden pallets where he had hidden a knife, held it to her throat, and told her to open her eyes when he counted to three. At three, she opened her eyes and he slit her throat. He pushed her forward and left her there until she quit moving and making noise; then he came back and violated her. Finally, he dismembered her, putting her remains into three garbage bags. All this before the first two known murders in 1989.

The investigators had known nothing of it until he confessed. MacKay was convinced that Archambault had also killed the women in the first two cases he had profiled, but the man refused to admit to them. Why, MacKay wondered, would he admit to three murders, including one the cops didn't know about, but deny two others that seemed so clearly to be his sadistic handiwork? The sadist's reply was as chilling as it was direct: "If I admit them, it'll never end." The implication was that there were still more dead bodies scattered near and far that the police didn't know about, and that he didn't want to talk about.

Séguin also remains convinced that Archambault killed and dismembered a 16-year-old girl who had disappeared a month before the Cordina murder and whose dismembered remains were found in three bags at a landfill site when a bulldozer operator spied an arm sticking out of a bag. But he can't prove it. He excluded another suspect, a neighbour, who passed his polygraph test.

Once convicted of the three murders, Archambault was designated a Dangerous Sexual Offender and jailed indefinitely. He was never charged with the others. No one may ever know how many more women he tortured and killed before the police took him off the streets. In November 2001, alleged serial killer William Fyfe claimed responsibility for the homicides in Ste-Adèle and Piedmont between 1987–89 that had been linked behaviourally to Archambault's murder in St-Calixte. His claim raised Fyfe's alleged tally to nine murders and police feel there are more victims, potentially surpassing Clifford Olson as the most prolific serial killer in Canadian history. He may well have been "the man on the hill."

Curiously, although Archambault met the FBI criteria for a serial

killer—three or more victims with a cooling-off period in between—
the SQ investigators interviewed in the press balked at the term.
They preferred "multiple murderer." Splitting hairs? Or was it a
clear sign that, more than a decade after Olson, now out of sight and
for most people out of mind, Canadian police still toiled in denial?
That they preferred to think Canada was safe from the predators
stalking America?

Séguin tried to share with MacKay the credit for solving the cases,
and duly advised the media that the investigation had included a
psychological profile. But the media drew their own conclusions and
heaped praise on the FBI.

It was just one more frustration in MacKay's battle for visibility
and credibility. Battered, bruised, and bloodied, he often stood
alone, but he refused to give ground or be beaten down by bureaucratic bunglers, short-sighted superiors who could not fathom innovation that did not come gift-wrapped in a policy or procedure, or
knuckle-dragging Neanderthal investigators who simply refused to
see any practical application for profiling. The media dozed through
it all, unaware of the revolution in policing being staged in Canada.

In fairness, perhaps they were just distracted. If, thanks to
MACROS, Snow, and Archambault, 1992 seemed a banner year
for MacKay, profiling, and serial-crime linkage, it was also a time of
excess. The best of times were marked by the worst of crimes: mass
murder in the Northwest Territories and a sexual sadist stalking
schoolgirls in southern Ontario's Niagara Frontier.

Moving back into the shadows, MacKay became the only cop
working behind the scenes on both of Canada's highest-profile
crimes simultaneously. Few people ever knew it.

8

Green Ribbon Task Force

The turbulent history of the first half of the 20th Century—marred by two world wars, the panic of global economic depression and a lethal influenza pandemic—eased into the prosperity of the 1950s. A postwar building boom shrank the world with a network of freeways. Suburbs beckoned with clear air and unlocked doors. Antibiotics eradicated killer diseases. Cops still solved 90 percent of murders by tracking traditional motives of jealousy and greed to the victims' killers, almost always someone they had known.

Then came the 1960s. JFK aimed for the moon and targeted Cuba and Vietnam. The bullet that killed him in Dallas also shot television past daily newspapers as the dominant medium, its unrivalled immediacy, the emotional impact of its marathon coverage of an assassinated president's funeral, and the searing image of his suspected killer being gunned down amid a phalanx of protective police—all broadcast live into our living rooms. Defining moments for a generation, but beyond those heady images lurked unseen and unimagined horrors.

Perhaps nothing shook our complacency like the heinous murder of Catherine "Kitty" Genovese. Attacked steps from her door returning from her duties as night manager at New York City bar, Genovese's pleas for help were ignored by 38 of her neighbours as she was repeatedly raped and stabbed. Her assailant left twice, returning each time to attack again and make sure she was dead. For nearly an hour, no one intervened. One man yelled at the killer from his upper-storey window to leave her alone; another called police, after first phoning a friend to ask what to do, 45 minutes after her first scream for help. The cops arrived within minutes but by then it was too late. Native New Yorkers, who seem to pride themselves on their rude nature and mental toughness, were stunned.

Like the September 11 attacks on the World Trade Center, the impact of the Genovese murder spread far beyond the boroughs of America's largest city. Shock and outrage was felt widely and deeply around the world. Innocence and trust died for many people along with Kitty Genovese that terrible night. Her killer later claimed to have murdered two other women, qualifying him as a serial killer nearly 20 years before the term was coined. From that instant, beginning with the onset of the first attack at roughly 3:20 a.m., March 13, 1964, the world made a little less sense, seemed a little more heartless.

Less than nine months later, on October 27, a baby boy born near Toronto was destined to make this cold, uncaring world an even bleaker, hellish domain. His sadistic rampage would destroy lives, dreams and deprive families of future generations, and alter crime-fighting in Canada, across North America, and around the world forever. The Bernardo family named their new son Paul.

Bernardo abused his first woman in the summer of 1984. He was 19. In May 1987, he sadistically raped his first two victims in Scarborough within a nine-day period. On October 17, he met Karla Homolka in a hotel corridor and swept the 17-year-old veterinarian's assistant off her feet. She had sex with the charming, handsome "older man" less than two hours after meeting him, only her second sexual experience after losing her virginity a short time earlier to a longtime schoolfriend who had moved to the American Midwest. Homolka would soon learn she wasn't in Kansas anymore. Bernardo seemed proud of his conquest until he later discovered she was not the 15-year-old virgin he had thought. But he continued to treat her nicely. For a while.

The Scarborough Rapist had been terrorizing the women of eastern Metropolitan Toronto when McCrary had profiled him after his eighth attack two days after Christmas in 1988. The toll had reached twelve before the attacks abruptly stopped in the spring of

1990. If McCrary's profile predicting a sexual sadist exhibiting escalating violence was right, there was no chance he had simply stopped
his rampage of his own volition. Three immediate scenarios
presented themselves with equal logic: he had been jailed for another
crime, he had died, or he had simply moved on. In any case, he was
likely now someone else's problem. Metro had plenty of other
violent crimes to pursue and, when there was the time and interest,
old cases to review like the still unsolved Alison Parrott murder.

The Scarborough terror resurfaced in the backyard of Niagara
Regional Police on April 6, 1991. At 5:30 that Saturday morning, a
14-year-old girl left home in the Port Dalhousie area of St.
Catharines to walk to rowing practice at nearby Henley Island.
Bernardo, emboldened by his success as a nocturnal predator in
Scarborough, routinely grabbing his victims in a blitz attack within
steps of their home, now gauged his victim and surroundings ideal
to strike again. The teen saw him following her and began walking
faster, alone on a deserted street. Moving quickly, he struck from
behind, clenching his hand tightly over the girl's mouth and nose,
and warned her to shut up as he dragged her across the street,
through a ditch to a path into nearby woods where he sadistically
assaulted her for half an hour. When the victim was interviewed by
the police, her details of what Bernardo did and said to her during
her ordeal were so strikingly similar to what had happened in the
Scarborough rapes that anyone familiar with both cases could have
linked them immediately. Sadly, no one did, and nothing existed to
help make that vital link. Bernardo escaped to strike again.

Next time, the horror would escalate to abduction, torture, and
murder. The cops would initially suspect another man.

On the evening of August 9, 1991, Jonathan Yeo, while on bail
awaiting trial for sexually assaulting a woman he had first threatened with a .22-calibre rifle, and having a history of psychological
problems, wrote a suicide note, pocketed a copy of his bail conditions, tossed that same rifle and ammunition into his car trunk, and

headed for the nearby border crossing into western New York. Questioned by U.S. Customs, Yeo claimed he was driving to Florida, an apparent violation of the bail-imposed order that he be home at his farm near Caistor Centre not far from Hamilton by 10:00 every evening. An inspection of his car turned up the rifle, ammunition, parole release, and suicide note. Yeo was turned back to Canada.

In the short time it took to drive back across the international bridge, a U.S. Immigration officer had alerted Canada Customs and regional police forces in Niagara and Hamilton-Wentworth to be on the lookout for a man he considered armed and dangerous, or at least nuts. All thanked him for his concern but said they had no power to seize a weapon that had not been used in the commission of a crime. Technically, Yeo had not left Canada when he had been turned around. Canada Customs agents were not "peace officers," nor had they Criminal Code power to arrest beyond the authority granted to them under Customs and Excise legislation. It's less clear why the police did nothing, but Yeo motored on, disappearing into the twilight shadows a little after 7:00 p.m.

Two hours later, Nina de Villiers, 19, vanished while jogging alone along a footpath around her father's athletic club in nearby Burlington. A massive search produced no clue to her disappearance. Nine days later, her body was found in a marsh outside Napanee, near Kingston in eastern Ontario. She had been raped and shot in the back of the head with a .22-calibre rifle. Yeo had disappeared, but he resurfaced two days later in Moncton, New Brunswick, where he promptly raped and murdered Karen Marquis, 29, shooting her in the back of her head with his rifle.

Then he vanished again.

Sergeant Mick Riddle, of the Niagara Regional Police Organized Crime Intelligence Unit, was among those who felt certain that Yeo would inevitably return home to his wife. Well versed in electronic surveillance, he had watched Detective Greg Hyatt, a technician from his unit, hunt and peck through hundreds of wires bundled into a switch box until he found the right one, then tapped a D N R—dial number recorder—into Yeo's phone line. The D N R would monitor all calls to and from Yeo's home. It was cutting-edge technology in

1991, but it had limitations. It would alert police to all incoming and outgoing calls at that telephone, and record the time a call was made or received and how long the conversation lasted, but it could not identify the source of any incoming calls. That meant those monitoring the calls had to play the odds that Yeo would call home, then deduce which call had been placed by him.

There was no option to the potentially deadly game of cat-and-mouse. All the cops could do was wait and hope, aware that just three months before his current rape-and-murder spree, their quarry had been charged with sexual assault, forcible confinement, and uttering death threats for allegedly brandishing a gun and a knife while assaulting a Hamilton-area woman. He had been released on $3000 bail. No one had thought to ban him from access to firearms. Then the cops could have seized him at the border-crossing bridge for violating his bail and at least two young women could have escaped being raped and murdered.

Yeo eventually called home as expected. When he was spotted driving through Hamilton, police were alerted and a dramatic high-speed chase ensued, complete with wailing sirens and screeching tires. After several city blocks, nearly a dozen Hamilton-Wentworth squad cars finally cornered Yeo in a shopping mall parking lot. Ringed by officers, all pointing their guns at him and screaming at him to surrender, Yeo sat silently in his car for several moments, then shot himself in the head with the same rifle he had used to kill Marquis and de Villiers. Riddle got the news that night when he was paged aboard the boat he had chartered to take his father fishing for pickerel as a Father's Day gift at Port Burwell, south of Tillsonburg.

Yeo's suicide was a golden opportunity for the cops, anxious to close as many unsolved crimes as possible, to link him to other unsolved violent crimes. It was standard procedure. With no opportunity to interrogate him, no chance for him to confess or deny responsibility for any of them, who was to say he hadn't committed others? More homicides were going unsolved longer. No cop on the planet wanted an open case on his desk that just kept growing colder and dustier with no new leads. If Yeo had raped and murdered two young women half a country apart, it seemed logical to assume he'd committed others.

And there were plenty of others. There were 17 murders in and around Hamilton in 1991, second only to the 19 killed in 1983, a record loss dating back to 1801. Alarmingly, the victims were getting younger. The average age in 1983 was roughly 45; in 1991 it was about 30 and included several teenagers, including the high-profile disappearances of de Villiers in April and Leslie Mahaffy, 14, of Burlington, in June.

The latter murder had been particularly troubling.

On Friday, June 14, 1991, Mahaffy had stayed out late with friends at an informal wake for schoolmates killed recently in a car accident. She missed her 10:00 p.m. curfew and came home to a locked house early next morning. She wasn't seen again until her dismembered body was discovered in shallow Lake Gibson near St. Catharines two weeks later. Police had no real leads, certainly no evidence linking Yeo to the murder, but Niagara Regional Police Inspector Vince Bevan was convinced Yeo had killed Mahaffy and obtained a warrant to search the dead killer's property—farmhouse and outbuildings including a slaughter house and the surrounding acreage—for evidence tying him to her murder. The exhaustive search produced nothing, virtually eliminating Yeo as a suspect. The last doubt faded the following spring when Kristen French, 15, was abducted in broad daylight, and in front of several passing witnesses, while walking home from school.

April 6, 1992, the day before Good Friday, was a slow news day. The first reporters were on the French case almost as soon as the cops. The media circus had begun.

Just days prior to the disappearance of Kristen French, Ontario Deputy Coroner Dr. James Young convened an inquiry to review the abduction and murder of Nina de Villiers. Those who had thought the terror in the Niagara Frontier had died with Yeo now grudgingly accepted the possibility that Yeo may not have killed Mahaffy. French's abduction underscored what no one wanted to admit, that, against overwhelming odds, there were likely *two* sexual predators stalking the same area at the same time. To their knowledge, that had never happened before. There were no manuals or policies for this situation and no one now expected the horror to end anytime soon. To admit that publicly would be to invite public panic, media hysteria, and career meltdown. The priority became immediately twofold: catch the predator and console the French and Mahaffy families through the dark days ahead.

The toughest job in the world likely falls to the cop who goes to the door of strangers to tell them they've lost a child. It is hard when it's an accidental death; tenfold harder when it involves violence or foul play. From that moment, the investigators want nothing more than to find the killer, not just out of a sense of justice, but out of a desire to be able to go back and knock on that same door and talk to people who are no longer strangers and tell them they have found the predator who killed or hurt their child. In fact, the hunt for a killer or a rapist or a kidnapper often has less to with some ephemeral notion of "justice" than it does with "family."

With Yeo dead, it would be bad enough for another lone predator to abduct, rape, and murder, but, if the eyewitnesses were right, this time there were two, operating as a team. An early FBI profile alerted the cops to expect to find a "dominant" predator and "subservient" accomplice. No one suspected they were a couple— that the devil they were chasing had taken a bride who was helping him abduct teenage girls.

There was no panic, not yet. Some people, notably teens who consider themselves invulnerable and immortal, took few precautions to avoid joining the list of victims. But the fear was palpable, almost choking, and the concern was not limited to the Golden Horseshoe. One irate caller to an Ottawa talk radio show angrily chastised some girls he had seen hitchhiking days after the French abduction in the same general area from where she had been taken. Had they no fear? No sense? Did their parents not know what their daughters were up to? Of course, they were just being teenagers—a singular reason why youth is such an inviting and vulnerable target for predators.

The police had very little to go on. From everything they'd learned from French's family and friends, she didn't seem the type to expose herself to danger. She was an excellent student, athletic, popular with her peers.

Among those dedicating themselves to finding Doug and Donna French's stolen daughter was Mick Riddle, an experienced and decorated major-crimes investigator, who, as an Intelligence sergeant, had tapped Yeo's phone line. This was a rare case that he took personally. As a father, as much as a cop, he wouldn't rest so long as this predator was stalking *his* backyard. He was no profiler, but experience had taught Riddle that this monster must be stopped. Now!

Mick Riddle grew up a cop's kid in Thorold, Ontario, not far from Niagara Falls. His father, Sandy, was a "scrapper," who rejoiced in his frequent dustups with the tough Cape Breton lads sailing through the Welland Canal. Sandy spent his entire career as a beat cop and loved every minute but discouraged his son from following in his footsteps. Still, the job appealed to Mick. He stayed in excellent shape playing hockey and baseball and had no problem growing up a local cop's kid, but drew the line at the thought of arresting old school chums. At age 19, he applied to several local forces right out of high school, and considered joining the OPP or Mounties. Anywhere but Thorold. Too many friends among the 8000 people in his hometown. Better to bust strangers.

Fresh out of high school, Riddle was shingling a house in July 1970 when the homeowner called him to the phone. It was the Thorold police chief calling. He had agreed to be a reference to help Mick get into the Law and Security program at Niagara College, but he had an unexpected vacancy, needed to fill it right away, and invited Riddle to compete for the position. It meant starting in his hometown, but he could transfer out when Thorold joined the new Niagara Regional Police in January. Riddle asked for a couple of hours to think it over. Back on the roof, he lost his footing and began sliding off. Sailing over the edge, he saved himself by grabbing the eavestrough on his way by. Dangling in midair helped clear his mind; policing couldn't be much more dangerous than roofing. He wrote the recruit exam that night, and was back on the roof, moving carefully, two days later when his mom called to say he got the job.

Over the years, Riddle had earned a reputation as a good investigator who spoke his mind. Despite his candour, he had risen to sergeant. When Bevan was named to head the Green Ribbon Task Force, created to investigate what was now recognized as the dual abductions of Mahaffy and French, he asked Riddle to join him and several other seasoned investigators working as an intelligence liaison officer and as an investigator. It put him at the heart of the case as the task force expanded to include the OPP and city and regional police forces east of Toronto to London in southwest Ontario.

If the miscalculation on how long Kristen French had been held captive was understandable, it was less clear how a golden opportunity to track the car she had been forced into was squandered. It was the first serious misdirection for the task force and came during a televised dramatic reenactment broadcast throughout the Golden Horseshoe with an appeal to the public to call in any tips or leads they had, no matter how inconsequential they might seem. FBI profiler McCrary appeared on camera and OPP Inspector Kate Cavanagh, his Quantico-trained counterpart, made her TV debut as a profiler, both of them intercut with studio interviews with Bevan and a Camaro parked on stage—a visual prop that took on a life of its own.

As all this occurred outside of Mountie jurisdiction, MacKay was relegated to a bystander. Had he been on hand, he might have pointed out what he later noted the first time he saw a tape of the program. While the program had been dubbed with eyewitness voiceovers describing the car used to abduct French as a Camaro "or similar" vehicle, the prop Camaro was the repeated focus. Thus, *a* Camaro or *similar to a Camaro or Firebird* became *the* Camaro by the end of the program.

The die was cast. In short order, cops in Niagara and Hamilton-Wentworth, the OPP, and city and regional forces patrolling northeast of Toronto southwest to London were stopping or visiting Camaro owners, inspecting their vehicles, and issuing them tags as proof they had been checked and excluded from the investigation.

No one bothered checking Bernardo's sporty Nissan, the "Camaro-like" car that he'd used to smuggle cigarettes into Canada, abduct Mahaffy and French to the home he shared with his new bride, Homolka, and transport their lifeless bodies to preselected drop sites.

It was no doubt an honest oversight under trying circumstances, but the police, by droning on about the Camaro, had excluded other makes of sports cars in the minds of the public, the press, and, worse, the investigators.

If Bernardo had watched the program, it must have reinforced his belief that those chasing him weren't bright enough to catch him, a typical trait of a sexual sadist. If they couldn't get the make of his car right, what chance did they have of following his trail of brutalized rape victims from Scarborough, east of Toronto, west to Mississauga, then south to the Niagara frontier? He had matched the police artist's composite drawing of the Scarborough Rapist, and had volunteered his DNA for testing when asked by Metro Police, fully aware it could link him to the Scarborough rapes but apparently willing to take that calculated risk, another trait of a sexual sadist. He had been among the thousands of suspects interviewed by Metro Toronto and Niagara Regional and had walked. They had found Bernardo's first murdered victim's remains on his wedding day as he prepared to honeymoon in Hawaii, then exhumed them for forensic testing after finding his second. Nothing had happened. No one came to his door. All the cops had was the wrong car and in describing his accomplice, no one on TV had once uttered the word "she."

For their part, the cops were overwhelmed with tips and leads that poured in after the TV reenactment. As with Olson a decade earlier, there was no shortage of suspects. Bernardo was on their list, and they had interviewed him. But he was one of thousands. With no prime suspect, and there was certainly no evidence at that point to rate Bernardo a prime suspect, they could not afford to exclude anyone. If an investigation was complicated or heinous enough to warrant a task force, it meant that the police faced the dismal, time-consuming prospect of sorting through an apparently endless list of suspects unless they lucked out: got a confession, a DNA match, or someone walking through the door claiming to know the identity of the killer *and* able to prove it. Anything less was little more than by guess and by golly. The veteran cops were savvy enough to know they had probably interviewed the killer, sat across the desk from him, and let him lie his way back onto the streets. To Riddle, it was as frustrating as it had been nearly two years earlier to watch Greg Hyatt search through hundreds of wires to find the right one to install the DNR on Yeo's home phone line. It was no easier to pick the right guy now than it had been to pick the right wire then.

Tragically, the problems plaguing the police were twofold: information overload on the one hand and failure to pass on potentially vital information on the other. Despite Bevan's pleas to police outside the task force to immediately forward any suspicious incidents involving young women, it didn't always happen. A young woman had accurately described Bernardo, his car, and his licence plate in her complaint to police that he was following her. That was after the Henley Island rape and eight months before the French abduction. Two young sisters later complained to police that a man was videotaping and following them. The older sister tracked him to Bayview Drive on the weekend two days after French was taken. She called in the information again, citing the report number from their earlier complaint. She had one digit wrong on the licence plate. The complaint was dismissed; the information was never passed on. And inside 57 Bayview Drive, Kristen French spent her last night alive. The next day, Easter Sunday, she defied her captor, refused to comply to his sadistic demands and drove him into a murderous rage by declaring, "Some things are worth dying for." He killed her.

Then he went with his wife to her family's home for Easter dinner.

Not yet aware of the costly breakdown in communications that had cost them their last and only chance to rescue French, the cops pulled out all the stops on all other fronts. At one point they summoned a psychic who duly conjured up a vision of a body. The cops found it right where she had predicted, but, to their dismay, it was a victim from another murder they had known nothing about.

Out of desperation or inspiration, Bevan made a bold gesture on a virtually unprecedented scale. While small groups of investigators routinely meet formally or gather informally to review cases and share information, Bevan threw the doors wide open, inviting anyone and everyone he thought could help solve the Schoolgirl Murders. High on the list were behavioural experts who could review the case in a new light. MacKay was soon working closely behind the scenes with Cavanagh, Collins, and McCrary.

The skeptics also arrived in force.

Whatever its formal title and aspirations, the gathering of veteran cops was commonly referred to as the "Think Tank." Opinions were shared, disputed, and defended. More than once, the discussions continued over a late-night drink, a less formal arena which encouraged frank exchanges between the emerging factions of veteran investigators who debated whether they were chasing one killer or two.

Many of the traditionalists argued that the cases were as different as night and day. Literally.

Leslie Mahaffy had disappeared late at night from what should have been the relative safety of her own home, or at least her neighbourhood. She had not been held captive long. Her dismembered remains, concealed in concrete and underwater, indicated no clear time, cause, or place of death. Kristen French, on the other hand, had been abducted in broad daylight on a busy street in front of witnesses, held captive for nearly two weeks (as they believed then), then abandoned in a public place, her long hair cut short but otherwise intact. Whoever had abducted her had had an accomplice, and there was simply no evidence that was the case with Mahaffy. The differences were just too great for it to be the work of the same killer, the traditionalists argued. Too many differences and loose ends to connect the cases.

MacKay disagreed.

Applying his profiling skills to what he knew of the cases, the Mountie was equally sure the same predator had abducted, tortured, and murdered the two girls. Everything he knew about the cases pointed to the handiwork of a sexual sadist. Once a victim was in his grip, it was almost impossible to escape. A sadist wanted power, not pleasure, and forcing his helpless victims to endure deviant sex was just his way of savouring his absolute control over their life and death. By the same token, he didn't kill them to prevent his victims from identifying him; he killed them because he enjoyed it. This was no Jonathan Yeo wacko who blitzed, raped, and shot his victims, then fled.

The Schoolgirl Murders were the prolonged, deliberate, scripted work of a disciplined control freak, driven to extreme deviance by insatiable fantasy. While that core fantasy, and the killer's ritual, would remain constant, his changing MO was revealed in how he had disposed of his victims' bodies. He had taken great pains to ensure that Mahaffy would never be found. When she was, he deliberately dropped French's body where it could be found in a different jurisdiction that he believed would distance himself from his crimes and lead the cops down the wrong dark paths and cold trails. Quite simply, when his first attempt failed, he learned from that experience and adapted.

MacKay and McCrary, Collins and Cavanagh all agreed the killer was leaving a false trail, trying to lure the cops in the wrong direction. He had no sense of grief or remorse for the anguish he had inflicted on the families of the victims, nor the horror he had unleashed on the community. His one and only concern was for himself—that he not be caught. Everyone else, including his subservient assistant, was expendable, to keep him free.

The three profilers and Collins, the forensic psychiatrist, were unanimous in their view that they were chasing a sexual sadist. That rarest breed of sex offender commonly wreaked havoc and headlines beyond all proportion to their numbers. They were the most brutal, the most cunning, the most organized predators stalking the planet. Sadists revelled in the suffering of their helpless victims. They got their kicks by inflicting physical and psychological pain, savouring the anguish of their victims and their absolute control over them, extending to their power over life and death in the end. They lived out their deviant fantasies through domination, control, humiliation, pain, injury, torture, forced sex, and violence. It was all scripted, instructing their victims verbally or in writing, what to do, what to say, how to please them, how to praise them, often recording their suffering to relive later.

Sadists are as predictable as they are cruel and cunning. They use a ruse, some innocent pretense, to make first contact with their victims, and then gain their confidence and put them at ease. With their quarry off guard, the sadist would turn on them suddenly, threaten or beat them into submission, and then abduct them to a preselected destination, often his home, a forest, or an equally remote haven, perhaps even forcing the victim into an elaborate homemade cage or coffin-like box—any place that offered solitude to the sadist and little chance of escape or rescue for the victim. Once they had their victims in their power, they would take their time, subjecting them to sexual bondage and brutal sexual deviance, raping them anally, orally, and vaginally with foreign objects like bottles, plumbing pipes, or branches. Whatever caused pain and terror.

When the sadist wearied of torturing his victims, he almost always killed them. Death marked the end of the fantasy, the final control over the victim. Most strangled them with their hands or a ligature, believing it more "intimate" than a gun or knife. They would keep incriminating evidence as trophies: secret calendars, maps, diaries, drawings, letters, manuscripts, photographs, audio- and videotapes, media accounts of their crimes, their victims' driver's licence, jewellery, clothing, and photographs.

Reviewing the evidence from the Schoolgirl Murders before leaving to profile another murder in Truro, Nova Scotia, MacKay saw an opportunity to add a new twist to the task force. The cops were planning a massive door-to-door area canvass, and he worried that without focus, it would be more costly and time-consuming than helpful. Insisting that "where" the trail led was as significant as "how" the crimes had been committed—Mahaffy had been abducted in Burlington, her remains found in Thorold, Riddle's hometown near St. Catharines; French was taken from St. Catharines, found in Burlington—MacKay urged Bevan to bring in Constable Kim Rossmo, of the Vancouver Police Department (VPD). Rossmo had spent years of his own time and wads of his own money to devise a computer program that could predict with mathematical accuracy where to look for a serial predator. His research had determined that human predators were no different than the lions of the Serengeti or shoppers on a spree when it came to choosing their hunting grounds, search routes, and targets.

Rossmo had even devised a catchy name for his program: "geographic profiling." No one else had heard of it.

MacKay had been introduced to Rossmo as someone he should get to know on November 22, 1990. The Mountie had been lecturing on profiling and VCAS at the B.C. Justice Institute and, over lunch, Rossmo explained how he had programmed a computer to show the most logical place to look for a serial criminal. MacKay was immediately intrigued, thought it had merit and saw its potential. But could Rossmo's theory be applied to actual cases? That was the test. In a way, it was Rick Mather all over again. MacKay and Maile had seen no immediate need for profiling until Olson brought "stranger" murders to Canada with a vengeance. Now, as then, MacKay was willing to believe, provided Rossmo could satisfy his sole criterion: "Show me."

Rossmo did just that. A heartbreaking child abduction in Alberta converted MacKay to the power of geographic profiling and forged another vital alliance in the war against serial predators.

In June 1991, while taking his promotional road show to Yellowknife, Edmonton, and Calgary, MacKay sat in on Rossmo's lecture to a class of detectives in that last city. He was overwhelmed by the brilliant presentation on two counts: Rossmo was clearly a genius, and the cops in the crowd didn't have a clue what he was talking about.

Chatting later, he urged Rossmo to use less technical language— smaller words—for his police audiences, and clarify his presentation by using a case study. Rossmo considered MacKay an experienced "realist" and took his advice to heart. Once he had simplified his presentation, and the detectives understood how geographic profiling could help locate serial predators, their resistance cracked. Not all were converted, many dismissed it as "voodoo," but a growing number of detectives spread the word.

Rossmo stressed to his audiences that it would still be like finding a needle in a haystack, because geographic profiling, like behavioural profiling, would never solve a case, never identify the killer or rapist. It was an investigative tool, no more, no less. Though no substitute for a thorough investigation, it could help avoid wasted effort and lost time, save money and lives. In short, in complex or bizarre cases, it could help lead to an arrest sooner rather than later or never. A geographic profile offered a variety of new investigative strategies to help solve major cases. Confronted with a field full of haystacks, Rossmo could mathematically predict the best haystacks to check first.

Given his background, it was no surprise that Rossmo had been talking over the heads of his audience without ever meaning to or possibly even realizing that he was.

He had been a high-school math whiz kid in Saskatoon, Saskatchewan, a boy genius bored by homework who could calculate complex trigonometric tables faster in his head than his classmates could copy their completed assignments onto the blackboard. To his annoyance, the teacher didn't marvel at his abilities but docked him marks for not doing his homework. For a lad who had taught himself calculus in Grade 10, and was studying Grade 12 "trig" in Grade 11, it seemed unjust. A frighteningly brilliant teenager is no less a teenager for his brilliance and Rossmo sought retribution the following year. He had the same teacher for Grade 12 algebra and, after the first week of classes, won permission from his principal to write the provincial final exam. He scored 100 percent—and another free period, excused from algebra class.

Like Maile and MacKay, Rossmo had no early police aspirations. Unlike MacKay, whose fighter-pilot aspirations were flamed by trig, and Collins, the forensic psychiatrist who had battled numeric dyslexia from childhood (adding "Rain Man" to his OPP nicknames) and claimed to be the only physician in Canada with only Grade 9 math, Rossmo envisioned a career teaching university math. He was particularly fond of topology, the study of "geometri-cal properties and spatial relations unaffected by continuous change of shape or size of figures" according to the *Oxford English Dictio-nary*. In plain English? Rossmo could predict where Jack the Ripper lived. Or worked. Most likely.

Rossmo's career epiphany hit while he was staring out his window during math class at the University of Saskatchewan. Worried that an academic life would not be exciting enough, he craved a different challenge. He took a year off to work as a private eye, and continued the job when he returned to his studies. His girlfriend back then suggested he study criminology. Still in his early twenties, with a B.A. in sociology, he checked out the Mounties, city forces across Canada, and the Royal Hong Kong Police Force. Toronto and Vancouver were the clear leaders; both had universities that offered a Master's degree in Criminology. He'd lived part of his childhood in Vancouver and loved the city, but had never learned to swim, a requirement for cops there.

With his hopes for Toronto dashed by budget cuts, he called the YMCA and took the plunge—literally—and learned to swim. Never a man of half-measures, he later learned to scuba-dive well enough to make night dives in the Caribbean and open-ocean deep-water dives. After joining the VPD, and completing the three-year Police Academy training program, he enrolled in the Master's crimi-nology program at Simon Fraser University (SFU).

Rossmo enjoyed patrolling the streets, particularly the roads and alleys of Vancouver's Skid Row. From the earliest days, he had a sense of the geography and local movement patterns of life on the streets, ranging from areas of high-traffic volume to preferred corners staked out by local hookers. He also had a creative knack for resolv-ing disputes. Patrolling with Toby Hinton, a young new partner he was "breaking in," Rossmo was called to settle a tenant problem at a seedy hotel on Hastings Street. The owners were sprucing up the building, trying to clean up its image, and clear out the least savoury tenants, to elevate it to a respectable Skid Row flophouse. That meant evicting their criminal clientele, but the property conversion put it under the control of a different bylaw. Instead of the usual 24-

hour notice to evict, tenants had 30 days. That presented a problem with one resident who, that morning, had physically threatened another tenant. His victim was too intimidated to talk to the cops.

Rossmo and Hinton assured the manager that they'd talk to the man alleged to have issued the threat. They went up to the fourth floor and knocked on the door of a large pimp, well known to the cops for his violence, and his druggie hooker girlfriend. Both were streetwise; neither was in any way intimidated by the arrival of the two cops. The pimp waved the eviction notice in Rossmo's face and smugly declared he had 30 days to party hearty, which the cop interpreted as a thinly veiled threat to be problem children for their neighbours and management in the coming month.

While Hinton diligently recorded the man's information and ran a check for outstanding warrants that could resolve the apparent standoff with an arrest, no "wants" came back.

Rossmo asked to see the eviction notice and the large man smugly handed it over. While he continued to rant, Rossmo studied the clause, "You must vacate the premises by the end of 30 days." After a few moments of deep thought, he took out his pen, stroked out "days," wrote in "minutes" and handed it back without comment. The pimp and the hooker were stunned into silence. Hinton stared in wide-eyed disbelief.

The pimp finally asked, "Can you do that?" Rossmo shrugged, and replied "I just did." The "streetwise" couple rushed around the apartment, cursing a blue streak as they tossed their meagre possessions into plastic garbage bags. Half an hour later they were walking down the street looking for a place to live. Only then did Hinton ask Rossmo if he really could do what he did. Well, said Rossmo, he *could* do it, but it sure didn't mean anything.

It was stellar police work. In street poker, you needed to know when to bluff and when to hold. Hinton laughed—and may have caught the theatrical bug that day, going on later to his own creative fame with the Odd Squad and their National Film Board Production of Skid Row drug life, *Through a Blue Lens*.

His gift for persuasion also helped Rossmo talk his way into the Ecology of Crime course taught by Professor Paul Brantingham,

Chair of Graduate Studies in the SFU Criminology Department, and later convince the faculty he could handle a full-time Ph.D. program while still working the streets and going to court as a patrol cop.

Paul Brantingham, who would later become Rossmo's academic mentor, and his wife, Professor Patricia Brantingham, had devised a "Foraging Theory" that indicated where criminals were most likely to operate on the basis of their activity space—where they lived, worked, played, and the travel routes between. Rossmo was fascinated. He had never been exposed to anything like that before and quickly saw how what he learned in the classroom applied to the streets. Patrolling the core area around Hastings, Main, Powell, and Water streets, Rossmo observed that the hookers had favourite corners and drug dealers their market areas. In foot chases, he noted the fleeing felon often followed a specific route and tended to turn in predictable directions.

Rossmo was intrigued and challenged. If that academic theory was validated by reality on the street, how else could it be used? Turning his attention to predators, he studied the "Foraging Theory" as part of his doctoral research and found the concepts could be applied to everything from the hunting patterns of the lions of the Serengeti to the shopping patterns of suburban housewives. In all cases, whether killing or buying their dinner, they had to find their target, minimize the time and effort to catch/buy, and avoid obstacles that could range from the police to traffic jams to a larger, meaner animal. It all led to Rossmo theorizing that if the Brantingham model worked to predict a criminal's hunting grounds, the reverse, finding his home or workplace on the basis of where he had committed his crimes, should be possible. When it came to human predators, he believed that, having first linked the crimes, for example proving that seven rapes in the same geographic area were the work of one rapist, not seven, you could apply mathematical algorithms to indicate where he most probably lived or worked. That concept became his doctoral thesis and the genesis of geographic profiling.

In May 1991, while researching Japanese policing methods, an inspiration came to Rossmo while he was riding a Bullet Train south of Tokyo. He scribbled his idea onto a couple of napkins, took them home, and spent the next nine months learning to write a computer program that would allow him to profile a geographic area as he had long believed he could.

By then, his simplified presentations had MacKay a believer. But Rossmo was still thinking only in terms of colourful 3 D map overlays until Vancouver Staff Sergeant Doug MacKay-Dunn, his boss at the Coordinated Law Enforcement Unit (CLEU), a multi-force unit in British Columbia designed to investigate all aspects of organized crime, suggested it could also be an excellent investigative management tool. By the time he got the call from Bevan, he could offer geographic-profiling help in several areas that might benefit the Green Ribbon Task Force:

1. *Suspect lists.* Help prioritize individuals for follow-up investigation by identifying suspects located in the high-profile areas.
2. *Patrol saturation and static stakeouts.* The high probability areas identified in the profile can help target patrols and surveillance. Because many offenders return to their residence or workplace after committing their crime, the results can also help the police to monitor the most probable residence after subsequent crimes.
3. *Neighborhood canvasses.* Help prioritize areas for door-to-door canvassing, grid searches, information/sign posting, community cooperation campaigns, and postal distribution of leaflets.
4. *Police information systems.* These contain important information on known offenders and reported suspects, and can be prioritized by street address, zip/postal code, and area telephone number.
5. *Outside agency information.* Outside agencies, including parole, probation, mental health, social service, and even private businesses, have geographically based databases which can include relevant investigative information.
6. *DMV database searches.* If a suspect vehicle colour and general type has been identified, Department of Motor Vehicles (DMV) databases may be searched for matching vehicles registered in

the high-profile area. The DMV database includes vehicle registered owner address files (including zip and postal codes), which can be prioritized through a geoprofile. Thus the search for a particular vehicle type can produce significant results by quickly focusing on limited areas of a manageable size.

7. *Forensic information/bloodings.* Focusing on the area of highest probability, police can minimize the number of suspects, resulting in a more effective and less expensive DNA screening procedure.

8. *Task force/major case management computer systems.* Prioritizing suspects and tips by street addresses, zip/postal codes, and telephone numbers can reduce system overload.

9. *Sex offender registries.* A list of addresses of known sexual predators living in a given area can be used with geographic profiling to help prioritize suspects in sex crime cases.

By the time Rossmo arrived in St. Catharines, the task force was awash in a quagmire of tips and suspects. Quickly concluding that the killer was trying to lead the police back toward Burlington, Rossmo prepared a geoprofile which included maps of St. Catharines. He also agreed with MacKay that the two schoolgirls had been killed by the same man, that he was changing his MO, not his ritual, to draw the cops off his trail. Like the psychological profilers, Rossmo would focus on the dominant offender; the presence of an accomplice was no huge complication.

There seemed little doubt that the killer had not wanted Mahaffy's remains to be found. Since they were, however, he had gone out of his way to drop French in a dumping ground where she seemed sure to found by salvagers. Her daylight abduction on a busy street was far more high-risk for the predator and seemed planned and deliberate. By contrast, Mahaffy's night abduction from a suburban neighbourhood seemed a crime of opportunity, a case of being in the wrong place at the wrong time—in a predator's hunting ground when he was foraging. If the killer had not specifically stalked French, there seemed little doubt he had prowled the area around her high school, Holy Cross, for similar potential victims. As with Olson's victims more than a decade earlier, if it

Ron MacKay, Royal Canadian Mounted Police,
1981, the man who envisioned ViCLAS.

Fred Maile, the Mountie who was instrumental
in breaking Clifford Olson.

Fred Zaharia, retired R C M P Staff Sergeant who, with Jim Hunter, fought to have the Crown prosecute Clifford Olson on sex charges.

Jim Hunter, the first Mountie to lay sex charges against Olson.

Mert Mohr, the former Mountie who conducted the internal review of the Olson investigation in the early 1980s.

John. J. Burke, Deputy Assistant Director of the FBI Academy, presents Ron MacKay with his diploma. Next to MacKay is John Douglas, unit chief of the National Center for the Analysis of Violent Crime (NCAVC).

Brian Sargeant, a young fraud cop who had to flee B.C. with MacKay to escape alleged murder contracts on them.

Ron MacKay and his colleagues from his course at the FBI Academy course at Quantico. The photograph was taken on the grounds of the Canadian embassy in Washington. (*l. to r.*) back row: Special Agent Mike Prodan, South Carolina Law Enforcement Division; Detective Sergeant Jim McCormick, New Jersey State Police VICAP/ViCLAS Unit; Special Agent "Gus" Gary, Bureau of Alcohol, Tobacco and Firearms; front row: Special Agent Steve Amico, U.S. Secret Service; Captain Diana Sievers, Illinois State Police; Inspector Ron MacKay, RCMP.

(*above left*) Ron MacKay with Assistant Commissioner Denis Farrell, who represented the RCMP at MacKay's graduation.
(*above middle*) Jim Wright, MacKay's mentor and FBI contact.
(*above right*) Steve McCarthy, Sergeant in Charge of VICAP, the U.S. forerunner to the Canadian system, ViCLAS. McCarthy was also instrumental in creating NERV, a formal alliance of northeastern states dedicated to pooling VICAP information.

The first symposium of Canadian Criminal Profilers: (ground): OPP Sgt. Kate Cavanagh (the first woman profiler in Canada), S.S.A. McCrary, Insp. MacKay, Cpl. Johnson; (row 1): Cpl. Roberts; Cpl. Urbanowski, Sgt. Seguin, Lt. Tremblay; (row 2): Cpl. Ash, Sgt. Doyle, Det. Burns, Sgt. Galianos, Sgt. Landry; (row 3): S/Sgt. Erfle, D/Sgt. Bowmaster, D/Sgt. Gentle, D/Const. Moores, Sgt. Turcotte; (row 4): D/Sgt. Pitfield, D/Sgt. Lewis, Det. Curwain, D/Sgt. Bladon, Sgt. Olver, Sgt. Morris.

Gus Gary and Ron MacKay ready to descend the Yellowknife Giant Mine during the investigation of the mass murder of nine miners in February 1993.

Gregg McMartin, the RCMP polygraphist whose interrogation of Roger Warren led to his confession as the Yellowknife Bomber.

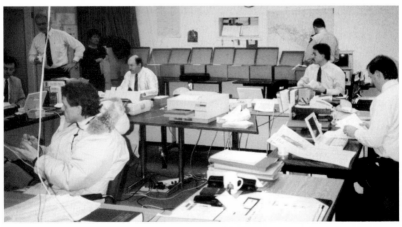

The Giant Mine investigation Task Force office.

Kim Rossmo, the Vancouver cop who devised geographic profiling which uses mathematical algorithms to predict where a serial killer or rapist probably lives or works, based on where he has struck.

Peter Collins, the only forensic psychiatrist in Canada with a Master's degree in Criminology and the first to work full time with police.

Roy Hazelwood, the FBI agent who specialized in the study of deviant sex and devised the theory of "compliant victim" that was a major factor in the review of the deal between the Crown and Karla Homolka.

Gerry Seguin and Ron MacKay arranged for a training session for all ICIAF understudy candidates in February 1996. (*l. to r.*) front row: MacKay, Kate Lines, Nicole Neirop, Roy Hazelwood, Seguin, Janet Oliva, Sharon Pagaling, Bob Urbanowski, John Yarbrough; second row: John Lang, G.W. Hildebrand, Jim Van Allen, Glenn Woods, Keith Davidson; back row: Karl Anglin, Mike Rundles.

CP PHOTO

Retired Justice Patrick Galligan, foreground left, listens to a question during a news conference in Toronto in March 1996. Galligan endorsed the controversial plea bargain deal with Karla Homolka.

CP PHOTO

Justice Archie Campbell answers questions from the media at a news conference in Toronto, July 11, 1996, about his findings on the Bernardo investigation.

Justice Casey Hill was the Crown
Attorney who oversaw the meticulous
preparation of the warrant application
to search the home of Paul Bernardo
and Karla Homolka.

Peel Region Deputy Police Chief Ron Bain and Staff Sergeant Jennifer
Dineen, who did the investigative legwork for the Campbell Report.

Lieutenant Claude Tremblay, a veteran polygraphist with *Sûreté du Québec*, was the first cop from that province to recognize the importance of profiling. He and Sergeant Gerry Séguin met with MacKay to discuss its use in Quebec—a vital link and ally to the unilingual, English-speaking Mountie.

ViCLAS programmer Paul Leurey, who devised the technology with Algonquin College computer-science classmate John Ripley, Sergeant Greg Johnson and Sergeant Gerry Séguin.

Ron MacKay, Keith Davidson and Greg Johnson at a February 1995 ViCLAS training session at the RCMP Academy in Vancouver, B.C.

(*l. to r.*) Peter Collins, Kate Lines and Ron MacKay, in Quebec, 1995.

The first international ViCLAS conference in Vancouver in 1995.

Assistant Commissioner Joop Plomp (*standing*) with Assistant Commissioner Murray Johnson (Vancouver) lending their support to the ViCLAS project.

Assistant Commissioner Joop Plomp and
Commissioner Phil Murray at the opening of the
Technical and Protective Operations facility in
June 1996, the new home for the Violent Crime
Analysis Branch and ViCLAS.

Superintendent Glenn Woods,
who replaced MacKay as head
of RCMP Behavioural
Services Branch in 1997.

Mike Woods, Glenn's older
brother, worked with MacKay
at the North Vancouver
detachment.

Martine Fourcaudot, who spearheaded mandatory compliance for SALVAC in Quebec.

Henry Derkach, RCMP ViCLAS coordinator.

Sergeant Larry Wilson, senior ViCLAS specialist.

Nancy Noel, the longest serving member of the Behavioural Sciences Branch.

The new profilers: (l. to r.): Keith Davidson; Jim Wright, FBI; Ron MacKay; John Lang (GBI); Eric Witzig (Quantico).

Peel Region Superintendent Dave Hazelton, Greg Johnson's early partner.

Vic Matanovic, former Detective Sergeant with Metro Toronto Police.

S/Sgt. Christine Wozney, who was in charge of the Vancouver RCMP ViCLAS unit.

Detective Jim Van Allen, OPP profiler.

Shelley Hassard, Francis Roy's parole officer, wrote a detailed report listing clear reasons why the Toronto police should re-investigate Roy for Alison's murder.

CP PHOTO

Lesley Parrott, mother of Alison Parrott, who was murdered in 1986, looks on at a news conference on July 31, 1986, as Metro Toronto Police Staff Inspector Ken Cenzura announces that an arrest has been made in connection with the 10-year-old murder case.

Ron MacKay

hadn't been them, it would have been someone else possibly very much like them. In this case, two teenage girls in Burlington and St. Catharines are alive because Leslie Mahaffy and Kristen French are not. By their deaths, they spared other innocents.

The French abduction was the most recent case, making the catchment area around Holy Cross, from where it drew its students, the logical focus of Rossmo's geographic profile. With too few locations to run the main algorithm, he modified its principles and theories slightly to produce three maps, factoring in the "encounter" sites where the girls had been abducted and the "drop" sites where they were later found. The profile included three key maps:

1. The probable area of offender residence, which included the Port Dalhousie neighbourhood where Bernardo and Homolka lived.
2. The regular commuting routes of the killer, near Holy Cross High School.
3. On the basis of what the Task Force believed was the "last known reliable sighting of the Camaro," an area of central St. Catharines where French was most likely taken after her abduction.

That last known sighting proved unreliable and that map, while logical, was wrong, being based on the incorrect information. The other two proved to be right. The theory worked.

The Green Ribbon Task Force marked the first time that all the new Canadian behavioural crime-fighting talents then in existence worked together in the same place at the same time behind the scenes of a major crime. While it cannot replace what the grieving families of the victims lost, it may console them to know the lengths to which the police went to avenge their daughters and to know there are women and children alive today, and from generations yet unborn, because of what was learned and applied in the Niagara Frontier.

But it was Karla who cracked the case.

9

Search and Seizure

On January 5, 1993, Karla Homolka was admitted to hospital. She had been savagely beaten with a heavy flashlight and stabbed with a screwdriver by her husband, Paul Bernardo. Her injuries were so grievous that the attending physician termed her the worst case of wife battering he had ever seen in his many years working in the emergency department. Severely bruised, her swollen legs too painful to walk, or even touch, she had been struck with such force on the back of her head that her brain had crashed into the front of her skull, causing classic "racoon" eyes from pooled internal bleeding. Released from hospital five days later, she stayed with an uncle and aunt in Brampton, Ontario. On January 25, she contacted Legal Aid and a divorce lawyer.

Ten days later, Metro Toronto Police investigators approached Karla's parents for help to arrange a meeting. They had some questions they'd like to ask about her husband.

The worm had turned on Bernardo on February 1 when the Centre of Forensic Sciences in Toronto had alerted the cops that they had matched his DNA to a semen sample from one of the victims of the Scarborough Rapist. There were several more matches to other victims over the ensuing weeks but the cops hadn't waited. They had put Bernardo under surveillance immediately, neglecting to advise Bevan at the Green Ribbon Task Force or Niagara Regional Police that they had found their man and were intruding into their jurisdiction. Metro had been excluded from the task force that by now had expanded to nearly a dozen police forces and hundreds of officers in various capacities, and their deliberate intrusion marked the opening salvo in a turf war that would seriously jeopardize the quest to solve the Schoolgirl Murders. Bevan was finally briefed on February 8, on the eve of the meeting scheduled for the next day between Homolka and investigators from the Metro Sexual Assault Squad. If he was unhappy to learn he'd been deliberately kept in the dark, he hadn't seen nothin' yet.

At their meeting the next day, Homolka limited her comments and information to her hubby's violent abuse. Bernardo had taught her well. Besides beating her to a pulp, he had pounded into her head that if she ever found herself involved with police, she was to tell them nothing until she'd called her lawyer. After the cops had left, Homolka confided to her aunt and uncle that Bernardo had abducted and murdered Mahaffy and French. That he had told her on their wedding night that he was the Scarborough Rapist. That he had her on videotape having sex with the schoolgirl victims. Two days later, she called lawyer George Walker for an appointment. He assumed it was to discuss assault charges against her husband. She had met him when he brought his dog to the veterinarian clinic where she had worked and he had always seemed like a nice guy. Walker agreed to meet her the next day.

If he was shocked by her appearance, still sporting her racoon eyes more than a month after the assault and seeming to weigh no more than 85 pounds, he was stunned as she recounted in lurid detail Bernardo's sadistic rapes and murderous toll, her sordid role in the torment of the murdered schoolgirls, and the accidental death of her youngest sister, Tammy. Homolka had drugged Tammy and presented her to Bernardo for sex as a Christmas present in 1990. She had videotaped him raping her unconscious sister, then he had taped her performing oral sex on her. The assault had ended abruptly when Tammy vomited and aspirated. Her death had been ruled accidental, but from that moment on, Bernardo had enjoyed total control over her, she said, threatening to expose her to her family if she did not do whatever he demanded, whenever he had demanded it. Their sex had grown kinkier and more painful and his assaults more frequent and violent, to the point that he had nearly killed her this past Christmas.

Once he had recovered from his shock, Walker wasted no time. He met the next day with Crown Attorney Ray Houlahan who in turn promptly referred him to Murray Segal, the director of Crown Law Office (Criminal), then briefed Bevan on the dramatic turn of events.

Finally, on February 12, 1993—six years after his name was first raised with police as a violent sexual predator who openly discussed his rape fantasies with friends, was alleged to have drugged and raped at least one woman, allegedly threatened others with a knife and attempted to assault them in his car, at his home, and at friends', and was confirmed by his DNA as the Scarborough Rapist—Paul Bernardo became the prime suspect in the Schoolgirl Murders.

It was not that there had not been early tips, but systemic and human errors, a sloppy paper-filing system, and failure to pass along or follow up on information had doomed investigators' efforts to tag him a prime suspect. He had been classified both a strong and a weak suspect—likely to be excluded—by different investigators, and had been one of only five suspects asked to give blood, hair, and saliva samples by Metro investigators; yet he had languished in the pack of 40,000 tips and 3200 suspects.

Even now that he had been identified by his DNA as the Scarborough Rapist, there was absolutely no evidence linking him to the Schoolgirl Murders. All eyes shifted to Homolka.

Murray Segal was a skilled and proven deal-maker, well respected for his ability to negotiate the exchange of a suspect's evidence without giving much away; for him it was routine for a murder accomplice to provide information, knowing he or she would still be charged with murder. Walker recounted to him what Homolka had told him, adding details never made public by the police such as the black bra and basketball shorts French had been wearing under her school uniform the day she had been abducted, and the jacket of the Henley Island rape victim that Bernardo had brought home, then later burned in the fireplace.

The information was convincing, the best and only evidence they had to link Bernardo to those crimes, and Walker asked for total immunity for his client. Segal refused to even consider that, even though he knew a deal might be the only way to get a sadistic predator off the streets. But it was a starting point for the negotiations that would last for months between two able adversaries.

Segal wasn't going to give anything away until they had had a chance to search Bernardo's home at 57 Bayview Drive in Port Dalhousie, which was located within the five-minute drive south of Holy Cross high school that Rossmo had pegged in his geographic profile. Only his third map, based on a faulty eyewitness report of the fleeing Camaro (which Homolka now revealed was a Nissan), had been wrong, suggesting Bernardo had taken his victims somewhere other than his home.

When Rossmo first got involved in the Green Ribbon Task Force, he estimated the split at only 60–40 in favour of the theory that the same predator was responsible for abducting, torturing, and murdering Leslie Mahaffy and Kristen French. But there seemed no doubt now that MacKay had been right in his prediction. The cops' earlier "hot" suspect was now excluded and Bernardo elevated to prime suspect. It was Olson all over again: while his name had appeared on several police suspect lists a decade earlier, the cops back then, too, had cultivated a better and more "logical" suspect in the murder of nearly a dozen B.C. teens than the man who actually killed them. Although Olson had finally confessed in return for cash payments to his wife, that was a highly unlikely scenario this time around. Unlike Olson, who talked himself into prison, a sexual sadist like Bernardo was unlikely to admit to anything.

While Segal and Walker continued to duel over the terms of any agreement to be offered to Homolka in exchange for her testimony against Bernardo, work began on the search-warrant application on the weekend of February 13–14. The plan was to complete that application first, in fact to get separate warrants for Metro and the task force to search at the same time for evidence linking the sadist to his rapes and the Schoolgirl Murders, then arrest Bernardo at home and take him to Halton Regional Police headquarters, which was appropriately midway between Metro and Niagara Regional jurisdictions and boasted an excellent audio- and videotape studio. MacKay and Collins, the forensic psychiatrist, suggested early morning or late evening as the best time to arrest Bernardo. They predicted he would ask to call his lawyer immediately and he was to

be allowed to do so to avoid any later Charter of Rights and Freedoms challenge in court. Ideally, the interview teams would be
briefed and well prepared for their interview with the killer even
before he was in custody.

On paper and in theory, the plan looked good. But when a cop
leaked the pending arrest to the media, actually identifying Bernardo
by name, it compromised the plan and jeopardized all that had been
arranged and accomplished. The police were ordered in; they
arrested Bernardo at home and when he asked to contact his lawyer
they told him he could call from the police station. A bad start that
quickly got worse.

Detectives Steve Irwin, of the Metro Sexual Assault Squad, and
Gerry Beaulieu, of the Green Ribbon Task Force, were to be the first
team to interview Bernardo. Beaulieu was to lead the interrogation
with questions about the murders as the most recent crimes and
most serious charges. Irwin would follow up with questions about
the Scarborough rapes. MacKay and Collins had hoped to discuss
tactics at length, but Beaulieu hadn't wanted to meet without Irwin,
who was working on the search warrant and said he had no time to
meet, despite repeated requests over several days. Irwin did,
however, have time to talk to his superior, Staff Inspector Steve
Marrier, who suggested he ask Metro homicide investigators how
best to proceed with Bernardo, judging from their experience inter-
rogating other suspects. Trouble was, none of them had likely ever
met or successfully interrogated a sexual sadist.

Beaulieu had earlier chatted briefly with MacKay and Collins,
enough to realize how vital it was that he and Irwin be totally
prepared to interview a man they had been warned would be a
master manipulator who would try to control the interview. But the
media leak, and the frenzy to "scoop" the story, changed everything.
As the press erected their satellite dishes across the alley from Green
Ribbon headquarters, MacKay and Collins conferred hastily and
briefly with the two investigators over a takeout Chinese meal. The
time for proper preparation had passed. About the best they could do
now was to remind Irwin and Beaulieu that no sexual sadist was apt
to confess anything under interrogation. The trick was to ask open-

ended questions that avoided yes or no answers. Rather than ask, "Do you like to torture women?" ask "What do you like to use to torture women?" MacKay predicted Bernardo would feel intellectually superior to the police. He had talked his way across the border while smuggling cigarettes, risking detection and apprehension each time, and had eluded the Metro rape investigators for years, even after volunteering blood, hair, and saliva for DNA testing. Under no circumstances, MacKay and Collins warned, should they provoke him or risk a confrontation. Such an approach would invite disaster.

No one else knew what was going on behind the scenes or that Metro had come up with its own agenda for the interview. Consequently, when the media leak forced Bernardo's rushed arrest and detention, Beaulieu walked into the Halton Regional police interrogation room, midway between Niagara Regional and Metro jurisdiction, expecting to ask the first questions. He was stunned, as were MacKay, Collins, and the investigators monitoring the interview in a separate room on a closed-circuit system, when Irwin immediately launched a verbal barrage at Bernardo. The Metro bully-boy tactic disintegrated into a debacle as Bernardo alternated between baiting Irwin and asking to speak to his lawyer.

Unaware that Bernardo had not been allowed to call his lawyer from home as planned but was promised he could make the call from the police station, and wrongly advised by Inspector Marrier (the senior officer present at the time in Bevan's absence) that questioning could continue until Bernardo *demanded* to speak to his lawyer, Irwin persisted in what Beaulieu called the worst day of his life. Partly because of MacKay's and Collins' urging to keep asking questions—explaining that while Bernardo was unlikely to say anything concrete or admissible, his physical and verbal responses to questioning about certain rooms in the house could indicate the best places to search—the interview lasted eight hours, ending about midnight.

It produced nothing. A later review determined that no one seemed to be in charge, no one was accountable for the disastrous interview that "began badly, degenerated into an argument [between Bernardo and Irwin], continued badly and ended badly."

The case against Bernardo now hinged strongly on what police would find in the house he had shared with Homolka at 57 Bayview Drive. One misstep, one misstatement in the search warrant that could be challenged in court by a judge or defence attorney, could invalidate any evidence found in what had become known as the Ken and Barbie Killers' "House of Horrors" and collapse the prosecutor's case like a house of cards. Long gone were the days when a few pages stapled together were going to withstand the scrutiny of Criminal Code and Charter challenges. The warrant had to be right, airtight, the first time it was submitted to a Justice for approval.

For the first time in Canada, a "behavioural" section was included in a high-profile case. Before Green Ribbon, only MacKay and Kate Lines (formerly Cavanagh; the OPP profiler had married Metro biker cop Bob Lines) had applied that aspect to search warrant applications to a handful of equally horrific but far less publicized crimes. The pre-Charter days when police could secure a warrant with little more than declaring, "I have reasonable and probable grounds to believe . . ." were long gone. The behavioural section was considered vital to finding the videotapes of Bernardo torturing, raping, and possibly killing his victims that MacKay insisted would be there if they could only find them. Its inclusion was unprecedented in an Ontario crime, just one section in an exhaustive application that ran to more than 1000 pages, and there must have been some anxiety about how it would be viewed by the issuing Justice. They needn't have worried; the application was reviewed and approved almost overnight.

With the behavioural aspects so new, and so vital, it was logical to designate McCrary as the front man, capitalizing on the image of FBI profiling that had been boosted by the Hollywood blockbuster *The Silence of the Lambs* a year earlier. It wasn't that the Canadian profilers, MacKay and Lines, or Collins, the forensic psychiatrist, couldn't have done the job equally well. All played their crucial role, but they simply weren't as recognizable as the FBI. Perception, not ego, jurisdiction, or professional competence, was the key.

While McCrary and Bevan spent endless hours on the phone in the days after Bernardo's arrest, hammering out the details and best language to promote their case, MacKay compiled a list of what to include on the search warrant for Bernardo's home, which was indeed within the small area of Rossmo's geographic profile. In particular, he stressed the need to unearth the videotapes he suspected would be there, a visual testament to the suffering, and perhaps murder, of the sadist's victims. He did not rule out the possibility that there could be more victims than the two murdered schoolgirls Homolka had tied to her former spouse, nor did he limit his input to the videos. He added other records and mementos, photographic equipment, tape recorders, reverse telephone directories, weapons or other instruments used to elicit suffering, pornography, detective and mercenary magazines, bondage paraphernalia, women's underwear, and sexual devices.

It was all a far cry from the one-page search warrants of MacKay's young cop days that could be sidestepped with a cooperative hotel night manager. But this time there was no alternative. They had one kick at the can and couldn't risk a Charter challenge at trial. There could be no shortcuts. In the end, their painstaking efforts proved time well spent, producing a comprehensive five-page, single-spaced appendix to the search-warrant application (see Figure 9.1).

Figure 9.1
APPENDIX TO THE BERNARDO
SEARCH-WARRANT APPLICATION

Niagara Regional Police
In the case of Paul BERNARDO
57 Bayview Drive, Niagara

I. ANALYSIS OF OFFENDER CHARACTERISTICS

I, the Affiant, have been given a report entitled "Analysis of Offender Characteristics" by Inspector Vincent BEVAN of the Niagara Regional Police. Through my discussions with Inspector BEVAN he has advised me that he has consulted with Supervisory Special Agent Gregg O. MCCRARY of the Federal Bureau of Investigation. MCCRARY's report is summarized as follows:

Supervisory Special Agent Gregg O. MCCRARY has twenty-three years' experience with the FBI and is a Criminal Investigative Analyst with the National Center for the Analysis of Violent Crime (NCAVC) at the FBI Academy in Quantico, Virginia. NCAVC is a law enforcement oriented behavioural science and computerized resource centre which consolidates research, training and investigative support functions to assist law enforcement agencies with violent crimes which are particularly complex or bizarre. Since 1981, NCAVC has focused its research capabilities upon serial killers and severe sexual offenders utilizing behavioural science methodology to develop a reliable data base and analytical framework for use in law enforcement. The unit reviews and studies information contained in hundreds of cases which are submitted each year for consultation purposes. The foundation of its data base is empirical research into the case histories of some thirty-six serial killers (i.e., three or more killings in separate incidents), forty-one rapists (each responsible for at least ten such offenses), fifty arsonists, seventeen child abductors/molesters and thirty sexual sadists. Refer to the article "The Sexually Sadistic Criminal and His Offenses" which is included as Appendix G to this Information. This research project has included an exhaustive review of the investigative files, in-depth interviews of each offender, and selected interviews of surviving victims.

Gregg O. MCCRARY, a Supervisory Special Agent with the Federal Bureau of Investigation, is assigned to the NCAVC ... [and] serves both as a consultant to law enforcement agencies and a research project coordinator. He entered on duty as a Special Agent ... in 1969 and served in various investigative capacities throughout the United States. He has been associated with the NCAVC since 1985.

He consults in the investigation and prosecution of such crimes as serial murder, serial rape, sexual homicides, kidnappings, and child abductions/molestations. His duties also include supervising 3 other Supervisory Special Agents. MCCRARY is a contributing author to the *Crime Classification Manual* published in 1992 by Lexington Press. This work is the first to systematically classify homicides, sexual assaults and arsons.

He has provided expert witness testimony before Select Senate Committees on Sexual Violence as well as in homicide trials in the United States.

He has consulted on thousands of cases throughout the United States, Canada, Central America, Australia, England, Austria, Italy and China. Agent MCCRARY has provided consultation or instruction to the Central Intelligence Agency, Federal Bureau of Investigation, Drug Enforcement Administration, Royal Canadian Mounted Police, National College of District Attorneys, National Criminal Intelligence Service of the Netherlands and numerous other local, state, federal and international agencies.

Agent MCCRARY's work in serial murder has been highlighted in a Public Broadcasting System documentary entitled "The Mind of a Serial Killer" and he has provided expert commentary to Cable News Network (CNN) television regarding serial murder.

Agent MCCRARY's formal education includes a Master's degree in psychology from Marymount University. He is a featured speaker to legal, medical, law enforcement and private sector audiences throughout the world.

Special Agent MCCRARY and his colleagues at NCAVC studied the available information (most of which is provided herein) about the first eight (8) offences of a then unknown offender called the Scarborough Rapist. During those offenses the rapist displayed several sexually sadistic characteristics and was becoming more and more violent as demonstrated by his punishing and beating of the victims. As a result of the behaviour of this offender, Mr. MCCRARY was able to predict that the danger posed by this person would escalate. The use of force beyond that necessary to subdue the victims, together with the psychological abuse, assisted in identifying this offender as a sexual sadist.

Special Agent MCCRARY is of the opinion that as time passed the sadistic component of this offender's actions would continue to grow. Research has demonstrated that such an offender will not stop of his own volition. He only stops with the exertion of external forces, that is he either dies or is in custody. The offenses may stop in a given area because this type of offender moves, but Mr. MCCRARY would expect to see the offender act out in the area to which he has relocated.

In the case of Paul BERNARDO, he moved from the Scarborough area and the offenses attributable to the Scarborough Rapist stopped. Within nine (9) weeks of BERNARDO's arrival in St. Catharines, a rape occurred in close proximity to his new home. This rape clearly demonstrated the same *modus operandi* used by the Scarborough Rapist as described elsewhere in this document. This pattern is predictable in the case of the sexual sadist. Mr. MCCRARY would expect to see another offence in close proximity to the offender's new home and the cycle would start all over again.

Mr. MCCRARY predicted an escalation in the nature of offenses based upon a lifestyle change. In the case of Paul BERNARDO, while living in Scarborough, he was in a home which was controlled by his parents. Once he moved to St. Catharines, he had a home of his own over which he was able to exert complete control. This change in his circumstances aids him in the escalation of his offenses to the point where he can now bring his victims home.

Abduction is a predictable progression for the sexual sadist. However, abduction of a victim virtually guarantees that murder will result. If the sexual sadist has held a victim he feels in his own mind that he can't possibly let them go. As his fantasy escalates he needs more control and gains that control through abduction and forcible confinement of his victims. The ultimate fantasy of a sexual sadist is to totally possess his victims, both physically and psychologically. He seeks to achieve control over their life and ultimately over their death as well.

In the expert opinion of Mr. MCCRARY it is predictable that some of the Scarborough Rapist's victims would be killed by this point in time. Rapists identified as sexual sadists are statistically less than 2% of all of these types of offenders. Therefore, the probability of having more than one of these type of offenders in the geographic area and population we are concerned with is statistically very remote. There is a high probability that the Scarborough Rapist and the sexual sadistic murderer of MAHAFFY and FRENCH is the same offender.

Further, sexual sadist tendencies when combined with a very rare phenomenon where hair is collected from victims, as BERNARDO did with two women in Scarborough, and as happened with Kristen French, is a strong indicator this is the same offender. The taking of hair satisfies BERNARDO's need to punish, degrade and disgrace his victims. It also serves as a trophy.

Special Agent MCCRARY and his colleagues at NCAVC studied the available information on the murders of Leslie Mahaffy and Kristen French and concluded that they are likely victims of a sexual sadist. Paul BERNARDO demonstrates almost all of the characteristics which are typically found in the sexually sadistic serial killer. The constellation of characteristics which NCAVC research has consistently encountered in such offenders includes each of the following:

- Male
- White
- Parental Infidelity or Divorce
- Physically Abused in Childhood
- Sexually Abused in Childhood
- Married at Time of Offence
- Incestuous Involvement with Own Child
- Known Homosexual Experience
- Known Cross-Dressing
- Known History of Peeping, Obscene Telephone Calls or Indecent Exposure
- Shared Sexual Partners with Another Man
- Education Beyond High School
- Military Experience
- Drug Abuse
- Suicide Attempt
- Excessive Driving
- Police "Buff"

The following characteristics, from the police investigation described above, apply to Paul BERNARDO:

- *White male.* Same.
- *Above average intelligence.* Investigators have established that BERNARDO completed a four year University Degree in three years.
- *Neat and well groomed.* Surveillance has established that BERNARDO presents himself very well in a social setting, especially during daytime. However, during the hours of darkness while stalking potential victims, his appearance changes.

• *Parental conflict.* Family members report that BERNARDO expresses hatred for his mother and thinks she is crazy. At age 14 years BERNARDO learned that who he had thought of as his father was actually his step-father since he was a product of his mother's affair with another man.

[PARAGRAPH REMOVED TO PROTECT
THE CONFIDENTIALITY OF THIRD PARTIES]

• *Will select an occupation which makes him an authority figure.* When asked about employment, BERNARDO told his wife's parents, who have been interviewed, that he was involved in a secret "project." He currently claims to be involved in writing "rap" music and has told his sister-in-law that he will be the white "M. C. Hammer," a popular black rap musician.
• *Fascination with weapons.* Several people have reported that BERNARDO has a "special" knife that he usually keeps in his car under a seat. A prior girlfriend, who also became a victim, describes this knife as having a personal inscription on the blade. A knife has been used in numerous offenses. Family members have disclosed that BERNARDO has purchased a "Stun gun" and normally keeps it under his bed.
• *Compulsive driving.* Surveillance has established that BERNARDO for several days in a row drove an average of 650 kilometres.
• *Initially presents the image of a sincere, caring, loving and attentive individual.* Past girlfriends and his wife's family all report that BERNARDO, during the early stages of his relationships, showered the women with gifts and attention. He maintained an outward appearance of being loving and attentive.
• *Dominating personality.* Family members report that BERNARDO told his wife how to wear her hair and chose her clothing. Over the course of time he isolated her from her former friends. A close friend of BERNARDO, Van SMIRNIS, disclosed that he observed many occasions when BERNARDO treated his wife with a total lack of respect. In January 1993, after charges were laid against BERNARDO for beating his wife, she disclosed a long history of physical abuse.
• *Obsession with sexual sadism; suffers from an overpowering compul-*

sion to inflict pain upon and totally dominate any sexual companion. A former girlfriend has disclosed that BERNARDO was unable to achieve an erection unless he frightened or inflicted pain on her. With that woman, BERNARDO used ligatures around her neck while engaging in anal intercourse. He also used foreign objects including bottles and sticks by inserting them into both vaginal and anal cavities of his victims. Further, any non-compliance on the part of his victims or willing sexual partners resulted in violence.

- *Compulsively collects and uses pornography.* A friend, Van SMIRNIS, has reported that BERNARDO made a videotape of himself having sex with an unknown woman. He then showed the video to his wife. SMIRNIS also reports that BERNARDO disclosed that his wife had been searching their home for a videotape that recorded her having sex with another woman. Further, BERNARDO is known to own a video camera and playback equipment. He, as a matter of habit, videotapes people and events and collects these.

- *Collects and keeps as trophies and mementos personal items belonging to past victims (e.g., undergarments, shoes, jewellery, wallets or identification); such trophies then serve as a source of perverse gratification and enrich the offender's sexual fantasies.* Investigation has revealed that each victim has lost an item during the attack which could be characterized as a "trophy." Trophies include photo identification, articles of clothing, jewellery, head and pubic hairs.

- *Selects victims who are particularly vulnerable—favours the young.* Most victims are young women found alone at the time of the attack. Victims all have the appearance of being between 14 and 18 years of age.

- *Married at time of offense.* Paul and Karla BERNARDO lived together from February 1991 at 57 Bayview Drive. They were married June 29, 1991. Therefore they were in at least a common-law relationship at the time of MAHAFFY and FRENCH.

- *Known history of peeping or obscene telephone calls.* In at least one of the Scarborough Rapist offenses BERNARDO told the victim he had watched her inside her home. One other victim reported receiving telephone calls after her attack. In addition, the victim in the Henley Island attack also reported phone calls.

- *93% of sexually sadistic serial killers plan their crimes carefully.*

Surveillance has established evidence of stalking victims during both the daytime and night-time. The method of disposal of the body in the MAHAFFY case is indicative of planning. The condition of the body in the FRENCH case also indicates planning since the body was cleaned to remove trace evidence. All rape attacks occurred in dark areas where there was some sort of cover. Also during the rapes he forced victims to swallow semen in order to destroy biological samples.

According to Special Agent MCCRARY, the NCAVC research found that the sexually sadistic serial killer exhibits a high degree of predictability in his criminal behaviour. Accordingly, Special Agent MCCRARY believes that it is not a question of whether, but when, Paul BERNARDO will offend again. Since there is no limit upon his appetite for sadistic gratification, it is only a question of time until his next victim does or refuses to do something which he perceives as a threat to his control over her. When that happens, he will react as he has always reacted. The documented case histories demonstrate conclusively that offenders like Paul BERNARDO cannot stop raping and killing of their own volition. They stop only when they are stopped by external forces.

Offender activity may be suppressed for a time. Close brushes with law enforcement would lead to a period of inactivity. In BERNARDO's case, he was interviewed as a suspect in the Scarborough Rapist case in November 1990. No offence was committed in that area after that time. This behaviour is consistent and predictable. However, this quiet period will consistently be followed by renewed activity by the offender. Hence the offence in St. Catharines in April 1991.

Special Agent MCCRARY agrees with those who attended the case review conference that Paul BERNARDO will react as predicted.

Finally, with respect to the likelihood that tangible evidence will be recovered through additional searches, Special Agent MCCRARY indicated to the Task Force in the month of May, 1992, that he believed that such evidence does exist and can be recovered for the following reasons:

- Supervisory Special Agent MCCRARY relates that a prime characteristic of the sadistic offender is to keep and conceal journals, graphic materials and particularly audio and videotapes which will feed his fantasies and enable him to relive the exhilarating moments of his past offenses for continual gratification. Indeed, 53% of the sexually sadistic offenders studied by NCAVC actually memorialized their offenses in some tangible form. Depending upon the particular offender's living arrangements and how secure he feels in any particular location, this collection of memorabilia may be hidden but will be somewhere within reasonably easy access. Paul BERNARDO should feel relatively safe in his home because although he was a suspect in the Scarborough Rapes and provided biological samples, 27 months have elapsed since he gave those samples and nothing has happened to him. He has no reason to believe that he is currently the target of any police investigation. Hence, he is likely to have his stash of "trophies" and mementos of the kind described above concealed in his home or in a related storage area, the location of which a thorough search of the home should reveal.

- The high risk nature of the abduction of Kristen French was a predictable action of a sexual sadist such as Paul BERNARDO. Since he believes he was not detected when biological samples were collected from him in November 1990, his confidence has grown and he has developed a sense of invulnerability. He will begin to think he won't be apprehended and therefore he indulges in more high risk offenses.

The opinions and information above described, provided by Special Agent Gregg MCCRARY, have been reviewed by Peter I. COLLINS, M.C.A., M.D., F.R.C.P. (C). Doctor COLLINS concurs with the opinions offered by Mr. MCCRARY. Rapists who are also sexual sadists are rare. Doctor COLLINS is the Consultant Psychiatrist, Violent Crime Analysis Section of the Royal Canadian Mounted Police.

Doctor COLLINS has further referred me to the following excerpts from the Diagnostic and Statistical Manual of Mental Disorders (3rd ed.) revised (1987) at pages 287 and 288:

AMERICAN PSYCHIATRIC ASSOCIATION
DIAGNOSTIC AND STATISTICAL MANUAL
OF MENTAL DISORDERS
3RD EDITION—REVISED 1987
302.84 SEXUAL SADISM...

Sadistic fantasies or acts may involve activities that indicate the dominance of the person over his victim (e.g. forcing the victim to crawl, or keeping the victim in a cage), or restraint, blindfolding, paddling, spanking, whipping, pinching, beating, burning, electrical shocks, rape, cutting or stabbing, strangulation, torture, mutilation, or killing. . . .

Differential diagnosis. Rape or other sexual assault may be committed by people with this disorder. In such instances the suffering inflicted on the victim is far in excess of that necessary to gain compliance, and the visible pain of the victim is sexually arousing.

Similar evidence relating to sexual sadism was recently held to be admissible in evidence as going to the issue of propensity to commit the offence: Regina v. Pierre Malboeuf (February 24, 1992), unreported judgment of the Ontario Court of Justice (General Division). The following holding of Mr. Justice MCWILLIAM is relevant:

For the reasons I have outlined, I have concluded that evidence from the alleged crime scene, the apartment of the accused, including drawings and art work found there, and evidence of his past relationships may indicate sadist sexual interests on the part of the accused. In my view its probative force outweighs the risk of a jury convicting the accused unfairly. Given the rarity, in absolute terms, of death caused by asphyxia in possible circumstances of non-consensual bondage, Dr. BRADFORD is right in my view when he says commonplace inferences in such cases might very well be misleading.

The search warrant was executed on February 19, 1993, and extended several times at the request of the police. They carted away truckloads of potential evidence, viewed more than 100 videotapes in the home until an amended warrant allowed them to remove them, but found only a 90-second clip of Homolka having sex with an unidentified female who appeared to be unconscious. At first the cops thought it was Kristen French, then realized it was yet another victim Homolka hadn't mentioned. The chilling videos they had expected and hoped to find to confirm his guilt in the murders of

Mahaffy and French were not found. A strand of hair similar to French's, and a tiny spot of blood that matched Mahaffy's DNA, were the only physical evidence to put them in the house with Bernardo, pretty thin circumstantial evidence to convict him of their murders.

The disastrous interview and failed house search had produced nothing to clinch a conviction. In any event, the refusal to let Bernardo speak to his lawyer despite his repeated requests meant anything that might have come out of the interview would have been inadmissible in court.

MacKay, though not one of the first to urge a plea bargain with Homolka, certainly favoured such a deal. Bernardo was by far the greater risk, the true sadist. MacKay and Collins suggested cops who would be well suited to handle Homolka and briefed them on how best to do it. MacKay also gave them copies of Roy Hazelwood's research paper on "compliant victims"—which no one had ever heard of and not everyone accepted—to better understand what made her tick.

While all this played out behind the scenes, Segal, apparently out of options, closed what many considered his deal with the devil. (See Figure 9.2.)

Figure 9.2
SEGAL'S DEAL WITH KARLA HOMOLKA

May 14, 1993
Mr. George F. Walker, Q.C.
Barrister and Solicitor

Dear Sir:

I am writing to confirm our mutual understanding respecting a proposed resolution as between the Crown and Karla Bernardo. It has been arrived at after lengthy discussions. If you are in agreement I would be obliged if you would confirm same in writing.

As I understand it your client, after receiving legal advice, has chosen to engage in a process that may lead to a resolution of certain investigations in her case. Your client's position is that she is permanently estranged from her husband with no immunity and is prepared to speak to the police and to testify regarding certain matters as described below.

The outline of the proposed resolution is that your client will provide an induced statement. If the authorities are satisfied at that stage, she will provide cautioned statements. At that point your client will be charged, waive the preliminary inquiry, plead guilty, and be sentenced to twelve years' imprisonment, subject to a judge's approval. I have now had the opportunity to discuss, in general terms, the proposed resolution with the families of the victims. I am totally satisfied that there exists admissible evidence respecting your client's involvement in the crimes for which pleas will be entered. I am in a position to proceed with the proposed resolution. The following represents the terms of our understanding.

(A) Induced Statement

- Your client will attend upon the police.
- The induced statement will not be used against her in any criminal proceedings.
- She will give permission for audio and video taping.
- It will be forthright and truthful. It will be complete, bearing in mind it is an initial statement.
- No assurances can or will be given respecting derivative evidence.
- Upon completion, the Crown and the police will assess it to determine whether they are satisfied that it has been given in a forthright and truthful manner.
- The police may decide that a second induced statement is required if insufficient time is set aside for the initial one.
- If the authorities learn through any means that your client has caused the death of any person, in the sense of her stopping life, any proposed resolution will be terminated at the suit of the Crown, regardless of the state the process is at.
- If any of the above matters are not to the satisfaction of the Crown, resolution discussions will be terminated and if no cautioned statement has been taken, the induced statement will not be used against her.
- The statement and any subsequent statement will be a full, complete,

and truthful account regarding her knowledge and/or involvement or anyone else's involvement in the investigations to the deaths of Leslie Mahaffy; Kristen French; . . . the death of Tammy Homolka; and any other criminal activity she has participated in or has knowledge of.

(B) Cautioned Statement(s)

- They will be under caution.
- They will be under oath.
- Permission will be granted to audio and video tape.
- They will provide no protection for a prosecution if it is discovered that she lied, including a prosecution for obstruct justice, public mischief, fabricating evidence, perjury, inconsistent statements and/or false affidavits.
- The video taped statement(s) will be used at any criminal proceeding if she recants, or if the Crown otherwise tenders them, or if a judge permits their use.
- They will be complete, full, and forthright.
- She shall fairly set out the roles or knowledge of all parties and witnesses to the crimes under investigation, including her role and knowledge.

(C) Other Assistance

- She will provide all reasonable and lawful assistance in permitting the police to recover real evidence, and providing written authority to police to recover real evidence relevant to their inquiries. She will assist the police in their inquiries relating to any real evidence in relation to anyone who is associated with the crimes under investigation.
- She will voluntarily provide fingerprints, handwriting, hair and blood samples, and like matters.
- She will provide a witnessed, written consent to the seizure of all items from 57 Bayview Drive, St. Catharines from February 19 to April 30, 1993, and such other consents respecting real evidence and information as may be requested by the Crown.

(D) Charge, Plea and Sentencing

- Upon conclusion of the receipt of voluntary cautioned statements at such time as the police require, she will be charged.
- She will be charged with two counts of manslaughter in relation to the Mahaffy and French homicides. The defence will consent to the reading in of facts of any other crimes as the Crown deems appropriate, the sentence of twelve years and twelve years concurrent taking into account any such additional matters.
- She shall waive the preliminary inquiry when the Crown deems appropriate.
- An indictment shall be presented.
- A joint submission shall be made for a total sentence of twelve years, comprised of two terms of twelve years concurrent with each other. A $100 weapons order will be requested.
- It is not the intention of the Crown to seek an increase in parole eligibility, given all the circumstances of these matters, including the total sentence that will be sought.
- The Crown is prepared to agree that your client be remanded out of custody, subject to the court's approval, for three weeks, but on satisfactory sureties and in an amount exceeding $100,000, and with such conditions as the Crown may require pending sentence.
- The acceptance of the pleas of guilty, the charge, the sentences, the period of parole ineligibility, and remand out of custody pending sentence are subject to acceptance by the trial judge.
- A refusal by a judge to accept the charges upon which pleas are to be entered, or the proposed sentences, will result in a trial being held on whatever charges the police and the Crown deem appropriate. In such circumstances, the admissibility of the cautioned statements is not affected.
- The Crown's position on sentencing of twelve years, and no less, will take into account any assistance given and proposed, the early pleas, and like factors. The Crown may read in such facts as the Crown deems fit. The Crown is prepared to receive any reasonable suggestions respecting such facts. The Crown will fairly describe to the court

the effect that the pleas and assistance may have, respecting all participants in the crimes.

- Her counsel will voluntarily provide at the first opportunity to inspect a copy of any psychiatric, psychological, or other medical reports.
- The Crown will in its discretion, supported by the defence, and subject to the approval of a judge, tender victim impact statements and related material, and/or move to call the parents of the victims at the sentencing hearing.

(E) Post-Sentencing Matters

- Your client need provide sworn testimony in any and all proceedings to which she is subpoenaed by the Crown arising from her cautioned statements and she will tell the truth.
- The Crown, on behalf of the police, is prepared to write to Correctional Services Canada and/or the Parole Board, attaching a full transcript of all proceedings and making full reference to any assistance offered and received in relation to interviews, testimony, and like matters, all of which will be for the exercise of the discretion of Correctional Services Canada and/or the Parole Board. In the event the accused applies for transfer for purposes of psychiatric treatment while in custody, the Crown and the police will leave such matters to the discretion of Correctional Services Canada and/or the Parole Board.
- Neither the Crown nor the police will make any other warranties respecting post-sentence custody or parole and like matters. The Crown and the police agree that such issues will be in the discretion of Correctional Services Canada and/or the Parole Board.
- While in custody, she will continue to fully assist the authorities.
- If released prior to the termination of all trials involving others implicated in the investigated crimes she will make herself available to be fully interviewed and to testify as required.
- If the sentencing judge imposes a sentence greater than twelve years, nothing prevents the defence from appealing against sentence to seek a reduction to twelve years.
- The Crown is prepared to confirm any aspect of this agreement to a

court or any government agency for the purposes of carrying out what
is contained in this agreement.

(F) Other Matters

- She will not give an account directly or indirectly to the press, media,
  or for the purpose of any book, movie, or like endeavour.
- She will not seek or receive, directly or indirectly, any compensation
  relating to the above, including any and all events and occurrences
  arising from the police investigations, criminal proceedings, or any
  statements given by her to the police. Thank you.

Yours very truly,
Murray D. Segal, Director

At the request of the Crown, the court imposed a media ban as
Karla waived her right to a preliminary hearing then pleaded guilty
to the facts read into evidence and was sentenced to twelve years
concurrent on two counts of manslaughter in the deaths of French
and Mahaffy. As for the death of her youngest sister, Tammy,
whether accidental or deliberate, it never happened as far as the
courts were concerned in Karla's case.

Despite the ban, word leaked quickly and widely and public
outrage was immediate and prolonged. The Crown requested, and
was granted, a preferred indictment by Ontario Attorney General
Marion Boyd to go directly to trial against Bernardo. It was a clear
sign the prosecution had a weak case, but it denied his lawyer an
early opportunity to discredit Homolka's credibility at a preliminary
hearing.

Though media lawyers unsuccessfully appealed the ban, the furor
of the O. J. Simpson media circus had spread to Canada as Internet
chat groups flourished, leaving the victims and their grieving families open to public view too often bordering on obsession. The
setbacks and disappointments seemed unrelenting. Then, when it at
last seemed that they would have their day in court, that justice
would be done for the rape and murder victims, Bernardo's lawyer,
Ken Murray, asked to be removed from the case.

Once excused, Murray offered to Murray the damning video-tapes, which he had removed from his client's home on Bernardo's instructions after the police search warrant had expired. John Rosen, Murray's successor, intercepted the tapes and after reviewing them, surrendered them to the police. For the first time since the Nuremberg War Crimes Trials nearly a half century earlier, the heart-wrenching plight of the victims of sadism and cold, calculated murder was broadcast in open court. Bernardo was convicted, pleaded guilty to the rapes, and was jailed indefinitely as a Danger-ous Sexual Offender.

MacKay wasn't there for the final triumph. He had left long before to profile the worst mass murderer in Canadian history—the Yellowknife Bomber—with help from Quantico classmate Agent Gus Gary, of the U.S. Bureau of Alcohol, Tobacco, and Firearms (ATF).

IO

The Yellowknife Bomber

On February 22, 1993, five days after Bernardo was arrested at home and three days after the search was launched at the house he shared with Homolka at 57 Bayview Drive, MacKay arrived in Yellowknife, Northwest Territories, to profile the worst mass murder on Canadian soil, second only to the Air India bombing, in Canadian history: the Royal Oak "Giant" gold mine bombing. It was a sign that his message was being heard as the request for his profiling services by the Mountie investigators in Yellowknife made him the only investigator directly involved at the same time in Canada's two most publicized, most heinous, and perhaps most baffling murder cases.

He was accompanied by ATF Agent Gus Gary, his former Quantico classmate from Alabama. The veteran bombing and arson investigator from America's Deep South arrived determined to help catch a mass killer in Canada's Far North, an optimism born of his own life experiences.

If major-crimes investigators routinely pride themselves on having heard and seen it all, most had probably heard and seen less than Gary in his formative years. Born in Mobile, where his father built Liberty transport ships, Gary grew up in York, a small town near the Mississippi state line, and had a front-row seat to the drama of the American civil rights movement of the 1950s and 1960s. At age 17, he had watched the Alabama National Guard escort Freedom Rider buses through hostile crowds. It was a violent era in the South and opposition to nonviolent civil rights protest was often swift and brutal. In an era of racial beatings, bombs, burning churches and crosses, lynchings, and murdered children and civil rights workers,

Alabama politics extended to the college gridiron. When fan passions flared against a black player with the USC Trojans who seemed to be single-handedly savaging Bear Bryant's all-white Crimson Tide at the University of Alabama, an enduring bastion of segregation, Gary recalled with awe how Bryant had crossed the field at the end of the game, thrown a protective arm around the player, and escorted him safely off the field.

Motivated by the youthful ideals espoused by John Kennedy's presidency, Gary remained proud of his rebel heritage and had retraced the steps of an ancestor killed defending Richmond, Virginia, capital of the Confederacy, whose 1864 death notice remains a family heirloom. A century after that bitter civil war to save the Union and free the slaves, black churches across the South were torched and bombed, culminating in the murder of three young black children attending Sunday school in a Birmingham church basement. That tragedy haunted Gary, and the alleged killers are only now being brought to justice nearly 50 years later.

Steeped in "service to country" and nurtured by relatives and family friends serving in the military and law enforcement, Gary was drawn to a job that promised action. The ATF was the only agency hiring when he graduated with a degree in history and political science from Tuscaloosa. More than a job, it had allure, tracing its roots to Eliot Ness and his famed Untouchables in the Bureau of Prohibition. Sworn in as a Special Agent in 1967, the 23-year-old satisfied his yen for action and history, working alongside oldtimers who included Ness' former Chicago clerk and Sam Posey, legendary for chasing the Purple Gang in Detroit and plying the Great Lakes to stop Canadian liquor from entering America illegally during Prohibition. Gary's debut as a "revenuer" may have offered less glory, but there was risk equal to that of the Capone days. Outsiders approached the moonshiners in the Freedom Hills of northern Alabama at their peril and sawed-off shotguns were routinely seized with the bootleg booze. Shots were often fired and high-speed chases topped 130 miles per hour.

A year after he joined the Bureau, the 1968 federal Firearms Law authorized ATF agents to handle commercial explosives for the first time. His U.S. Army training qualified him to blow up, rather than seize, the rudimentary stills in the hills. By 1972, Gary could dismantle and defuse explosives at the Army's Hazardous Devices School and had been trained by the ATF in post-blast investigative technique. Death had become a constant companion. In one instance, only half of the six sticks of dynamite set to blow the pilings of a Mississippi bridge had exploded. Gary retrieved the remaining three to test them for latent prints; but while he was handling them—without protective gloves or clothing—nitroglycerin leached into his pores and he was rushed to a hospital cardiac intensive care unit. He nearly died, but rallied and was soon investigating bombings in Alabama's strike-torn coal strip-mines. In 1979 he was named to the newly created ATF's National Response Team (NRT), and crisscrossed the country probing deadly fires and explosions, playing his own vital role in helping the NRT to solve 92 percent of the hundreds of cases it investigated.

It should have surprised no one when Gary agreed, even before arriving in Yellowknife, that the Giant gold mine bombing was highly solvable. His conviction was underscored by piercing eyes—some said they could unnerve even the innocent—that belied by his sense of humour. In Ottawa, he ragged on MacKay for taking him so close to the Arctic Circle in January instead of July but his engaging smile was long gone when he stepped off the plane in Yellowknife to help identify a mass murderer.

Five months earlier, on September 18, 1992, the simmering violence of a prolonged labour dispute had literally exploded in an underground blast that killed nine miners who had crossed a union picket line to go to work. The victims had included three "scab" replacement workers from distant mines and six local union brothers who had recently returned to work after manning the picket lines and rocking buses transporting workers past the strikers.

The Mountie investigators had identified two of the union miners as their chief suspects and hoped MacKay's profile could help them narrow that down to one. MacKay had turned to Gary for help for several reasons. Practically, Gary was very good at what he did and very experienced with bombs and bombers; he had a proven and distinguished track record. Psychologically, nothing grabbed attention like the arrival of an American profiler on the scene. After two years of promoting his skills across Canada, MacKay had accepted that he had less visibility on either side of the Blue Wall than FBI or ATF profilers and sagely concluded that including Gary would create a larger media fuss and be more apt to smoke out the bomber.

MacKay wanted it known well in advance that Gary was heading north, hoping it would give the killer, and anyone who knew or may have conspired with him, something to think about. It might even defuse the tensions between the striking miners and the local cops they denounced as the "Royal Oak Mounted Police." The psychological groundwork was laid in a newspaper article that had run on page 3 of a Saturday edition of the *Edmonton Journal* early the previous December. The article, datelined Quantico, Virginia, ran under a six-column banner headline, "U.S. expert creating offender profiles in Yellowknife bombing."

RCMP investigators have tapped the expertise of an American crimefighter to help identify suspects in the September 18 bomb-blast deaths of nine miners at the Giant Mine in Yellowknife.

Gordon P. "Gus" Gary, 48, a 25-year veteran with the Alcohol, Tobacco and Firearms (ATF) Bureau of the U.S. Treasury Department, has been enlisted to help. His speciality is creating "offender" profiles to track down serial arsonists and bombers.

His pioneering work in the art of probing minds helped crack the case of a tragic fire at the Dupont Plaza Hotel in San Juan, Puerto Rico, which killed ninety-seven people. He has been based at the National Center for the Analysis of Crime run by the FBI since 1989. The FBI behavioural sciences service was showcased in the film *Silence of the Lambs*.

Based on interviews with more than one hundred convicted arsonists and bombers, Gary suspects the blast at the strike-bound gold mine owned by Royal Oak Mines, Inc., was murder. The targets were three outside replacement workers and six local miners who crossed union picket lines to return to work.

No matter how many people were involved with the planning, execution and possible cover-up of the events at the gold mine, Gary predicts that a "dominant personality" will emerge.

"The behavior exhibited is usually that of the dominant offender," he says. "If there are multiple offenders, the actions of the lower echelon will reflect his demands [and personality]."

If a conspiracy exists to commit or cover up the killings, Gary expects solidarity to crack as it did in Puerto Rico where he helped identify the arsonists who torched a hotel on New Year's Eve, 1986.

Gary's profiles led police to six hotel employees, all members or executives of Teamsters Local 901, who voted to strike prior to the fire. Another union suspect committed suicide to avoid questioning.

Five men were sentenced to from 75 to 99 years for first-degree murder, largely on the testimony of a cleaner who admitted setting the fire with a can of cooking oil from the hotel kitchen.

Gary calls him "the last man on the bus," who realized his only hope for special consideration in court lay in co-operation.

Gary sees several striking similarities between the two cases— simmering labor-related confrontations that erupted into violence and "revenge-motivated" murder that are "inside jobs" where the victims are known to their killer(s).

He denies that he is targeting the striking Canadian Association of Smelter and Allied Workers, but has not ruled out an unsanctioned attack, noting that any group can have its "loose cannon."

While blast damage at the Royal Oak mine eliminated crucial evidence at the scene, Gary notes that the Dupont Plaza fire also consumed key evidence, but he was able to create profiles that led to arrest and conviction.

He agrees with RCMP statements that the Royal Oak blast is "highly solvable."

Forensic results from lab tests by the RCMP's post-blast team in Ottawa are imminent and will determine, with his own analysis, if Gary will visit Yellowknife. Although no plans exist, a visit to the murder scene has not been ruled out.

Whether the *Journal* article exemplified cooperation between the police and the media in a common cause for the greater good—catching a killer—or bordered on media manipulation, it served MacKay's needs well. It was a welcome contrast to the escalating hostility between some cops and reporters covering the Green Ribbon Task Force in southern Ontario, exacerbated by a ban on publishing any details of the Homolka guilty plea prior to Bernardo's distant rape and murder trials. The article left no doubt that Gary was a man on a mission, that he had the experience and credentials to catch the bomber and that he agreed with the Mountie investigators that the case was "highly solvable." MacKay was never named so as to focus on the higher profile of the American agent from the ATF.

Despite what they had told the press, there was never any doubt that Gary and MacKay would visit the murder scene. The carnage in the bowels of the Giant gold mine was a classic setting for the profilers to do what they do best: see what the killer saw, hear what he heard, smell what he smelled, sense what he'd sensed. While there was always other important evidence to consider—investigators' notes, crime-scene photos, medical and investigative reports—they were no substitute for visiting the actual scene.

After reviewing case files and absorbing the forensic and trace evidence, Gary and MacKay went down and stood where the killer had stood, turning slowly in a circle, trying hard to put themselves in his shoes at the moment he set the bomb. As his final act to recreate as nearly as possible the exact environment the killer must have had, MacKay asked for the lights and ventilation fans to be killed. Engulfed in total silence in a void so dark it seemed choking, the two profilers knew at once that the bomber had to be a miner, familiar with his surroundings and explosives. No one else could have done this under these conditions.

As always, the profilers were not there to solve the crime, but to help point investigators toward the type of person most likely to blow apart nine men on their way to work. As always, victimology was a vital clue: how the killer selected his victims, whom he killed, and how he did it could tell them a great deal. Were the victims specific or random? Why use a bomb? How did he bomb? Similarly, post-offence behaviour could prove significant. Whether a lone bomber had killed the miners or he was helped, the subsequent behaviour was fairly predictable and would likely become more pronounced as the risk to the offender escalated. It would affect even the most callous individual, and the distress he felt for himself or his victims would magnify any existing personality disorders. For example, a drug or alcohol habit would grow more pronounced. An introvert would withdraw more deeply into himself; an extrovert would grow more bombastic. He could change his circle of friends. Or he could fabricate a reason to suddenly leave town. Possibly he had already left town before the profilers arrived.

It would be the same for any accomplice or co-conspirator. No matter how many people were involved in the bombing, or knew who was, a dominant personality would emerge. He would manipulate others to his own ends and, if he even suspected he was at risk, would sacrifice them without a second thought. His one goal was to escape detection and apprehension. To accomplish that, he considered all others expendable. It would be vital to him to remain in control. That could be hard in a conspiracy. Others would know what he knew. When the first tile fell, the domino effect would threaten to take him down as well. Everyone would then be at risk.

In the Yellowknife murders, as in so many other cases, there were hundreds of suspects and no tangible evidence against any of them. The senior Mountie investigators had nevertheless narrowed the field to two suspects they strongly suspected had set the fatal bomb. As in the Green Ribbon investigation, in which eyewitnesses had

reported two people had abducted Kristen French, the profile of the
Yellowknife Bomber was based on the dominant suspect:

> The dominant offender in this case will be a white male with an
> estimated age in excess of thirty years. His childhood years will
> reflect a disruptive rearing environment. He will have a deep-
> seated need to seek respect. While he may present a face of
> confidence, he suffers from well-hidden insecurities.
>
> The anger which perpetrated this offence is mostly deperson-
> alized and is directed at "Scabs" generally and not toward indi-
> vidual persons. . . . The victims represented not persons, but
> objects upon which he could focus his anger while carrying out
> an act that would demonstrate his importance to his peers.
>
> The prerequisites required to complete this crime would be
> extensive knowledge of mining operations generally and long-
> standing experience and geographic familiarity with this mine in
> particular.

Few still doubted that the killer was a miner, most likely one of
the CASAW strikers: a lone wolf. Even the close-knit community of
miners had begun to accept grudgingly that the killer was one of
their own—that the local victims had likely known their killer. The
profile predicted he would demonstrate an observable change in his
behaviour that would grow more erratic as the noose tightened. He
might skip town; maybe he had already left. But the community
knew him, even if they didn't suspect he was the bomber. If it was a
conspiracy, and more than one person was involved in planning or
triggering the bomb, the first domino would eventually topple. That
would be the weak link, and when the investigators found it, everyone involved would be at risk. Then, the only way out was to deal
for a lesser sentence and, as Gary was fond of pointing out, there
was only room for one on that bus. All others would be facing first-
degree murder charges and long, hard time in prison.

The profile excited the media more than the investigators, who
seemed to feel it told them nothing they didn't already know or

suspect. There was nothing in it to deter them from pursuing their two prime suspects, but the Crown Attorney insisted that no charges be laid against them until the "lone wolf" theory was dismissed and that suspect excluded.

That task fell to veteran interrogator Sergeant Gregg McMartin, who was brought in from Calgary RCMP. Reviewing the case file on the "lone wolf" suspect, including the transcripts of his 11 earlier interviews with investigators and sessions with two respected polygraph operators, McMartin was convinced that his previous statements—what he had not said as much as what he had—raised serious suspicions. His refusal to exclude him without a chance to interrogate him himself did not endear him to the senior investigators.

MacKay and Gary's profile had also twigged something for McMartin. While it fit several miners, including the two prime suspects, in general, several specific predictions dovetailed nicely with his statement analysis of the third strong suspect. For example, they predicted the killer would have never anticipated the deep public abhorrence to his violence, and his inner turmoil, conflicts, and demons would be reflected in his answers under interrogation. He'd be both proud and ashamed of murdering the nine replacement miners.

McMartin, already convinced the third man was the killer, saw it more simply. His suspect was lying through his teeth. He'd killed nine men and he'd be forced to confess no matter how long it took. The Mountie sergeant was a proven interrogator with a reputation for results. Equally effective with or without using a polygraph machine, he also had a rare ability to play both the good and the bad cop role all by himself to wring a confession from the most stubborn suspect. While the senior investigators discounted the profile as being too general to be of much help, McMartin was a bit more sympathetic, seeing it for what it was—one more weapon in an arsenal to get a confession.

And in the end, while the profile didn't determine his approach to the ensuing interrogation of the "lone wolf" suspect, its behavioural predictions were borne out under the pressure he exerted. But MacKay was long gone by then, stopping briefly to consult with the Green Ribbon Task Force in southern Ontario before moving on to profile other cold cases and the most bizarre and violent crimes across Canada.

The dismissive attitude of the senior Yellowknife investigators toward the profile was nothing new to MacKay. The rules of the game were simple. If a profile helped lead to a suspect, an arrest, and a conviction, the glory went to the investigators. That was fair. But what was discouraging was the lack of even a kind word for profiling that might help promote the service to other cops. The behavioural work was performed behind the scenes, and never was the adage more true: Out of sight, out of mind. If profiling helped, and MacKay felt he had proved repeatedly by this point that it could, then it should be used by everyone whenever appropriate. But how to get that message out when too many cops across Canada, especially outside the RCMP and OPP, didn't know it existed?

Still, despite the lack of formal recognition, MacKay's phone continued to ring. He had the distinction of being the only cop in Canada to work simultaneously on the two highest-profile murder cases of the era—of the century according to some media—committed half a continent apart. And horrific as those murders were, Yellowknife and Green Ribbon were simply the deadly tip of the iceberg. Many, many others, just as vicious and heartrending, had occurred across Canada, less well known because they had been committed far from the English-language media base in Toronto. Sadly, MacKay had no shortage of work.

Yellowknife was not the first time MacKay and McMartin had collaborated on a case. Although they have still never met in person, they first worked the same case in early 1991 when they reviewed the unsolved murder of Lucie Turmel, a female cab driver in her early twenties who had been found brutally stabbed to death the previous spring in Banff, Alberta. She had moved from Quebec in

1987, one of millions of vacationers, transients, and job seekers who flock every summer into the world-famous tourist town of 8000 people nestled amid the majestic beauty and serenity of the Rocky Mountains. Turmel had a job, a fiancé, and no apparent enemies.

Once again, investigators had no shortage of suspects in an unsolved murder and no evidence to charge anyone. They were, however, able to trace the victim's final minutes. At about 1:30 a.m., May 17, 1990, Turmel had shared a few moments with her fiancé in her idling cab before heading off to pick up one last fare and calling it a night. She had picked up a man and two women at the Banff Springs Hotel. The women were never identified, and it's unknown where they got out, but it is known that Turmel drove off alone with the man. Ten minutes later, another cabbie spotted her taxi passing by, driven by a man he could not identify in the dark. Suspicious, he tailed the stolen cab down a dead-end road to a remote wooded area. Running out of road, the driver bolted out of the cab into the woods and disappeared. The cabbie never saw his face.

Turmel's bloodied body was found dumped in the middle of a Banff street about a block from her fiancé's home. Her slashed carotid artery showed how she had died and the defensive wounds on her gashed hands bore mute testimony to how hard she had fought to live. The evidence suggested a violent struggle; the clock suggested it had been tragically brief. The windows and steering wheel of the abandoned cab were smeared with blood which they assumed was the victim's, but aside from a few coins on the floor there was no sign of the money she had made that night. Robbery was considered the motive for the attack.

The first surprise was the result of the blood testing at the crime lab. Although blood tests back then were primitive, they were sufficient to type and identify as male or female. The cops were told the blood was a man's. It was the first link the cops had to her killer but they still had no one to match to it.

The shock of the first murder in Banff in nearly 30 years faded over the months the police spent trying to find the killer. Although they had found a bloodstained 11-inch hunting knife in a nearby driveway on the morning after the murder, and confirmed through forensic testing that it was indeed the murder weapon, it bore no fingerprints or any other evidence to help link it to the killer. A photo of the knife ran in the local media and led to some tips, but still no killer.

Among the scores of suspects interviewed by the police was Ryan Love, a transient part-time worker from British Columbia. In his hotel room they found an empty knife sheath, and he admitted the murder weapon was his knife, but claimed it had been stolen a month earlier and he'd never thought to report it. Ryan wasn't excluded, but a stronger, more logical prime suspect had emerged.

He was a known violent criminal with a long record who had escaped custody in Calgary and arrived in Banff the day before the murder. Banff was a favoured hangout of his when he wasn't in jail. The local Mounties asked him to provide samples for DNA testing, something that didn't exist at the time of the murder. Although the man denied any involvement with the murder, he refused, and the Criminal Code back then gave police no power to compel his cooperation. But the cops overcame that apparent roadblock by recovering a hair from his brush in an undercover "sting" operation.

To everyone's amazement, the result from the crime lab was negative. The cops had to eliminate their prime suspect. They were back at square one.

In frustration, they asked MacKay, 18 months after the murder, to profile the case. As he probed the "victim-offender interaction," MacKay was immediately intrigued by the short time span involved. Less than eight minutes had elapsed from the time the young woman had picked up her fares and the time of her murder, and that was unique in MacKay's experience. There was no evidence that the attack had been in any way sexually motivated, confirming robbery as the motive. Nor did the murder appear to have been planned. The attack had been hurried, impulsive, and brutal. MacKay surmised that the woman's resistance had caught her killer unawares, that he had probably believed waving a knife or other weapon in her face would be enough to make her hand over her money. When it hadn't, armed robbery had abruptly, unexpectedly, and tragically escalated to murder.

MacKay's profile suggested the killer was new to Banff because anyone who knew the area well would never have driven to a dead-end road. There was no exit off the road before it ended, a known fact to long-term residents. But he had seemed to be familiar with the main streets and was probably employed part-time in the town. Banff resorts hired hundreds of students from across Canada for the tourist season, packed into cramped living quarters dubbed "student ghettos." Whoever had jumped out of the cab that night had picked an ideal spot—the short distance across country to the Banff Springs Hotel where he could dissolve into the crowds of student workers and hotel guests. The killer would have found an excuse to leave Banff soon after the murder.

By the time police interviewed his roommate, Love was long gone. The cops found a knife sheath but the roommate said it wasn't his, couldn't remember seeing the knife, and no one made the connection to the murder weapon nor tied the evidence to Love.

At about the same time, a young investigator asked McMartin to review the transcripts of some early suspect interviews. He had heard McMartin's lecture praising statement analysis as an investigative tool to separate liars from those telling the truth and wondered if he could help on the baffling Banff murder. Although never officially part of that investigation, McMartin happily agreed to help. He was immediately struck by Love's statements, stumbling over the pronoun "she" five times and later blaming her murder on the victim.

The case demonstrated the power of two separate investigative tools that shared at least one characteristic: it was not necessary to have access to the suspect. Both were equally adept at pointing a finger by reading the signs, whether it was ritual and signature or vocabulary and syntax. While profiling made no effort to specify a suspect, just tried to refocus an investigation and steer investigators to the type of person who most likely could and would commit the crime, statement analysis dealt in individuals, and McMartin was positive that Love was the killer.

A review of airline records had also confirmed another aspect of MacKay's profile: Love had indeed left town right after the murder.

The investigators learned that his family had sent him an airline ticket to attend an out-of-province reunion, but that he had been otherwise broke. The profile had suggested a personality type who would like to be the centre of attention. It would make sense that Love had taken two women for a ride in a cab to impress them, then left alone in the taxi, planning to rob the cabbie. But it was all circumstantial.

A second covert sting operation was mounted, involving two undercover policewomen spending the evening with Love in his hotel room. They left early, leaving him alone in his room and hopefully so sexually frustrated that he would "take matters into his own hand." The next day, another undercover cop, posing as a chambermaid, searched his room but found nothing that could produce a DNA sample for testing.

Another was arranged. Love was to guard a hotel room while undercover cops pretended to leave to stage a robbery. Though all they got from his room the next day was a tissue he'd used to blow his nose, there was sufficient mucus for a DNA test. Love's sample matched perfectly the extremely rare swab taken from the victim's taxicab. At the time of his arrest, police found he still had a newspaper clipping about the murder and a photo of the knife in his wallet, small signs that he took pride in his "accomplishment."

At trial, Love's lawyer argued that to admit DNA evidence would call the administration of justice into disrepute; the judge ruled that it would bring the administration of justice into disrepute to exclude the evidence, given the violence of the murder. Love—proclaiming his innocence to the end—was convicted and sentenced to life in prison.

The Banff murder was a classic example of a truly significant case that changed the law of the land without the sensational media reporting of self-styled "Crimes of the Century." Beyond its impact as one of the first cases to accept DNA evidence, it was a factor in later amendments to the Criminal Code of Canada that empowered police to compel suspects to provide hair, fluid, and blood samples for testing.

The Banff tragedy was also a reminder of the elevated risk that women face at night.

In October 1991, Keith Davidson had hosted Project Eclipse in Vancouver. For eight days, Rossmo from the Vancouver Police and profilers from the RCMP, the OPP, the FBI, New York State Police, and the South Carolina Law Enforcement Division gathered to review the murders of 25 prostitutes and young women to try to behaviourally link as many of the homicides as they could. MacKay linked four deaths, and all agreed they were probably the work of a single killer. His efforts did not lead to immediate arrests, but what was significant was that for the first time ever, an international murder workshop, hosted in Canada, drew the best and brightest of the behavioural experts into one room to help solve a series of brutal crimes. Profiling and linking the crimes, it was hoped, would be the first step to catching the killer(s).

In the spring of 1993, from March 20 to April 1, the process was repeated with Project Kayo, in Edmonton. Once again, an international cast of behavioural experts gathered to review 14 unsolved murders, including those of two Calgary prostitutes who had simply disappeared.

The first body had been recovered by accident, turned over by a bulldozer at a construction site. The second had been found in the woods, on top of the ground. Here too there were signs that the killer had tried to bury his victim, but he had apparently given up because of the many tree roots that blocked easy digging. Like most sexual predators, the profilers concluded, this killer had been a "lazy sucker." MacKay's profile matched a man whom Calgary police later charged with the attempted abduction of a woman. They had caught him trying to stuff his victim into the trunk of her car, alongside a shovel they believed he had placed there to bury her with later. He was jailed for that offence, but was never tried for the prostitute murders.

Hookers weren't the only victims that tragic spring in Edmonton. In May 1992, a three-year-old girl was abducted from a playground near her home. She was found alive and suffering from exposure the next morning by horseback riders in a remote rural area several miles north of the city. She had been strangled and left for dead, and the trauma of that experience—both physical and emotional—

coupled with her young age made it almost impossible for her to give the city police investigators any information.

That September, following a police press conference, the *Edmonton Journal* reported that a city detective had lamented the lack of results despite a thorough investigation. It was hoped that the girl might be able to provide more details when she got older, but until then or until the police got new evidence or a lead from elsewhere, the abduction would remain unsolved. There were other crimes to investigate and they had to push ahead on those.

Four days after that story ran, a six-year-old girl was abducted from her backyard while playing with a four-year-old friend behind her parents' condo. A man simply walked up, carried her away, and drove off in a van. The girl's body was found at an Edmonton truck stop. She had been sexually assaulted and then carefully redressed after being killed.

MacKay's profile linked the two abductions behaviourally, but the Edmonton police insisted publicly that they were investigating the two abductions as parallel but separate crimes. They had no problem with MacKay telling the media that he believed they were linked, but it seemed to him that they had no intention of admitting that a serial predator was running free in Edmonton grabbing children with impunity and that they had no idea who he was or how to stop him. Amid private fretting behind the scenes by some that the *Journal* article may have somehow emboldened or provoked the killer to strike again, this time with fatal consequences, MacKay saw the media as a good way to generate new leads.

The dramatic recreation of the Kristen French abduction in southern Ontario had led to a flood of tips to the Green Ribbon Task Force and it was hoped the same would happen here. Someone must have seen something that could help find the roving sexual predator. Two competing TV stations, ITV and Global, quickly agreed to air a simulcast called "Somebody Out There Knows." (The CBC, Canada's national public television broadcaster, declined to participate.) It produced no helpful leads, nor did a later reenactment on the popular American television program *Unsolved Mysteries*, but when host Robert Stack dubbed him "Canada's foremost criminal profiler," MacKay got more publicity and recognition than he'd mustered across Canada in nearly three years.

It was time to put Kim Rossmo's theory to the test. MacKay urged the Edmonton police to bring him in to perform a geographic profile—the first time they worked together on a case.

Back in British Columbia, MacKay met with Rossmo and Keith Davidson in his hotel room next to Vancouver's City Hall to discuss the case. He asked Rossmo if a geographic profile could be used to prioritize postal codes in the criminal's hunting area: a simple but powerful idea. The prioritized postal codes could be fed into Alberta's Department of Motor Vehicle (DMV) record system, along with the vehicle type ("van") and colour. It was estimated that a three-parameter search of DMV files (vehicle type, colour, and registered owner's postal code) in a city the size of Edmonton would produce only about 65 suspect vehicles—a manageable number for a major crime investigation.

MacKay's idea opened up a whole new range of options for geographic profiling. Not only could maps be produced to show the likely area of an offender's residence, but spatial data of any type could be prioritized. The potential was exciting, as an estimated 85 percent of records contain an address, the "handle" that can be used to manipulate data.

Rossmo completed the Edmonton profile, and after learning more than he ever wanted to know about postal codes, he and Davidson spent hours listing and prioritizing hundreds of them by hand. The latest geographic profiling software, Rigel, can now accomplish this task in just a few seconds, but in 1992 the system was not so powerful and Rossmo and Davidson's combined efforts were complicated by other problems. For example, the man who had abducted the murdered girl was reported to have driven a van. But evidence at the scene where they had found her body suggested a front-wheel-drive vehicle such as a K-car. While it might seem a simple matter to search the DMV database, that information is stored in a way that does not lend itself to "data mining." There was also a technical problem in that each province had its own system.

An inability to retrieve information quickly or easily requires a new computer program to be written. That takes time and time is of the essence in a fresh serial or major-crime investigation. Also, writing a new program to enable an outside agency—or any combination of federal, provincial, and municipal jurisdictions—to access government data raises special political and legal implications of privacy and access to information. It's always a "tomorrow" issue and tomorrow never comes. By the end of an investigation, when there might be time to write a completely new computer program, another case rears up and everyone moves on. MacKay put it on his "to do" list for when he retired.

Meanwhile, nothing· worked. The *Unsolved Mysteries* episode aired several times over the next few years with no result. The abductions of the young girls have never been solved. Two more cold trails astride many, many dark paths.

Profiling so many deaths was grim work, and any distraction was welcomed. Two of those reviewing the cases of Project Kayo, Gerry Séguin, from Quebec, and Henry Derkach, the RCMP coordinator for Saskatchewan, slipped away to watch a couple of NHL hockey games. Edmonton Oiler owner Peter Pocklington had traded superstar Wayne Gretzky to Los Angeles and the hometown fans had expressed their dismay, it seemed to Séguin, by cheering harder for the visiting Toronto Maple Leafs and Montreal Canadiens than for the struggling hometown crew.

After one of the games, Séguin and Derkach visited a local pub. Besides the few patrons, there was an unhappy publican lamenting an Australian wine he had purchased in bulk and that no one would drink. Pressed for details, the bartender confessed that the wine tasted "like horse piss." Séguin found that hard to believe and cheerily accepted a free sample. A sip confirmed the diagnosis. Not just any horse—this one had been ill! Nevertheless, Séguin surprised the owner by promptly ordering a bottle, negotiating a vastly reduced price. The publican cheerfully pocketed the five dollars and probably thought Séguin as crazy as Derkach must have.

Séguin sought out FBI profiler Jim Wright. As the most seasoned among the international cast gathered in Edmonton, and the man MacKay had asked to be his Bureau contact when he had returned to Canada from Quantico, Wright seemed the logical choice to present a thank-you gift to their host at the end of the project. When Séguin explained the story of the wine, Wright gleefully agreed to present the bottle to MacKay.

On April 1—appropriately enough—after suitable kind words, the wine was presented and poured. MacKay took a swig. For five or ten seconds, which must have seemed an eternity to him as the wine curdled in his mouth, for he was too gracious to spit out the odious brew, the audience of profilers from across Canada and the United States watched with straight faces as long as they could. When they finally exploded in laughter, MacKay promptly, and no doubt with great relief, spit the wine back into his glass with his patent comment for all disasters: "Oh, good."

A few months after Project Kayo, MacKay was summoned to Buctouche, New Brunswick, to help the local Mounties solve the murder of Marcel Cormier and the disappearance of his teenage girl-friend, Marcia LeBlanc. The evidence suggested that the couple had been parked, unaware of the killer as he approached them from behind. Firing his Lee-Enfield .303 rifle through the rear window, the blast killed Cormier in the driver's seat of his father's car and blew out the front window. The driver's side rear door window had also been broken and the cops believed that LeBlanc had been forcibly abducted; the killer had either pulled her through that broken window or reached in, unlocked the door, and crawled in after her.

The investigators, who had been frantic to find Marcia, had discovered a cartridge at the scene which they believed had been ejected when the killer loaded another round. With that as their only evidence, they had canvassed the area, visiting all known owners of a Lee-Enfield .303.

This group had included a man named Roger LeBlanc, no relation to the missing girl. LeBlanc admitted owning that type of rifle and offered to bring in a shell casing the next day. The cops had him fire a round into a woodpile and took the casing for analysis. The ploy had forced his hand and, in the few days it took to test the evidence at the crime lab and confirm through ballistics that LeBlanc's gun had fired the fatal shot, he had fled.

That was the situation greeting MacKay when he arrived. He faced two pressing questions that required immediate answers: Was the girl still alive and if so, where was she? Calls had come in to police reporting the sighting of the abductor and his victim in Halifax, Toronto, Maine, and elsewhere. MacKay analyzed the case and concluded it was unlikely that the missing girl was still alive. He also believed it possible that her killer was also dead by his own hand.

The cops located the fugitive's abandoned vehicle and launched two massive searches with help from the military. Neither the suspect nor the missing girl was found.

MacKay described geographic profiling to the local Mounties who, at his urging, brought Rossmo, now promoted from constable to acting detective inspector, into the investigation.

After being briefed on the details of the crime and told about MacKay's belief that the missing girl was dead and that her killer may have committed suicide, Rossmo identified two areas where each body was likely to be located, although he had too few geographic points to use his computer algorithm. He theorized that if the Catholic killer was suicidal, he might not want his body found lest people learn he had taken his own life; he'd just want to disappear. Rossmo urged local investigators to look within his prioritized areas for sites from which LeBlanc's body could disappear after he'd shot himself, such as bodies of water or high points near inaccessible ravines. An RCMP sergeant pointed out there was a railroad trestle over a stream right in the peak area of the profile, and asked if that was the sort of place Rossmo meant. Indeed. That spring, when the snow melted, LeBlanc's rifle with an spent cartridge in the chamber was recovered under the trestle, and his shirt, still buttoned, was found snagged on a tree after the runoff.

The theory was simple: The killer had shot himself, and his body had fallen into the river and washed out to sea.

A third search was launched and the missing girl's body was found in the secondary area Rossmo had specified.

On the evening of October 16, 1993, MacKay was called at home by an investigator in Yellowknife who told him that the suspect they'd arrested for the mine bombing fit his profile. Recalling the two contending prime suspects, he asked which it had been. Neither. It had been suspect number three, the "lone wolf." He had confessed under McMartin's interrogation. It was the first time MacKay heard the name Roger Warren, later convicted of murdering the nine miners.

MacKay was pleased the case had finally been solved and happy for McMartin's success, but he had other things on his mind. In less than two months, he planned to formally launch ViCLAS. Ever the diplomat, he set up the debut of the revolutionary new program to link serial rapes and murders at the Ontario Provincial Police Academy in Brampton.

11

ViCLAS

From December 11 to 17, 1993, Canadian investigators from 23 city, regional, and provincial police forces; and RCMP detachments from St. John's to Vancouver; and members from four major American crime-fighting agencies gathered at the Ontario Provincial Police Academy in Brampton, near Toronto, to mark the official unveiling of the long-awaited Violent Crime Linkage Analysis System: ViCLAS. It had been more than 18 months since MacKay's first public reference to his vision for revolutionizing police investigations at the University of Windsor's first annual conference on serial, mass, and spree murder, and almost as long since Keith Davidson had transformed that dream into reality with the spectacular success of his MACROS prototype linking within minutes the brutal rape of a Surrey teen to several other assaults nearby and in distant Prince Rupert.

Unveiling ViCLAS at the OPP Academy was politically astute, allowing MacKay, ever the pragmatist, to underscore his message to the assembled investigators, senior police brass, and awestruck journalists that ViCLAS was to be shared with all police forces, heralded by the slogan provided by Metro Toronto Police as a revolutionary system "created by Canadian police for Canadian police." Although the OPP was out in force, including Commissioner Tom O'Grady, a former Mountie troop mate of RCMP Commissioner Norm Inkster, and profiler Kate Lines, who had done most of the organizing, they kept a fairly low profile, allowing the spotlight to focus on the Mounties who had conceived and produced the system—MacKay, Davidson, and Johnson. It was perhaps the greatest example of interagency cooperation since OPP Inspector Moe Pilon had been named the first, and only, non-Mountie ever to head the Canadian Intelligence Security Commission (CISC)—the federal government's watchdog on organized crime.

The official unveiling was staged at a press conference on December 16. No one in the room that day was prouder than Johnson, the self-confessed "techno-dolt" who had journeyed the road less travelled, reviewing American systems, adapting what worked, avoiding what didn't, to create a computer system so simple even he could use it.

But no one was going to use it quite yet. While the technology now existed, the cases did not. The ceremony in Brampton was the first of three phases that promised a fully operational and interconnected system would be up and running by the end of 1995 and resolved MacKay's chicken-and-egg dilemma whether to wait until the database had enough cases to link before launching ViCLAS, or present the technology in the hope that ensuing publicity would help convince investigators to submit their cases. When the forms, designed with input from Collins to ensure they captured behavioural details that would satisfy both criminal and medical criteria, were approved and printed at the end of November, MacKay quickly gauged the timing was right to push ahead.

Beyond ensuring the behavioural integrity of the questions from a medical point of view, Collins, the forensic psychiatrist, played one other crucial role, suggesting the Latin motto—"*Non omnis moriar*" ("Everything does not die")—for the analysts who would actually run the system, analyze the data, and make the links. It was originally the motto of a heroic underground hospital in the Warsaw Ghetto obliterated by Hitler's storm troopers.

The Canadian Association of Violent Crime Analysts (CAVCA) was launched at the same time as ViCLAS, spearheaded by Davidson, who talked MacKay into serving as vice-president and Jim Moores of Metro Toronto, who had coined the ViCLAS made-in-Canada slogan, as president. The analysts, all veteran investigators, had a mandate to:

- Encourage and develop cooperation among all accredited police organizations in the professional and ethical use of

Criminal Investigative Analysis (psychological profiling) and
related techniques.

- Encourage and develop cooperation among all accredited police
  organizations in the professional and ethical use of ViCLAS and
  related computer systems.
- Advance the scientific, professional, and public acceptance of the
  contributions of Criminal Investigative Analysis and related
  techniques in the promotion of public welfare.
- Promote and maintain high standards of ethics, integrity,
  honour, and conduct in using profiling and related techniques.
- Advance the knowledge, skill, and status of those engaged in the
  field of profiling by providing a clearinghouse for ideas and
  experience, as well as promoting and participating in research
  and discussion on all aspects of violent crime analysis.

In short, the analysts would do whatever it took to make it work,
saving time, money, and lives in the process. The immediate hurdle
now was to convince every investigator of the need to submit all of
their solved and unsolved cases going back five years. The logic for
unsolved cases was clear, but the need to enter solved cases was the
result of a hard lesson learned by the Americans.

Among the U.S. models Johnson had reviewed was the Washington State Homicide Investigation Tracking System: HITS. It had
linked one solved murder behaviourally to two others in a particularly bizarre series of homicides. Using circumstantial and similar-
fact evidence, the District Attorney had tried to link the killer
convicted in the solved murder to the two others, arguing that no
similar crimes had been committed in Washington. Under cross-
examination by the defence, the State Police admitted they had not
"captured" all homicides. The similar-fact evidence was excluded
and the killer convicted of one murder, not three. The only way to
avoid similar disappointment was to ensure that *all* homicides,
solved and unsolved, were logged into the database.

A clear American presence at Brampton underscored their role in
helping Johnson adapt the best their earlier systems had to offer.
Besides the well-known FBI VICAP, lionized by the Hollywood

blockbuster *The Silence of the Lambs*, there were delegates from both the New York and the New Jersey State Police and the Iowa Sex Crimes Analysis System. Johnson had found all these systems to be superior to the Major Crime File, which had never linked any of the nearly 800 cases that were ultimately entered into its database. By comparison, MACROS, Davidson's prototype for ViCLAS, had, within 18 months, made 57 linkages among the 584 cases in its database. Unlike the MCF's "narrative" forms, based on "open-ended" questions, all of the American systems made extensive use of check-box questionnaires with "closed-ended" questions that provided more continuity and similarity in case details that could then be more easily formatted for automated search and comparison. ViCLAS did the same.

Despite all their similarities, Iowa stood alone as the sole state in the Union to enjoy total support from the investigators in the field. As a result of the early efforts of the Iowa Division of Criminal Investigation to heed the opinions of those agencies who would feed information into their database, the state boasted 100 percent compliance. Everybody was using it, leaving no holes or gaps through which sexual predators could slip undetected. That was in stark contrast to VICAP, a national database which at one point received cases from only 20 of 50 states in the Union and was riddled with huge, potentially lethal gaps. Adapting what worked, abandoning what didn't, Johnson had incorporated Iowa's focus on sex crimes into the traditional focus on serial murder, to give ViCLAS its unique ability to analyze and link the behavioural aspects of *both*. This, combined with its ability to accept reports in any language, gave ViCLAS a unique and truly international appeal. This revolutionary technology, created using off-the-shelf software, was designed to link:

1. Solved and unsolved murders and attempted homicides
2. Solved and unsolved sexual assaults
3. Missing persons cases, where the circumstances strongly indicated foul play and the victim was still missing
4. Unidentified bodies, where death was known or suspected to be homicide, and

5. All non-parental abductions and attempted abductions.

Any doubt that ViCLAS could do all it claimed paled beside the concern that it would never get a fair chance to show what it could do. Compliance was voluntary, and while many said they would use the system there was no guarantee that police forces would go beyond lip service.

Johnson was a big fan of decentralized cooperation and hoped that would help motivate cops across Canada to "buy in" and use the system. One of the first things he had noticed about the FBI VICAP system was how centralized it was; everything was done through the NCAVC at Quantico. He had wondered aloud whether allowing the field offices to play a greater role in at least collecting, if not analyzing, crime data might not pay off with more cases being submitted by state, county, and city police forces. In his view, things always worked better at the local level of enforcement where investigators and FBI agents who knew each other, trusted each other, might more willingly share information. That, he was informed, was *not* the FBI way.

It was, however, how ViCLAS would work. Although all information eventually found its way to the mainframe computer at RCMP headquarters in Ottawa, it was funnelled there from 22 coordinator/analysts across the country, a logical extension of the 18 profiling coordinators across the land. MacKay's promotional road shows had resulted in RCMP coordinators in Vancouver (responsible for British Columbia and the Yukon), Edmonton (responsible for Yellowknife and the Northwest Territories), Regina, Winnipeg, Fredericton, Halifax (responsible for Nova Scotia and Prince Edward Island), and St. John's. Lieutenant Claude Tremblay and Sergeant Gerry Séguin had been instrumental in persuading the Sûreté du Québec to base a coordinator at their headquarters. Kate Lines' profiling in Ontario was coordinated outside the OPP through designated officers at Metro Toronto and regional forces in Peel, Durham, Hamilton-Wentworth, and Ottawa-Carleton. While profiling and ViCLAS were promoted as "distinctly different but complementary" as a tactic to defuse investigator resistance, the latter also promised enhanced security to investigators worried about their evidence being leaked to the press or otherwise gone amok.

Designed to be extremely user-friendly, allowing easy data entry and quick responses, ViCLAS had the unique capability to protect any "key-fact" or "hold-back" evidence that was identified as such by the submitting investigator. That was crucial. The greatest single impediment to sharing information is distrust and a genuine fear that information leaked to the wrong person, even inadvertently, will destroy an investigation, collapse a case in court, and allow a killer, rapist, or pedophile to walk free.

That had been the exact case with Bernardo. When the Green Ribbon Task Force had finally learned from Karla Homolka whom they were chasing, the news was promptly leaked to the media by an insider, presumably a cop, forcing them to arrest Bernardo long before they had any evidence aside from Homolka's testimony. (Olson too had been arrested before the cops had evidence linking him to the victims in the Vancouver area, but that was in response to a perceived threat to two young girls in his company while he was under surveillance.) Both cases were resolved by widely denounced "Deals with the Devil."

ViCLAS could track anyone requesting key-fact or hold-back evidence. If it was leaked, an audit would immediately identify the delinquent, devious, or just plain stupid cop who did it. A permanent record was to be maintained of all queries for that type of information and it would also identify which of the 22 coordinators or analysts had accessed the data. There were even more security features in those cases where such information was printed out.

The enhanced threat of discovery went a long way to easing investigators' concerns for security and evidence integrity. But did it go far enough? Would it be sufficient peace of mind to compel them to faithfully submit their solved and unsolved cases to ViCLAS? That, in the end, was all that mattered.

Not every case qualified for ViCLAS, no more than every case called for profiling. But if a case required either, it would logically benefit from both. In an effort to boost compliance, to get as many cops as possible completing the forms, both MacKay and Lines made it known that once the system was up and running, all requests for profiling had to be accompanied by a completed ViCLAS booklet or, where circumstances warranted, a shorter eight-page form containing 83 questions culled from the 262 in the 36-page long form. It was estimated that each long-form booklet could take up to two hours to complete.

In addition to documenting conventional investigative information—details of the crime, the crime scene, the predator's MO, victimology—ViCLAS was designed to capture also the behavioural factors within each crime—what the predator said, what he did, and in what order.

That had proven vital to helping investigators solve violent serial crime dating to the MACROS debut on the Surrey rape. For what little comfort it might offer that young victim, her suffering had not been in vain. Four women had been attacked before her; none after, because MACROS had linked the predator to his other crimes, allowing the investigators to contact those jurisdictions, get a photo of a suspect who had not been charged due to lack of evidence, have the Surrey teen identify her attacker from a photo lineup, and help send him to prison for eight years. This case carried the highest profile of the 18 confirmed linkages MACROS had made; roughly one-third of all 57 linkages made in its early days.

Quite simply, ViCLAS offered a new focus on old, cold, and complex cases. Profiling was based on reviewing the behavioural "ritual" of a crime; ViCLAS, too, while retaining the ability to store information on the "how" and "what," also incorporated the "why" of the crime, the predator's "signature."

But ViCLAS, like profiling, was a tool, not a solution. There was no SOLVE button on the computer. That message was never lost on those who championed ViCLAS. From its conception to its inception nearly two years later, it was never forgotten and hammered home relentlessly by the behavioural experts: ViCLAS, like any tool in any occupation, exists to help do a job, not steal it away. As MacKay was fond of reminding investigators from all jurisdictions whenever he felt tensions needed defusing, "There's glory enough for all."

The message was kept simple for the benefit of the reporters who would write the story and the cops across the country who would read it:

- ViCLAS is more than a computer system. It is also a communications tool to get police talking to each other and sharing information, leads and suspects.
- ViCLAS combines specialized technical analysis with an understanding of the offender's psychology and predictable behaviour.
- ViCLAS will reduce violence against society's most vulnerable victims—women and children.

The true mark of success for ViCLAS would be to accomplish more than linking serial crimes. It also had to change traditional police mentality, giving the investigators a new impetus to do what they should have been doing all along—sharing information with other investigators. Most didn't, and Ted Bundy loved them for it, declaring shortly before his execution in the United States: "Jurisdictional boundaries and the inability of law-enforcement agencies to communicate with each other allows transient killers to avoid identification and detection."

Getting caught was the sole fear of organized serial sexual predators like Bundy and Bernardo. For them, the inability or unwillingness of police to get along and work together was a godsend. Even the stupid and disorganized predators would run free long enough to wreak havoc on their innocent and unsuspecting victims so long as the cops spent as much time and energy obstructing each other and withholding information as they did beating the bushes for a suspect.

It was a tough enough job trying to find a prime suspect among the hundreds or thousands who could surface in a stranger murder or sexual assault where the victim did not know her attacker. Profiling could narrow the field to a behavioural type, and ViCLAS could trace their travels.

But the odds were still heavily in favour of the serial predators during the early phase of their attacks. Unlike the police, they knew exactly who and what they were looking for. To Bundy, who preferred young and young-looking women with their long hair parted down the middle, it had been little more than a deadly game of cat-and-mouse for him and others like him: "We were just hunting humans. I guess because we thought they were the hardest things to hunt, but humans are the easiest things to hunt. Sad to say, but it's true."

ViCLAS could change that, *would* change that—if it was used. MacKay was convinced of it, and his optimism was contagious. A growing band of adherents believed that ViCLAS was their best response to Bundy's chilling warnings. But ViCLAS was only as good as the data it received. The investigators had to take the time, make the effort to properly complete the forms. If they did that, were able to answer each question, they would at least have the satisfaction and peace of mind of knowing they had conducted a thorough investigation. If their predator had struck earlier or elsewhere, ViCLAS would find him and link him to their case and hopefully speed his arrest. Investigators in the field would be able to get him off the streets sooner and keep him off longer.

ViCLAS and profiling could simply help them do their jobs faster and more efficiently, saving millions of dollars on complicated cases and scores of lives. Every time they locked up a serial predator, they didn't just end his reign of terror, they prevented other women and children from falling into his clutches and adding to the toll of victims. The technology now existed to do that. To ignore it or refuse to use it was unconscionable.

There was no way to protect the first victim; that was a tragic fact of life and death. But if the cops refused to do something as simple as fill out a ViCLAS booklet, they might as well have started listing "investigator arrogance" as a cause of the ensuing rapes and deaths.

In any occupation, but particularly in a conservative workplace like policing, there are suspicions, fears, resistance, and outright obstruction to any innovation, and ViCLAS was more revolution than evolution. Hopefully, resistance would pass with time, but how many women and children would suffer and die before then? That question haunted MacKay and the others who championed behavioural analysis.

To his Brampton audience, Johnson cited the Major Crime File as proof that good intentions are not enough:

> We can ill afford a second failure from an operational, political, or image perspective. . . . We must be fully committed to making ViCLAS work and this can only be achieved by having *all* police forces with appropriate cases fill out the form and have the case entered on the system. Should we fail to do so, we stand to be severely criticized within the police community, from women's groups who represent the majority of the victims we seek to help, and ultimately the public at large.

He went on to state that the most difficult homicides to solve are stranger-to-stranger sexual homicides, adding that rapists who go on to murder—and there was growing evidence that many of them did—would show similar behaviour in both types of crimes. The Americans had systems for tracking serial rapes *or* murders, but ViCLAS was the first to do both. Regarding the horror that had stalked Ontario's densely populated Golden Horseshoe, Johnson dropped a bombshell on the assembled media:

> Had [Paul Bernardo's] 1988 rapes been entered onto a system such as ViCLAS, it is highly likely that the sadistic behaviour exhibited in those crimes would have been identified in his first murder, that of Leslie Mahaffy, in Burlington, and perhaps his second victim, Kristen French, would have been spared.

When MacKay had taken that claim national in a CBC interview, Mick Riddle had driven him to the studio. The Green Ribbon disclosure officer had been asked to attend the ViCLAS unveiling by taskforce commander Vince Bevan. Although he and MacKay were both heavily involved behind the scenes of the Bernardo investigation, this was really the first time they had been able to relax and get to know each other. Each sensed a kindred spirit in the other—both were proven investigators, open-minded but demanding that anyone who promised to make their job easier had better be able to prove it. Riddle was hooked. ViCLAS was the real deal as far as he was concerned. He was determined to get Niagara Regional Police involved as soon as possible, and he wanted to head the unit.

He knew a system like ViCLAS not only could have linked Bernardo's crimes but also could have done it even before Mahaffy was abducted and murdered. Riddle was stunned to learn that, in hindsight, the Henley Island rape, so brutal and devastating to the young victim, had been the warning flag. She was the last of Bernardo's victims to survive him. Henley Island was the crossover case. Riddle dedicated himself to the system so that such a blatant sign that a rapist's violence was escalating would never be missed again.

Riddle was determined to ensure that the Henley Island victim had not suffered in vain. The push for ViCLAS in the Niagara Frontier was due to her. Other women and children would benefit, be less at risk, because of what had been learned from her misfortune.

The launch was a success, even though the system existed largely in name only. ViCLAS was championed by the media, and MacKay, finally shedding the anonymity that is the lot of a profiler, was hailed as the driving force behind what one reporter dubbed a "super computer" that promised to make the world a safer place. The computer was, in fact, quite ordinary; it was the software application that was amazing. Now it was up to the investigators. If they submitted their cases, ViCLAS would work; if not—well, no one wanted to think about that just yet. All MacKay could do was keep fighting the good fight to get cops talking and sharing information. Hopefully sooner than later.

Meantime, the grisly body count of innocents mounted across Canada.

In July 1993, a half-year before ViCLAS made its debut in Brampton, MacKay had met with Corporal Bob Urbanoski to discuss how best to stop a stalker in Dauphin, the Manitoba VCAS coordinator's old hometown. While the concept, even the term "stalker," was quite new, Urbanoski knew a problem when he saw one and this problem was menacing, with great potential to get worse.

Known widely as "Turbo," Urbanoski was featured in a bestselling book and a nationally televised movie that detailed his role in solving the murder of Helen Betty Osborne 16 years after the teenage Cree student had been abducted off a main street in The Pas by four white youths, sexually assaulted, and stabbed to death with a screwdriver. Apparently it was common knowledge in the community who had been involved. The problem was that, on their lawyer's advice, the four suspects refused to talk to the cops; there was no concrete evidence against any of them beyond the hearsay evidence of several people who claimed to have heard one or more of the quartet bragging about their feat.

Urbanoski had arrived on the scene and run an ad in the local newspaper asking people to come forward with any information they had on the case, no matter how irrelevant it might seem. Tips flooded in, and information from wiretaps and surveillance poured in. In the end, two of the four were charged with murder and one was convicted. Urbanoski would later be a star witness at the provincial Aboriginal Justice Inquiry of Manitoba into the Osborne murder and other instances of violence against Native peoples.

Urbanoski had come late to the Mounties. Like Johnson, he was judged too short on his first attempt, and by the time the minimum-height requirement was relaxed for single candidates, he was married. But when that impediment was also waived, he was quick to join the force he had admired from boyhood.

After agreeing to a strategy to handle the Dauphin stalker, MacKay returned on a later trip to visit the scene of a chilling crime that Urbanoski feared might have been part of a series.

MacKay reviewed the case materials and found that Lennie Pomfret was already in custody for the abduction and rape of two 14-year-old females from a foster home and the attempted murder of their 15-year-old male friend. After driving them to party in the woods about 30 kilometres east of Winnipeg late one Saturday night, he had smashed the boy's head with a baseball bat and left him for dead. MacKay found it particularly significant that after tying up the girls, he had shaved their pubic hair, raped them repeatedly, and tortured them for hours, pausing only to videotape and photograph his terrified, naked young victims. Meanwhile, the boy had revived, stumbled to the road, flagged down a car, and called the police.

The next morning, Sunday, the cops had searched the scene with tracking dogs and found Pomfret's truck cleverly concealed nearby. Expanding their search perhaps another 20 metres beyond where the two young teens had been raped, they found skeletal remains that investigators believed belonged to Tina Franks, a 15-year-old girl who had been reported missing roughly six weeks earlier. She had been a friend of the teens Pomfret had raped the night before. Because Franks had had a history of running away from home, Winnipeg City Police hadn't suspected foul play.

MacKay agreed that Pomfret had likely killed Franks, and would have killed the two girls in the woods had police not arrived. He was proved right later, when the cops found an earring with a small tag of flesh attached to it under the seat of the truck Pomfret had used. They also recovered sequentially numbered fishing licences, issued one right after the other in his name and Tina Franks'. DNA tests confirmed that the flesh on the earring was Franks', and Pomfret was convicted of her second-degree murder.

While most of MacKay's time was consumed by his behind-the-scenes work with the Green Ribbon Task Force—consulting with Metro Homicide and the Metro Sexual Assault Squad, preparing an affidavit on sexual sadistic behaviour—Project Kayo in Edmonton and Pomfret in Winnipeg were proof to him that the Niagara Frontier had no monopoly on sex killers and sexual sadists. In May, he was back in Edmonton with the filming of the dramatic reenactment of the two abducted children for the popular television show *Unsolved Mysteries*.

With ViCLAS launched and word spreading on his profiling achievements, demands for MacKay's skills grew heavier than ever. In January 1994, he arrived in Prince George, B.C. to profile the murders of two women. Marnie Blanchard, a young white woman in her twenties, had disappeared just prior to the first snowfall back in 1992. Snowmobilers discovered her skull in woods north of Prince George. Police found the rest of her body and her clothing and managed to get a DNA sample from their suspect, but there was nothing left to compare it to; the skull and skeleton had been picked clean by animals. Theresa Umphrey, a Native woman in her mid-to-late thirties, had vanished two years later. Her body was found perched atop a snowbank beside a plowed logging road 30 miles south of Prince George. She had been raped and murdered, then dragged behind a vehicle, virtually skinned. Her killer had wanted her to be found. DNA, presumably from her killer, was extracted from semen found in Umphrey.

MacKay, called in after the Umphrey murder, linked the cases with an earring found by police at the Blanchard murder in the middle of the opening to a clearing frequently used by hikers and bikers until the first snowfall. He had learned from wildlife experts that studies of lynx kills of caribou with ear tags in the Yukon showed they always eat around the tags, allowing them to drop directly to the ground from the head—the "dainty" eating style of a cat rather than the dog-like gulping of a wolf.

The evidence suggested that Blanchard's body had been displayed just like Umphrey's and would have been found just as quickly had it not been for the unexpectedly heavy early snowfall. The killer had displayed the bodies to degrade the victims and shock whoever found them. DNA evidence from one trial was admitted in the other when the court refused to sever the cases as the defence had argued. MacKay had explained the significance of his analysis so well that the prosecutor understood perfectly and didn't call him as an expert witness, despite the fact that he had prepared a "signature analysis" using "similar-fact" charts. MacKay was starting to get respect, but no exposure in open court to help promote ViCLAS and profiling.

It was not the only time MacKay remained unknown, unseen, and often unthanked behind the scenes. The Toronto Transit Rapist was a classic example.

In March 1994, police in Toronto had taken a suspected rapist into custody, believing he was responsible for as many as 11 sexual assaults on women on underground subway platforms. Victimology seemed a key clue on this case: 10 of the victims had been elderly East Indian women; the 11th was Brazilian but could easily have been mistaken for East Indian. After linking the attacks by this distinct similarity, MacKay viewed a security tape he had been sent by Metro Police and spied Orville Thompson, the man they had charged with one rape. He was standing in the background and clearly ignored a stunning blonde as she strolled past him and got on an elevator alone. But a short time later, he followed an older East Indian woman when she passed by and disappeared behind her off-camera. Moments later, he had dragged her down a stairwell and raped her.

The police had charged him, and were convinced they had caught the so-called Toronto Transit Rapist. They hoped MacKay might link him to other rapes. Citing the deep social and cultural aspects of the attacks, he explained that while rape is a degrading experience for anyone, victims within certain societies can lose all "value" if they are violated. That seemed a big factor in this case.

He was able to link 11 of the assaults behaviourally—and explained it so well that the Crown Attorney who prosecuted the case didn't have to call him to testify as an expert witness.

That June, he profiled Susan Aiston's murder in Richmond, B.C. She had been killed in her apartment and her body was found there a day later when water began leaking through the ceiling of the apartment below; she had been locked in her apartment with her baby and a tap was left running. The baby was unharmed. Aiston's apartment keys were found hidden in a culvert in a nearby park.

MacKay predicted the killer lived nearby and knew her. A neighbour who had lived on Aiston's floor was playing cards with her and his common-law wife in his room the night she had died, and had moved to Surrey soon after. He was arrested there and later convicted for her murder.

In mid-November, MacKay profiled a murder and an attempted murder in Saskatchewan before turning his full attention to the murder of Chantale Brochu in Montreal, a tragedy that hammered home the value of profiling in Quebec.

In September 1992, Brochu, a petite young coed, went dancing at a college pub with a girlfriend. She was approached and asked to dance by an attractive, well-mannered young man. As the evening wore on, her friend told her she was leaving but the man persuaded Brochu to stay with him. The next morning, her naked body was found in front of a nearby church, about 100 yards from the street and a third of a mile from the bar. Rain had destroyed much of the crime scene overnight but an autopsy confirmed she had been strangled and raped with a blunt object.

Montreal Urban Community (MUC) Police homicide investigators learned of the young man from Brochu's friend and promptly launched a public appeal for help to identify him. The cops got over 700 tips over the next two years for the man they dubbed "The Dancer," convinced that the attractive young man was her killer, on the basis of their own years of experience and a report from a forensic psychiatrist in Montreal who had assured them, "Find the Dancer and you'll have your killer." But the person was never identified nor caught.

After two years, Séguin prevailed upon his friendship with the lead Montreal investigator Jean-Claude Bergeron to have him ask his management for permission to have MacKay profile the case. Everyone seemed willing to set aside their egos and try anything that might solve the baffling murder.

To everyone's shock, and no little skepticism, MacKay's profile concluded it was unlikely that "The Dancer" was the killer. The evidence at the crime scene suggested to MacKay that the killer had ambushed Brochu in a blitz sneak attack from the bushes and he argued that whoever killed this young woman would never have had the social skills and confidence to approach her on the dance floor. It was possible the killer had been in the pub that night, but if he was, he would have been in the background, probably lounging alone in a darkened corner or against a wall. If so, he may have followed her when she left and attacked when she least expected it.

The profile hit the investigators with the impact of a sledge hammer. It was mind-boggling to them that they might have been chasing the wrong guy for two years. But even if the profile was right, it told them only the type of man to look for, not "whodunit." The break in the case came some time later in a phone call from Sherbrooke police who had a rape suspect in custody who had been identified by one of his victims from a police sketch broadcast on television. He was interrogated while in custody by sexual-assault investigators and denied everything; but after they had left he confided to a prisoner in the lockup that he had been worried that they would ask him about the Brochu murder. The prisoner duly informed the cops—it was Tip 735—and the MUC homicide investigators showed up to question him. They followed MacKay's advice, pretended to understand his feelings and establish rapport with him, and in their third interrogation the man confessed.

At a soirée to celebrate closing the case attended by several hundred investigators and journalists directly involved, Séguin was honoured with a plaque, but was more cheered to hear MUC management admit the killer had fit the profile nearly 95 percent. MacKay also received a certificate acknowledging his contribution and had been invited to attend but was buried in other cases. Ironically, the province he had worried most about penetrating was among the first to formally acknowledge his contribution to a major high-profile case and, in 2002, planned to legislate mandatory compliance requiring all Quebec police to submit cases to ViCLAS.

All in all, it had been a trying, emotional year for MacKay. Not only was he involved in profiling some of Canada's most horrific and bizarre crimes; his son was injured in a motorcycle accident and spent a week in an intensive care unit, his sister died while he was attending a conference in Halifax, and Clifford Olson kept phoning, trying to interest him in interviewing himself and a few others he could line up. But at least his emotional rollercoaster went up when on September 1 Bernardo was found guilty on all counts by a jury and he was later designated a Dangerous Sexual Offender and jailed for an indefinite term.

Between cases, marketing ViCLAS was intensified, not always with happy results.

On August 22, 1994, MacKay, Johnson, and OPP Constable Guy DeGagne were to make a joint ViCLAS presentation on the final morning of the annual Canadian Association of Chiefs of Police conference in Montreal. The presentation was postponed to 3:00 p.m., and drew a crowd of fewer than 20 chiefs and senior officers, mostly Mounties, from among the several hundred who had attended the conference. They had known the late hour would affect turnout but were stunned and more than a tad pissed off to see so few. While some of the absent brass may have had planes to catch, MacKay couldn't help fretting that many were squeezing in a final round of golf or chatting with colleagues in the bar over a final "cold one." It got worse. Peel Regional Police Chief Al Lunney, a former Mountie, concerned that the conference was running late, asked them to be brief. MacKay spoke first, followed by Johnson. DeGagne, already nervous about making his first public presentation—even a small audience of brass hats could be unnerving—had just begun speaking when Lunney held up a sign saying "TIME."

The ViCLAS presentation was a disaster in every way, a personal and professional low point for MacKay in his recent years plagued by bureaucratic indifference and investigator resistance. Not to mention the sandbags strewn in his path by one RCMP assistant commissioner who had stymied his every attempt to select and train his own replacement, accepting, then brushing aside, repeated memos for over 18 months. MacKay had emphasized the urgency, pointing out that it would take two years to train his replacement and he was due to retire in less than three. His boss just didn't get it, at one point suggesting it might be better to close MacKay's behavioural section and "cut our losses." But MacKay persevered, and when Joop Plomp arrived on the scene as his new boss, requests that had been blocked for years were approved within hours. Although the earlier delays had set back his retirement plans by a year, MacKay picked his successor and was instrumental in having three more Canadian profilers trained before he hung up his spurs.

None of that rankled as much as this keynote presentation being postponed, set back, and then rushed to its doom in front of an almost empty auditorium. A golden opportunity to showcase ViCLAS to those in command, who set policy, controlled budgets, and allocated resources, had not just been lost, it had been wasted and destroyed beyond salvation.

Happily, though, the devastated trio was not without friends in high places on that occasion.

Frank Palmer—the former Assistant Commissioner, Operations, and second-in-command in E Division, recently promoted to RCMP Deputy Commissioner, Operations, for all of Canada—was livid. British Columbia had been home at some point to every key Mountie player involved in the concept and creation of ViCLAS —MacKay, Davidson, and Johnson. It was E Division that proved ViCLAS could work, on the basis of Davidson's spectacular success with MACROS. It was where Olson had first proved Canada was not immune to the horror of serial murder and needed a better way to stop him and others like him.

Palmer did not mince words. As possibly the only person in the room more upset than the downcast presenters, and the only one among them with the rank to speak his mind openly, Palmer roared his displeasure, gave full vent to his rage, leaving no doubt just how disturbed, disappointed, disgusted, and downright pissed off he was. Palmer blasted the postponement and the senior cops who hadn't bothered to show up for what, to him, had been the most important presentation of the conference. It had been rushed to ruin for the handful of his colleagues with the brains to attend. How could any professional group claim to have public safety at heart and not show up to learn about what was perhaps the greatest single innovation in recent memory? When he had finished, Palmer had wheeled toward the trio standing within earshot and apologized for the treatment they had been accorded.

That, thought Johnson, was "pretty neat."

Palmer had salved their pain, but could not end their worry. If only a handful of the top police brass from across Canada had enough interest to show up to learn about revolutionary new developments for linking and nabbing serial predators, what chance was there of enlisting the support of grunt investigators in the field? It seemed clearer than ever to MacKay that, left to their own devices, few cops would ever submit their cases to ViCLAS.

But then things always seem darkest just before dawn.

By the end of 1995, ViCLAS was recognizable as the system promised by MacKay in Brampton at the end of 1993. There were already enough cases in the database for MacKay to estimate that there were 12 to 20 serial killers stalking Canada at any given time and God knows how many serial rapists. That was good for another headline as the system was launched.

The work had continued behind the scenes over the past year. The ViCLAS forms had been constantly reviewed and simplified. The number of questions had been reduced by 17, to 245, and the two hours originally estimated to complete the long forms was now actually closer to 45 minutes. There had been software glitches and other minor setbacks, not every deadline had been met, but progress had been relentless.

Also, there seemed to be a growing number of investigators who were willing to spend the time to take advantage of a system that could link and analyze in minutes what it could take months to determine using traditional methods. But the compliance rate remained abysmal. Cops still filled out the forms and submitted their cases as whim, or desperation, struck them. ViCLAS was still a porous database with ample room for serial predators to disappear.

But if MacKay and ViCLAS had yet to win the hearts and minds of the grunts in the field, they were clearly winning major battles in the public-affairs arena. Praise was immediate and universal. Mike Cryan, an FBI major-case specialist with VICAP, hailed ViCLAS as "the Cadillac system in the world." Dr. David Cavanaugh of Harvard University, and a consultant involved in upgrading that FBI pioneering system, was more explicit: "The Canadians have done to automated case linkage what the Japanese did with assembly line auto production. They have taken a good American idea and transformed it into the best in the world."

There was growing interest abroad as well, from Australia to Austria and elsewhere in Europe, where open borders, a common market, and diverse languages could all be accommodated by ViCLAS. Even diehard fans of the FBI openly admired the superior ability of the Canadian system to link and analyze sexual assaults and other serial crimes beyond the serial murders that had made VICAP's reputation.

ViCLAS was able to replace the traditional reliance on the notebooks and memories of investigators who would inevitably retire or move on. Nowhere was the danger of that clearer than in the case of Jack Unterweger, the Austrian "Prison Poet" and first modern-day international serial killer.

Though convicted of murder and sentenced to prison for life, Unterweger was freed early at the insistence of Austrian high society, the literati, and media, who cited his poems and other writings as a model of rehabilitation. An immediate celebrity, he proclaimed himself a freelance journalist with a particular interest in reporting the street life of prostitutes.

It never occurred to anyone that Unterweger—affable and popular, seemingly a very likable guy—might also be killing the hookers. When the toll reached eight victims, all women, nearly all prostitutes, and all strangled with their own underwear tied into a unique knot that could easily be manipulated with one hand, Unterweger disappeared, resurfacing in Los Angeles where three more prostitutes were soon found strangled in an identical fashion.

A transatlantic manhunt was launched when an Interpol request for assistance with the murder investigations in Austria and the Czech Republic ended up in the hands of FBI profiler Gregg McCrary, who quickly linked all 11 crimes behaviourally.

Just as Homolka had fingered Bernardo, the Prison Poet was

turned in by an unhappy girlfriend. Unterweger was arrested in Miami and extradited to Austria.

The only physical evidence against him was DNA from a single strand of hair of one victim, but with McCrary's testimony linking the crimes, Unterweger was convicted of 8 of the 11 murders. Vowing never to go back to prison, he hanged himself hours after the verdict, tying the same unique knot in the drawstring of his sweat pants that he had used to kill his victims. As one observer commented, "It was a bad day for Jack." The case marked the first time that FBI crime-scene analysis was accepted as evidence in an Austrian court.

Unterweger, like Olson and Bernardo, was never an early suspect. There was simply no evidence to link him to the murders. He didn't even have a driver's licence and the killer was obviously mobile as nearly all of the victims were found in isolated areas. It never seemed to occur to them that a serial killer, Austria's first, might be too preoccupied to worry about being ticketed for driving without a licence. Incredibly, Unterweger had even obtained a vanity plate.

Only pressure from a retired Austrian cop, who had failed in his bid to have Unterweger charged with a second murder when he was first convicted and imprisoned, had finally prodded the investigators to consider him a suspect. Thomas Müller, an Austrian criminal psychologist who had worked closely with the investigators, cited the case in praising ViCLAS: "How often is that going to happen? How often does someone come forward? How often does someone listen? But ViCLAS never forgets."

In June 1996, MacKay and ViCLAS were totally vindicated by an Ontario Judge with the wisdom of Solomon, who reviewed the Green Ribbon Task Force, savaged its systemic failures, and vowed that the young victims would not suffer and die in vain. This time, Peel Regional Police had played a vital role in that absolute vindication.

12

What Makes Karla Tick?

On August 7, 1996, MacKay escorted retired FBI profiler Roy Hazelwood to his interview with Karla Homolka at the Prison for Women—the P4W—in Kingston, Ontario. The two had become friends as well as professional colleagues over the years since their first meeting at the FBI Academy in Quantico when MacKay was training to be the first non-American profiler. All of his instructors had been impressive, but he considered Hazelwood to be the best teacher he had ever had for simplifying the complex. He also had a knack for raising the eyebrows of cops and academics with his theories on criminal minds and aberrant behaviour.

The interview room was as drab as the grey skies and teeming rain outside, making Homolka's entrance all the more notable, wearing a sundress as stylish as it was skimpy. Even without Bernardo telling her how to dress, what to wear, Karla knew how to dress to impress. Hazelwood had seen it all before; Homolka was the 18th of the 20 women he would interview to expand his study of women he had dubbed "compliant victims" of sexual sadists. He had found they all had projected a disarming "aura of helplessness," a femininity he associated with "50s feminism," and accorded Homolka that same sentiment. MacKay was a little more cynical in his view of her "Ellie May" outfit, a reference to the naive sex kitten on the 1960s TV series *The Beverly Hillbillies*.

Homolka was a willing participant, answering, as did all the interviewees, every one of Hazelwood's 448 questions, arranged by theme over 74 pages.

Her answers were so detailed that the interview had to be carried over to a second day. At the end of the first, as they prepared to break and resume the next morning, MacKay asked her what advice she would have for the police who would be dealing with the next person in the position she had found herself in with Bernardo. She replied with no hesitation: "Get her the hell out of the situation with the man right away. Don't let her make any contact with him because if she makes contact with him, your chances will go down right there. That's the biggest advice."

Hazelwood had made his name profiling the Atlanta Child Murders. At the time he was called in to profile the case after the seventh victim, many believed the case had ominous racist overtones, but Hazelwood soon proclaimed that the killer was black. That revelation had come while touring the neighbourhoods in a police cruiser with two black Atlanta detectives. There were no children on the streets, no kids playing or even hanging out. That seemed odd to him, but his escorts explained word had spread like wildfire that there was a white man in the vicinity. All the kids were hiding, safe inside. Digesting that tidbit for a nanosecond, Hazelwood realized that no white killer could ever get close enough to these children to grab one. The killer was black! It was a major turning point in the investigation that ended with the conviction of Wayne Williams, a local young black hustler who lured his victims with offers of recording contracts.

Beginning on April 27, 1992, a month after MacKay had first doodled "ViCLAS" on his notepad, he and Kate Lines worked with Hazelwood almost around the clock for three days and nights on an "equivocal-death" analysis of what had seemed to some an open-and-shut homicide. A man had been found dead near the foot of the interior stairwell of a three-storey above ground parking lot in Guelph, Ontario, about an hour northwest of Toronto. The victim's uncle, a retired OPP detective, suspected homicide and pushed for an inquest. Hazelwood, bearing the credibility and mystique of the FBI National Center for the Analysis of Violent Crime, and a proven profiler, had been brought in to testify, to present and explain the conclusions of their combined analysis.

Equivocal-death analysis was a new take on, and a new term for, what had once been called a "psychological autopsy," something employed to explore the state of mind and behaviour of a deceased when it was unclear whether the cause was homicide, suicide, or misadventure. The profiling trio had first discussed the case late into the night at the First International Conference on Serial, Mass, and Spree Murder at the University of Windsor in southwestern Ontario, where MacKay first referred publicly to ViCLAS. The media had lapped it up and MacKay had left a happy, if hungry, man. Reviewing the Guelph case that night, they became so absorbed they missed the banquet.

Resuming their review in Guelph, they sorted even more diligently through every scrap of paper in the box of case files and photos that Lines had provided. The task was greatly simplified by personal preference: MacKay preferred to start with the visual evidence of the photos; Hazelwood, the written reports. But it was still a wearing task. By the third day, as days and nights began to blur, Lines and MacKay began to weary, and their only break from analyzing the Guelph case over 72 hours was to verbally analyze another—the Blackburn murders that would be linked to David Snow—to OPP Detective Sergeant Ron Gentle over lunch. Sensing his colleagues' fatigue, Hazelwood urged them on, warning: "We can do 100 hours of analysis for five hours on the stand, or five hours' analysis for 100 hours on the stand." Point taken. They pushed on.

All reached the same conclusion. In their collective view, the man had leapt to his death. Unusual. Unorthodox. But suicide. Hazelwood presented their combined analysis to the inquest jury, who agreed, on April 30. The case marked the first time equivocal-death analysis was accepted as evidence in a Canadian courtroom.

If the verdict rocked conventional police wisdom, that was nothing new for Hazelwood, who had been raising eyebrows and raising hell since he was a slicked-down, combed-back Texas teenager more interested in avoiding the cops than ever working with them. A stint in the army as a military-police officer seemed a stabilizing influence. Hazelwood joined the FBI, transferred to behavioural science from investigating the Mafia, and became globally renowned as an expert investigating deviant sexual behaviour ranging from autoerotic fatalities—in which victims (mostly men, very rarely a woman) accidentally hang themselves trying to enhance their sexual gratification by using ligatures to reduce or cut off their oxygen supply—to sexual sadists who deliberately torture and kill for the same purpose.

Hazelwood has never claimed an ability to "get into their mind," but has demonstrated conclusively that he can think like deviants. He and profiler John Douglas once agreed to answer a written psychological test as they thought a paranoid schizophrenic would. After four hours writing in separate rooms, each set of answers was diagnosed by mental-health professionals as the work of a paranoid schizophrenic. A novel talent unlikely to appear on their résumés.

The point being, Hazelwood is not your average FBI stereotype but rather a living, breathing three-dimensional character who also happens to be a brilliant profiler, teacher, researcher, and writer. Those who work with him also consider him a true gentleman. His intense curiosity was evident from one of the first lectures he heard as a young army shave-tail MP. The instructor was detailing Harvey Glatman's penchant for calling women to pose for his camera—the identical ruse used to lure young Alison Parrott to her death in 1986—and he was intrigued. Hazelwood had never heard of a killer holding victims captive, tying them up, and posing them so he could take pictures of his fantasies before and after he killed them. Why had he done all that? Why keep photos that could be used against him as evidence? That didn't matter, he was told. All that was important was that he had killed three women. Hazelwood thought it likely did matter and spent the rest of his life proving it.

Hazelwood wasn't just right about Glatman; he was prophetic. His early questions, so quickly dismissed, were to become the basis of behavioural analysis. Glatman was the spark for VICAP, the FBI national database for linking serial murders, first envisioned by Pierce Brooks, the L.A. cop who caught Glatman and linked him to his other crimes through newspaper reports of similar assaults. Brooks joined Hazelwood at the FBI years later, the visionary for, and first head of, VICAP just as surely as MacKay later drove ViCLAS forward.

For MacKay and Hazelwood, both men of vision and insatiable curiosity, the Homolka interview was a natural progression. Splashing through the cold Kingston drizzle toward the drab, dreary, and soon-to-be-condemned P4W seemed a perfect prelude to the exhausting work that lay ahead. Homolka would be MacKay's first such interview, one of three Canadian women he had suggested were appropriate candidates for Hazelwood's study. Karla was the only non-American to be interviewed.

If MacKay was unsure what lay ahead, Hazelwood had no illusions. The interviews typically lasted anywhere from five to 15 hours over two days. All were emotionally draining. But the gain was worth the pain if they could glimpse the answer to the question searing so many minds: "What makes Karla tick?"

Championing a controversial theory like compliant victims was never an easy ride, even given the fact that it stemmed from Hazelwood's earlier collaboration with renowned behavioural co-authors Janet Warren and Park Dietz, *The Sexually Sadistic Criminal and His Offenses*, which had been warmly received, critically approved, and was soon the standard insight to the sadistic mind. Basing his ideas on descriptive research into 30 sexual sadists, most of whom were in prison, a throwback to Robert Ressler's pioneering work interviewing convicted serial, spree, and high-profile killers that led to profiling, Hazelwood had determined that inflicting pain and brutal aberrant sex were less the goal of the sadists than means to an end. The ultimate thrill for sexual sadists was the suffering of the victim combined with their own unbridled power. Initially, for many of them, this involved humiliating, degrading, and enslaving their wives and girlfriends. When that was no longer enough, they risked detection and capture to abduct innocents. They held supreme power of life and death over their helpless victims, and when they crossed the line to murder, there was no turning back. As one sadist confessed, "I never thought it would be so easy to kill a person, or that I would enjoy it. But it was easy and I was enjoying the feeling of supremacy. A supremacy like I have never known."

Their absolute power transformed them, in their minds, into gods who could not be defied. And could never be caught. Every new success fuelled their passion for more and their delusion that they were all-powerful, all-knowing, and undetectable supreme beings. The seized recordings of their crimes were so repetitive they became as predictable as other aspects:

- Careful planning
- Selecting strangers as victims
- Recording their abuses by various means (usually photographs, audio- or videotapes, a journal, or some combination of them all)
- Keeping personal items stolen from their victims (as reminders of what they had done and what they had gotten away with, and to help them relive the moment)
- Putting their victims into restraints
- Holding their victims captive for anywhere from 24 hours to seven days before killing or, rarely, releasing them.

While some sexual sadists were quite forthcoming about the grisly details of their crimes, none spoke openly about their sexual fantasies or patterns of sexual arousal that motivated or accompanied their crimes—abductions, rapes, tortures, and murders. It was almost by accident that Hazelwood and his colleagues discovered that many of the sexual sadists had ex-wives and girlfriends. These women, several of whom had conspired in the crimes, apparently had no compunction about detailing how their men had liked their sex—rough, rude, and often—and how easily, to their collective and individual utter shock and remorse, experimental consensual aberrant sex had become the norm, how quickly they had been transformed from normal, functioning, often successful women into sexual slaves and accomplices, co-conspirators, and participants in abduction, torture, and murder.

All of the first seven women Hazelwood interviewed came from middle- or upper middle-class families. All but the youngest had good jobs when they "fell" for their sadist, lured by the attention and affection he had initially showered on them. All had recognized their man's "darker side" early but perceived it as more exciting than dangerous. Most hooked up with men who were "beneath" them socially; typical pairings were as follows:

- A bank employee and an ex-convict/mechanic
- A fire-system engineer and a music sound mixer
- A business owner and an ex-convict/card dealer
- An insurance broker and a business owner
- A student nurse and an unemployed man
- A retail clerk and an unemployed man
- A teenager and a metal worker.

All of the women claimed they had been physically, sexually, or psychologically abused growing up, the last being by far the most common and hardest to define. All were transformed by the same carefully orchestrated and deliberate five-step process:

- Select a vulnerable woman
- Seduce her
- Reshape her sexual behaviour
- Isolate her socially from family and friends
- Punish her for not complying with insatiable demands (and, in the process, transform her into a subservient who would punish others for not complying).

No matter how good sadists' instincts—often very good when it came to culling the most vulnerable—their selection was still often at least partly by trial and error. Not every woman succumbed. But those who stepped onto the slippery slope found no easy exit. Even those presented with an opportunity to escape rarely fled their torment, paralyzed by palpable fear and psychological dependence. With the patience of a pedophile, the sadist would bide his time until he was sure he could manipulate the woman to sexually gratify him. Absolute subservience soon followed. A new monster was born, remade in the image of her creator.

All seven women claimed that their sexual experience prior to meeting their sadists had been limited to "normal" vaginal intercourse. All had consented to oral and anal sex, overcoming any early sense of disgust or fear of pain to make their men happy; forced fellatio, bondage, and sodomy had followed soon after. Six had endured the vaginal and anal insertion of foreign objects ranging from wine bottles to cylindrical lengths of wood; four had been photographed or taped committing lurid sex acts, those records being used to coerce and control them further with the threat of exposure. All of their men had preferred, in this order, anal sex, forced fellatio, vaginal intercourse, and foreign-object insertion. Sodomy quickly evolved from aberrant experiment to the norm as their men lost all interest in vaginal sex.

All seven claimed their men had been insatiable; they had been required to perform whenever and however they were directed. And scripted. The sleep deprivation, deepened sense of shame, and fear of exposure had gradually eroded all resistance and dragged them deeper into the abyss. Yet not even total compliance had saved them from the beatings, the insults, and eventually the shared belief with their tormentors that they deserved what they got, that no decent woman would do what they were doing on demand. There had seemed no depth to which their men could not drag them.

It was disturbing to learn just what these women had endured. Almost everything that would later happen to their victims had first happened to them: the scripted sex, captured on film or audio- or videotape, as well as the pain and humiliation of the whippings, the painful nipple and labia clamps, bondage, breast and labia biting or piercing, burns to body parts easily concealed by clothing, self-administered enemas and foreign-object insertions, and forced confinement. Two of the seven had been raped by their sadist's friends. Six had been strangled manually or by ligature during sex to the brink of unconsciousness. Four had been hanged, the same number forced to help procure, then have sex with, young victims later killed.

The unrelenting process of degradation was akin to "brainwashing" prisoners-of-war and cult "mind control." Isolated, degraded, beaten, manipulated by systematic deviance or reward and punishment for compliance or resistance, all had complied.

But was that a defence for helping to abduct, torture, and murder young innocents? All seven women had truly suffered, but none had been afflicted with any recognized mental illness that would excuse their actions. The "abused wife" defence exonerated women who turned on their abusers, and the Patty Hearst "brainwash" or Stockholm Syndrome plea granted the claim for diminished capacity. But these women—three married to sexual sadists for 2 to 13 years, four dating them exclusively for 3 to 18 months—just didn't fit the mould, classic square pegs in the round holes of justice. It was Hazelwood's goal to find out if they were slipping through those holes; not to condone or condemn them but to understand them.

Nothing Hazelwood discovered was meant to absolve the women who participated in the sadists' crimes—although his research convinced him that none of the seven would ever have dreamed they could sink as low as they had. Four of these women had served lengthy prison terms as accessories to murder. Hazelwood's sole interest was in understanding how it had happened so that it might help the next cops under siege to end the carnage sooner.

Having aroused enthusiastic and widespread interest in their initial study on sexual sadists when it was published in 1990, Hazelwood, Warren, and Dietz now submitted their findings in "Compliant Victims of the Sexual Sadist" to *Australian Family Physician* for publication at the request of a police officer whose friend edited that journal and wanted anything to do with research by the Behavioral Science Unit. That noble gesture of friendship and loyalty to a colleague came back to haunt them as critics of the Homolka deal railed that it could only make the pages of an "obscure" journal, a charge that was as false as it was fiery. At any rate, their findings were attacked or dismissed by vocal North American academics and mental health experts.

Not to worry. Hazelwood had been hit much harder by far scarier people. The important thing was that it was published and could now be debated. To several people working behind the scenes of the Green Ribbon Task Force, the theory had already been proven by its first application to a high-profile case.

Hazelwood had asked MacKay to review an early draft of the compliant-victim paper. The Mountie was intrigued by the strong similarities between the women's experiences—saw they were virtually identical—and sensed that the paper applied equally to Homolka, judging from her early statements to the Green Ribbon interrogators. With Hazelwood's permission, he passed his draft copy to the investigators to help them understand what they were dealing with to be better able to question Homolka. But at that point, few likely cared what Karla had endured as a teen; nothing, in their minds, could explain what she'd done.

Ensuing events would disprove that widespread sentiment.

On Tuesday, November 14, 1995, Ontario Attorney General Charles Harnick announced to the provincial legislature in Toronto that he had named Mr. Justice Patrick Galligan to conduct an "external independent review" of the plea bargains (there were two) negotiated by the Crown, the role of that office in determining what charges the police had laid or stayed, and report his findings on these and other "certain matters relating to Karla Homolka." The review would commence the day after Galligan retired from the bench on November 30 and was to be submitted no later than March 15, 1996. His mandate was specifically to find out:

1. Whether the plea arrangement entered into by crown counsel with Karla Homolka on May 14, 1993, was appropriate in all the circumstances.

2. Whether the advice given by crown counsel to the Green Ribbon Task Force in connection with possible charges against Karla Homolka arising out of a sexual assault on Jane Doe was appropriate in all the circumstances.

3. Whether in all the circumstances it is appropriate or feasible to take further proceedings against Karla Homolka for her part in the deaths of Kristen French and Leslie Mahaffy and the sexual assault on Jane Doe.

4. To inquire into such related matters, if any, which the Attorney General may from time to time direct.

Galligan's assignment was as limited as it was specific. Despite the potential to expand it as set out in the fourth point, that would be at Harnick's sole discretion.

The announcement was immediately attacked. What seemed to upset people most was that the review would be conducted in secret. Questioned in the Ontario legislature, Harnick said he'd "keep an open mind on the appropriate course to follow" when he received Galligan's report, but vowed to make it public: "The citizens of this province have a right to a complete explanation of the decisions made and the advice given by prosecutors in this case. I look forward to putting all the facts before the public through Mr. Justice Galligan's independent review."

Harnick, brand new to the job, had barely sat down before Annamarie Castrilli, representing the eastern Toronto riding of Downsview, waded in:

> People have been shocked, have been outraged, at the way in which this government has stalled on this matter. Now, at long last, we have some action. But . . . rather than lead, this government has shown a propensity this time to stall, and here we are stalling again. . . . A secret process . . . will not help to restore that confidence the public now seems to lack. The people have a right to know, and we have a right to ask, what is being hidden here? Why cannot this be held up to public scrutiny and why

should we go through a charade? I hope this is not going to be a sham. In the end, only the system of justice will lose if that is the case. We urge the minister to reconsider and to open the matter to public inquiry, as the people have demanded.

Former NDP Attorney General Marion Boyd, who had approved the Homolka plea bargains that Harnick and the Tories had inherited and honoured, was more supportive:

> The commitment always was . . . that once all the matters before the criminal court pertaining to Mr. Bernardo were complete, there would indeed be a full disclosure. . . . Mr. Justice Galligan is an excellent choice for this kind of an inquiry. Having practiced criminal law, he understands the concerns already being expressed very vociferously by those who practice criminal law in this province around the necessity, first, to build better public confidence in how the justice system works, and, second, to ensure that due process is accorded to every accused in this province and that indeed, whatever kind of public pressure is brought to bear on the Attorney General of the day, the legal process will be full of integrity and will in fact go forward in a way that does not prejudice the possibility of a successful conviction in a case of this magnitude. . . . I would say that I have every confidence Mr. Justice Galligan will be mindful of our need to ensure that the implications of any finding in this case are clearly laid out for us . . . to ensure that the integrity of the justice system is not questioned.

Harnick vowed that the review would be thorough and proper, and made public "in a timely way." Castrilli's anxious "God knows when that will be" was a symptom of the widespread pessimism throughout Ontario that perceived foot-dragging by the Conservatives had delayed justice and their secret review would deny it. Petitions had flourished—320,000 signatures to Queen's Park, 12,000 to the Senate of Canada—where Liberal Senator Ann Cools was already leading the charge to amend the Criminal Code section on plea bargains, retroactive to Homolka—beseeching:

> We the undersigned petitioners, residents of Canada, do humbly pray and call upon the Senate of Canada, to use its full powers to effect an inquiry into the negotiation of the Karla Homolka plea bargain agreement, including the activities of all Crown and law enforcement officials; and to pass the laws necessary to lengthen Homolka's sentence to fit her crimes; and to take such measures and pass such legislation as may be required to respond to these notorious events and restore public confidence in the administration of justice in Canada.

(While the more than a quarter-million petitioners found little favour with the Ontario government, another, less ambitious petition was received as the dust settled and debate moved on from the Galligan announcement. Derwyn Shea rose on behalf of the fine folk of High Park–Swansea and "proudly" added his name to the "thousands of constituents" who had signed to support "Tigger the cat" in his fight with health officials seeking to keep "this friendly feline" out of a local tea shop. Petitions are apparently like opinions in Ontario: everybody's got one.)

Galligan's selection troubled Cools and others, not because of questions about his integrity or ability, but for his ardent defence of the press ban invoked by Justice Kovacs that had barred the foreign press from the courtroom when Karla pleaded guilty to two counts of manslaughter, and muzzled the Canadian media from reporting any details beyond her conviction and sentence to protect Bernardo's right to a fair trial. Cools later testified at the Proceedings of the Standing Senate Committee on Legal and Constitutional Affairs, after Galligan had submitted his report:

. . . many different parties, including the media . . . appealed that publication ban. As time rolled by, that appeal was decided upon by the Court of Appeal of Ontario. The panel included the very notable and prominent judge Mr. Justice Dubin, as well as Mr. Justice Galligan. I put out that information for people to do with as they wish.

There is no evidence that Galligan's role in enforcing the press ban influenced his review of the plea bargain or the Crown's role in what charges were laid, and nothing in his track record to ensure that any future finding exonerating the deal and the Crown was a foregone conclusion. In fact, his background, experience, and lineage suggested quite the opposite. If he was on record as supporting the press ban, his record as an Appeal Court Justice was equally clear that he was not blindly loyal to the police and the Crown.

For example, in April 1994, Galligan and Mr. Justice Allan Goodman voted 2–1, Mr. Justice Coulter Osborne dissenting, to overturn on appeal the $200 fine levied three years ago against a woman for performing oral sex in a public place—a car parked in an almost empty bowling-alley parking lot, 100 feet from the entrance and 150 feet from the nearest parked car. Two Hamilton cops had watched a woman get into a car after a brief chat with the driver and followed it as it drove off. Five kilometres down the road, the car had pulled into the lot and parked. The cops had parked higher up the slope and one of them had slid down the treed slope, keeping to the bushes, snuck up on the driver's side, peeked into the window, and spied the woman performing oral sex. The woman, charged and fined under Section 173(1)(a) of the Criminal Code—"Every one who wilfully does an indecent act in a public place in the presence of one or more persons . . . is guilty of an offence punishable on summary conviction"—appealed.

Galligan upheld the appeal, writing: "There is no question that, had the police officer not sneaked up on the car to see what was going on inside it, no one would have seen or been aware of the sexual activity taking place." In his view, "surreptitious surveillance" did not turn anything done in private into a public act.

Goodman concurred, arguing that the law was "absolutely not intended to cover police officers who surreptitiously sneak up on people in the middle of the night," slide 20 feet down the Niagara Escarpment, through the bushes, then get up to "about a foot-and-a-half behind you then jumping up and yelling GOTCHA!" His concern seemed to span the generations: "Surely young couples conducting their courtships in automobiles in dark secluded (albeit public) places are not committing criminal offences simply because curious onlookers seek to approach and look into such vehicles to satisfy their curiosity."

Osborne, the sole dissenter, seemed to view the issue beyond the specific appeal, decried street prostitution as "evil," and praised the law for fighting it.

Galligan had demonstrated similar independence and moxie dealing with media lawyers who had appealed the press ban, clearly demonstrating that they bored or annoyed him at their peril. No one would ever suggest that Galligan was a pushover. He had no qualms about asking tough questions of men and women who asked tough questions for a living.

It was the Crown prosecutors who had to make the case against Bernardo, and while his DNA linked him conclusively to the Scarborough rapes, the only thing that tied him to the Schoolgirl Murders was the testimony of his ex-wife, Homolka. Yes, it was perplexing for many cops, and by extension the press and public, that Murray Segal, the Crown's top gun for negotiating plea bargains, was never known to have settled for less than a guilty plea to second-degree murder for an accomplice willing to testify in exchange for a reduced sentence. What, they wondered, was so special about Homolka? But it was likely that the plea bargain was a sign of just how tenuous the case was against Bernardo.

There had been no alternative. They had needed Homolka to get Bernardo, who everyone agreed at least was a killer and would kill again if released.

Even the heart-wrenching tapes which eventually surfaced after the deal were at best circumstantial evidence. All that was known was that, twice, three young people went into a room, and, twice, only two came out alive. Whether or not social conditioning or the circumstantial evidence led the jury to unanimously conclude that it was the man who was the killer—that no woman could do it—the videotapes and Karla's own testimony had painted an image of her as far from "the girl next door." But was that enough to overturn the plea bargain and lay further charges?

The Bernardo videos, eventually the heart of the prosecution, were debated by almost everyone in letters to the editor, newspaper columns, editorials, and Internet chat rooms *ad nauseam*. The media again sent their legal hired guns into court to challenge any thought of shielding them from public view, as always, in "the public interest" and the "interests of justice." When the courts compromised, allowing the public to hear but not view the tapes, many of the voyeurs streamed out of the courtroom with tears and cries of anguish at what *they* had to endure. It never seemed to occur to any of them what the *families* of the victims must have endured.

Only a handful of experienced investigative and mental-health professionals ever viewed the tapes, and even fewer—MacKay, Lines, Collins and a very few others—viewed them through a "behavioural lens." And what it projected to them was not Karla's "feral" enjoyment of her role in torturing innocent victims, but her resigned enactment of a role in her man's fantasy. To those few who spent much of their time and energy investigating sexual deviance and aberrant violent crimes, who had seen the work of sexual sadists elsewhere, Homolka was merely an actress playing a role, albeit to chilling perfection. After viewing the tapes, they were more convinced than ever that Bernardo, not Homolka, had killed the girls. The answer was on the screen. He *liked* it.

If indeed Homolka met Hazelwood's criteria for the compliant victim, had been systematically transformed and remade by her sadistic husband, something might be learned, perhaps change—too late for their victims, but to the benefit of other women and children. Hazelwood's study of compliant victims was designed to open minds, nurture free thinking, not free convicted felons. It was a hard sell to an audience whose collective mind was made up and wished not be confused by facts or opinions or theories. But if Homolka was a threat only in the company of a sexual sadist—and she had posed no danger before meeting Bernardo—then arguably, if she could stay away or be kept away from the Bernardos of the world, she was harmless. Self-absorbed, perhaps even vapid at times, but not deadly. Even she claimed to have limits, telling MacKay and Hazelwood she had refused his demand that she have sex with his pet rottweiler, claiming she'd rather die.

As Hazelwood and MacKay wound up their interview with Homolka near noon on the second day at the P4W, the Mountie accepted that she fit his colleague's criteria for a compliant victim. He also realized then that he had studied others, notably Lennie Pomfret's girlfriend, who had fled her relationship with that sexual sadist in Manitoba back in 1993. Why had Karla not done the same?

Galligan's mandate to review the plea bargains, and Mr. Justice Archie Campbell's subsequent and concurrent review of the police investigations of the Scarborough Rapist and Schoolgirl Murders, posed a formidable challenge that would test the wisdom of Solomon.

There was no doubt Galligan, a former criminal lawyer with extensive knowledge of the criminal justice system, had the necessary experience, and the broad respect and confidence of all sides in the adversarial criminal justice system. He was first appointed to the bench as a High Court Justice in 1970, and named to the Ontario Court of Appeal in 1989. He boasted an impeccable lineage: son of a long-serving county court judge and grandson of a member of parliament.

His devotion to public service was further underscored, if less

well known, by his activities as one of three Ontario Supreme
Court Justices who were fellow benchers and also fraternal brothers and prominent alumni of Delta Chi, the prominent law fraternity founded at Cornell University in New York State on October
13, 1890. Delta Chi evolved into a general fraternity in 1922, and
in 1929, amid the worst stock-market crash in history, it became
the first fraternity to abolish Hell Week and outlaw hazing. As
well, Delta Chi pioneered the volatile debate on the need for jour-
nalistic ethics.

The fraternity is obliged by their constitution to promote friendship and sound education, develop character, and advance and
uphold justice "in every facet of their life." Its registry reads like a
who's who of public service, big business, entertainment, and sports
across North America, including: Ontario Supreme Court Justices J.
Edward Eberle and Robert Rutherford; William Sessions, former
Director of the FBI; Robert Todd Lincoln, son of assassinated President Abraham Lincoln who sought equality for the negro in America; former Alabama Governor George Wallace, who did not; U.S.
President Benjamin Harrison and presidential candidates Henry
"Scoop" Jackson and William Jennings Bryan; author Russell Nye,
who won a Pulitzer and the Knopp Prize; space shuttle Commander
Henry Hartsfield; Secretary of the Navy James H. Webb, Jr.; Charles
Marshall, former vice-chairman of the Board for AT&T and press
secretary to President Richard Nixon; actor Kevin Costner; Pat
Gillick, general manager of the Baltimore Orioles; and NFL Hall-of-
Fame tackle Ron Mix.

One of the "basic expectations" adopted by the Delta Chi Board
of Regents on July 24, 1988—"I will exercise compassion and
understanding in dealing with all persons"—must have posed a
unique test for Galligan when he seemed one of the few people, in
Ontario or beyond, still trying to keep an open mind on Homolka
and her plea bargain.

Galligan's sole condition for undertaking his review was to have
a "top-flight" member of the Criminal Defence Bar as counsel.
David Humphrey, an experienced defence attorney and former

Crown Attorney, cheerfully rearranged his schedule to join Galligan, applying his "broad and thorough understanding of the criminal law, practical experience . . . good counsel, boundless energy and a keen sense of humour" that eased the tension of reviewing a horrific litany of crimes and the lonely task of seeking some good part of Homolka that could be understood. He found it, and the basis for defending the deal and the Crown actions, in Hazelwood's study of *Compliant Victims of the Sexual Sadist*, attached as an appendix to his 342-page report. It had earlier been attached to justify the search-warrant application for the home Homolka shared with Bernardo.

Galligan's report said, "I was very skeptical about her statements that she was subjected to violence and threats to the point where she was in such fear of him that she would do his bidding, no matter how monstrous, yet she still loved him and would not rid herself of him." But he went on to explain that Hazelwood's research, especially the account of the seven original similar documented cases, gave him pause, forced him to accept that she *might* have been telling the truth. It was harder to automatically assume she had lied, first to the police and the Crown, when she downplayed her role in the torment of the murdered teens and her own sister's death, then later when she said she hadn't told them about another videotaped "Jane Doe" rape of an unconscious teen in their home, because she simply "forgot."

As for the plea bargain, Galligan confirmed that there had indeed been two deals: "The first decision, to agree to a twelve-year sentence, was driven by sheer necessity and not by a desire to treat Karla Homolka differently than any other criminal." Galligan had "no doubt" that the Crown would have preferred to put Homolka in the prisoner's dock with Bernardo, facing first-degree murder charges, but without her testimony, at the time the decision was made, the police had no evidence to charge Bernardo with murder, "much less convict him." As for the second deal, made on May 18, 1995, he wrote:

(It) was not made for the purpose of benefitting Karla
Homolka. It was a considered decision taken to advance the
Crown's case against Paul Bernardo. . . . The risk that was seen
in charging Karla Homolka with the June 7, 1991 assault on
Jane Doe was that serious damage would be done to the case
against Paul Bernardo for the murders of Leslie Mahaffy and
Kristen French. . . . It was decided that the risk of charging her
was too great to be taken. I, for one, am not prepared to second
guess that decision.

As for any "unfair and unjust" implication that anyone had
offered Homolka a "sweetheart deal" or "preferential treatment,"
Galligan concluded: "It is entirely without foundation. I reject it
completely."

The deal stood. The government relaxed. The press and a broad
segment of the public howled its outrage.

And Galligan moved on to pressing personal problems.

On Wednesday, October 16, 1996, Sean Conway, representing
Renfrew North, rose in the House to ask Health Minister Jim
Wilson if he was aware of the plight of Ella Galligan, a 102-year-old
widow living in Pembroke, who had just been told by Wilson's offi-
cials that, effective November 30, 1996, "she will not only lose her
OHIP coverage but her OHIP card because, in the view of the
Ontario Ministry of Health, she is a refugee claimant."

Wilson admitted he knew nothing of the case but would get back
with an answer as soon as possible. Conway pressed on:

Minister, let me tell you a little bit about Mrs. Ella Galligan of
Pembroke, Ontario, who your department now thinks is a
refugee claimant. She's a 102-year-old citizen of our community. She is the daughter of a former member of Parliament. She
is the wife of our long-term county court judge. She is the
mother of Mr. Justice Patrick Galligan, recently retired from the
Ontario Supreme Court. She is a lifetime resident of the Ottawa
Valley, a distinguished citizen. Her family wants to know not
only that you're going to fix this, but how it is possible that

someone so distinguished ends up in the government computers of Mike Harris's Ontario as a refugee claimant.

Wilson, nonplussed, shot back:

> I would remind the honourable member that when the Liberal government sent out blank forms for people to get their health cards in 1986, parrots and dogs and cats and other family pets were issued health cards by that government. In fact, 12 million people were issued health cards for a population of 10 million. I have devoted most of my career to straightening out the health card system, and I'm doing that as we speak. I will take the question on notice and get back to the honourable member with the specific case and correct any errors that may have occurred, but I certainly don't need any lectures about inappropriate databases from the Liberals.

Whether or not the exchange let an elderly woman keep her health card, and no matter how yanking his mother's card seemed a rather bizarre "thank you" to Galligan for his years of devoted public service, culminating in retirement with his Homolka review, it was an encouraging sign that life was resuming, that once again one arm of government didn't know what the other was doing, that government had found a new way to target the elderly besides closing hospital beds, that what passed for reality among politicians, at least in the microcosm of Queen's Park, was alive and well. But there were more serious political exchanges to come.

A month later, Thursday, September 26, six months after Galligan had submitted his report, Cools, a Trudeau senator and one-time student radical who had occupied administration offices of Sir George Williams University in Montreal during the campus protests of the 1960s and 70s, expressed her dismay and disdain for Galligan's report to the Standing Senate Committee on Legal and Constitutional Affairs:

> I should like to call the attention of members of the committee

to a report by a former judge, Mr. Justice Galligan. It is a
lengthy report which I have read cover to cover. . . . This report
is very hollow and shallow. It whitewashes a terrible process on
the grounds that it was driven by necessity.

Nor was Cools much impressed with Hazelwood's research or its
impact on opening Galligan's mind:

I should also like to draw the attention of honourable senators
to a very questionable article which is referred to in this report.
It is supposed to have provided the fuel for the moral suasion
for the prosecutors who entered into their deal with Karla
Homolka. The article is found on page 334 of the report and is
entitled "Compliant Victims of the Sexual Sadist." I ask senators to note that this article was printed in the obscurity of
Australia. It is written and produced by the FBI Behavioural
Personnel and could only find expression in Australia. . . . This
is the article that all the respective prosecutors relied on for their
theoretical moral justification for the particular plea bargain
that they entered into with Ms. Homolka.
    Honourable senators, with all our understanding of human
error, it is quite easy to understand how the prosecutors went
down that road and got into the first plea bargain. It is not
acceptable or morally right; however, I can understand and
appreciate what happened. Terrible crimes were happening.
They were not sure what to do. To be quite frank, they had
spent $25 million. I have researched these figures. They were
eager to close the case. They came across this blonde with long
hair who batted a few eyelashes. What she said sounded reasonable to them because somewhere in our hearts we do not believe
that human beings can do the kinds of things that were done.
Because we are so abhorrent of such repugnant action, we
sometimes take comfort where we should not. Basically, that is
the road they went down.
    I cite this article as well because Mr. Galligan's report relies

heavily on it. I will revisit the whole concept of sexual compliance of psychopaths. My opinion, and the opinion of the learned people with whom I have spoken, is that Ms. Homolka was herself a psychopath. We had two psychopaths coming together—two monsters coming together to create in harmony a different monster, in combination.

Cools argued that Homolka's deviance resembled "hybristophilia," a sexual disorder—not mental illness—marked by arousal, gratification, and satisfaction from watching, or joining in, a partner's brutal rape, torture, and/or murder. Known in layman terms as the "Bonnie and Clyde" syndrome, it seemed to fit Homolka at least as well as the "compliant victim" syndrome. If so, why did none of the several forensic mental-health experts who examined her diagnose a single personality disorder? None. Zilch. Nada. Even after Galligan's exhaustive review, there were still questions.

Whatever the differences between Hazelwood, who believes you are not necessarily evil because you love or marry an evil man, and Cools, who sees two monsters merging to create a third, more horrible evil, Cools was one of the few to publicly address an oft-overlooked tragedy of the Homolka plea bargain:

Finally, I should like to come to one issue that has been extremely troubling to me. . . . Honourable senators, a travesty occurs in this process. There are two charges of manslaughter for the deaths of two teenage girls, Kristen French and Leslie Mahaffy. If you read the judgment carefully, you will see that the issue of Homolka's sister, the young girl called Tammy Lynn, and Homolka's culpability in the entire matter, are read into the record. The result of that, honourable senators, is that she will never be prosecuted for the death of her sister Tammy Lynn. There is also another result of that, which cannot be unintentional because these prosecutors are too skilled and too knowledgeable not to know that this circumvented the issue of a third murder charge. Were there to be a third manslaughter charge against her, she would then be in a new category, that of a serial killer. I find this disturbing.

Whether you find her logic reasoned or flawed, whether you accept or refute that an apparently accidental death can be included in the toll of serial murder, Cools speaks, however obliquely, for the family that lost more than any other. The Homolkas have twice the right to hate and curse Bernardo. In a case of unbound horror and grief and tears, when young women and loving families lost so much to pure evil randomly stalking the land, they lost *two* daughters to him. No matter how unlikely the world is to forget—nor quickly forgive—Karla, it has been easy to forget that Tammy was the first to die, her death acknowledged but, many argue, never truly avenged.

Only time will tell, after Homolka is released in 2005, if she will pick up the pieces of her life and move on, presumably no threat to society, or pick up with another Bernardo—in which case, God help us all. Perhaps the best that can be said of this stark tragedy that defies logic and decency is that lessons have been learned.

While it may offer little comfort, something good has come from all the suffering. Police and prosecutors have been shaken out of their denial and delusion that "it can't happen here" and will be better prepared for the next time. Sadly, there is always a "next time" to test what has been learned and applied, or ignored and doomed to repeat.

Four months after Galligan submitted his report, Mr. Justice Archie Campbell's review of the police investigations of the Scarborough Rapist and Schoolgirl Murders was made public. Its findings were total vindication for MacKay and ViCLAS and made the world a safer place for women and children.

But only in Ontario.

13

Vindication—The Campbell Report

The human spirit has a magnificent capacity for surviving extreme adversity, the most horrific tragedy, any natural or man-made disaster. All we ask is that some silver lining, some greater good, come from our anguish; that we learn from misfortune and make change to prevent it happening again. To learn nothing, to change nothing, invites the horror to return. From the foundering of *Titanic* early last century, where intelligence (ice warnings) was ignored, to the kamikaze attack on September 11, 2001 that collapsed the twin towers of Manhattan's World Trade Center, where security intelligence didn't exist, the result was the same: cataclysmic snuffing out of thousands of innocent lives, forever altering life for those who survived. Each spawned deep introspection, but change was mandated from without. Solutions were clear: sufficient lifeboats for all passengers and crew; better communication and information-sharing across jurisdictional lines. Anything less mocks the victims and invites further mass destruction and unconscionable loss of life. In all cases, lessons learned too late for many were applied for the greater good of many, many others.

Similarly, the systemic failures and human errors that had plagued the Bernardo investigations, where information was too often not shared or not passed on, and intelligence missed, misinterpreted, or ignored, spawned lessons that, if learned and applied, could glean some good from abject grief. Though it was too late to protect those who had innocently strayed into the path of a deadly sexual sadist, or to preserve their shattered and stolen young lives, there was ample opportunity to proclaim their dignity and nobility, so richly earned, by applying what could be learned from their misfortune to benefit others. Mr. Justice Archie Campbell stepped into the void to champion their cause and help ensure, "Never again!"

On December 13, 1995, Campbell was appointed to head the "Bernardo Investigation Review" and recommend to Ontario Solicitor General Bob Runciman ways to improve the much-maligned manhunt for the sadist who had raped, abducted, and murdered his way undetected across the Golden Horseshoe from Scarborough to the Niagara Frontier. Unlike Galligan's limited mandate, which should perhaps have been the focus of any criticism of his report, Campbell was to:

1. Review the role of the Green Ribbon Task Force and its investigation into the deaths of the victims, and the Metropolitan Toronto Police Service investigation into the Scarborough sexual assaults.
2. Review the involvement of the Centre of Forensic Sciences and the analysis of samples submitted for testing regarding the Scarborough sexual assaults.
3. Review the issues concerning the autopsies performed on Tammy Homolka and the police and coroner's investigation into her death.
4. Review the role of the provincial government in the provision of funding for the Green Ribbon Task Force.
5. Provide a written report to the Solicitor General and Minister of Correctional Services by March 31, 1996 comprising an identification of issues and recommended policies or procedures that would improve the responses of the police, the Centre of Forensic Sciences, and the Coroner's Office to effectively and efficiently deal with crimes of the nature investigated.

Campbell knew his way around the government system and was widely respected for his analytical skills. Before donning the judicial robes, he had been an assistant deputy minister in the Attorney General's office and a Crown Attorney. No one doubted his ability to wade through issues or find ways to make the world a safer place. He enjoyed two huge advantages over the investigators who had vainly tracked Bernardo's carnage for so many years: the clarity of hindsight and the power to pick his fights. If Crown Attorneys seem to enjoy some latitude in which cases they prosecute, the cops must play the hands they're dealt. Every problem, ignored or falling through the cracks of the agencies that exist to address them, is dumped in the lap of the cops. Most criminal cases invariably stem from social, family, financial, or health issues nurtured by systemic failures. Hindsight almost always shows that, had steps been taken by the appropriate agencies and those who staff them, the cops could have been spared involvement, allowing more time to clear the cases and the paperwork already burying them.

Campbell's approach to his review seemed based in the wisdom that you can mandate systemic change, but you can't legislate human nature. All government ministries, boards, agencies, and commissions were ordered to assist him "to the fullest extent," but it didn't take the wisdom of Solomon to realize this review could be no one-man show. Campbell was determined not to produce a "door stopper" that would sit on a shelf, paving another road to hell with its dust-coated good intentions and recommendations that would never be implemented. Whereas Galligan had been aided by a top litigator, Campbell needed an interrogator—a cop, not a lawyer—who could interview other cops on their roles dating from Bernardo's first rape on May 4, 1987, to his murder convictions on September 1, 1995.

After interviewing several highly recommended candidates, Campbell named Peel Regional Police Superintendent Ron Bain his "Chief Investigator" and, at Bain's suggestion, also recruited Peel Detective Jennifer Dinneen. The trio bonded into a blessed trinity to protect those most at risk—women and children—from serial predators.

Bain was a veteran homicide investigator with eight years' experience and had led the high-profile investigation into the tragic murder of Christopher Stephenson, an 11-year-old abducted from a

Brampton shopping centre west of Toronto and murdered by Joseph Fredericks, a paroled high-risk sex offender, in June 1988. Bain had been the case officer on both the investigation and the 1993 coroner's inquest, the first to issue its findings in report-card style to clearly show where the system and investigation had passed and failed, which led to the passage of "Christopher's Law" and the creation of Canada's first registry of convicted sexual offenders in early 2001.

Bain had joined Metro Toronto police as a cadet in 1972, moving to join the Parry Sound town force in the heart of Bobby Orr country before ending up at Peel in 1979. Although his maternal grandfather had patrolled the highways and byways between Port Colborne and Pickering on a motorcycle in the 1920s—before the OPP was even a glimmer in the Ontario government's eye—it was neither his lineage nor any romantic idealism that had lured him into uniform. Quite simply, he and several high-school pals had thought policing offered a challenge—an "interesting and imaginative proposition." Bain was the only one to follow through.

Though arriving at Peel too late for the Mississauga rail disaster and the largest peacetime evacuation in history, he retained unique memories of that night. Cops don't like surprises, nor are they big believers in coincidence, but the fact remains that on the same night a chlorine rail tanker tipped over west of Toronto, Bain, against all odds, found himself in charge of a toxic cleanup in Parry Sound where several tanker cars had tipped while shunting on a side rail. There had been derailments before, mostly new cars tipping off train flatbeds, but this was the worst in local history and could not have come at a worse time. As the spilled crude oil oozed into the pristine waters of Georgian Bay, threatening the environment and tourist dollars for a major mecca in Ontario's cottage country, Bain called vainly for salvage equipment but was advised that nothing was available. It was all racing toward Mississauga. Making do with what he had, he contained the spill with booms until more sophisticated equipment was freed and dispatched from southern Ontario.

While Bain was responsible for conducting, coordinating, and analyzing all interviews and case files from the Scarborough Rapist and Green Ribbon Task Forces, researching applicable policing and investigative issues, Dinneen offered her own invaluable expertise. She had earned an enviable reputation for excellence, and her proven investigative and people skills honed by investigating sexual assaults and treating the victims with compassion would prove invaluable as she interviewed the young women who had survived Bernardo's attacks and the families of the schoolgirls who had not.

While the Peel investigators completed their legwork behind the scenes, Campbell refined his strategy to take the high road, addressing systemic rather than human failures, believing that pointing fingers at individuals would accomplish less than fixing the system that had clearly failed the young women who had strayed into Bernardo's path.

Like Galligan's review, Campbell's was not a public inquiry and would also be conducted in secrecy. No formal evidence would be called, no sworn testimony nor statements taken that could be subject to cross-examination. The alternative, a public inquiry or Royal Commission, would involve a host of lawyers that could, it was feared, muddy the issues, cloud findings, and delay solutions. All agreed that the last thing anyone wanted or needed was an unnecessary administrative burden or bureaucratic nightmare at the end of a case that had spawned no end of headaches.

The best strategy was to keep it simple, thorough, and prompt. But even with a flexible mandate, mandated cooperation, and an outstanding pair of investigators, the deadline was unrealistic. Campbell requested and was granted an extension.

On June 27, 1996, he presented his findings to Runciman. The "Campbell Report" was made public a month later. Blunt, detailed, and forceful, it was also a masterpiece of clarity, brevity, and wisdom, concluding that the chaotic saga of the Bernardo investigations "is a story of systemic failure."

Admitting that serial predators like Bernardo posed "unique" challenges, Campbell insisted that the cops must adapt and systems had to change for any hope of stopping "a determined, organized, mobile, sadistic serial rapist and killer who demonstrates the ability" to strike anywhere, anytime. What seemed most alarming was that the problems that had plagued the Bernardo manhunt had earlier plagued the Olson and Bundy cases and others less well-known but equally deadly. As Campbell lamented, "And always the answer turns out to be the same—systemic failure. Always the problems turn out to be the same, the mistakes the same, and the systemic failures the same." These mistakes were being repeated across the country, the continent, and the world. That, Campbell insisted, had to change: "Ontario has, in its existing law enforcement agencies, the essential capacity to respond effectively to another case like this, but only if certain components of those agencies are strengthened and only if systems are put in place to coordinate and manage the work of the different agencies."

Campbell further cautioned that not all problems could be fixed simply by political will and tons of cash. Improved systems and better training would be wasted if attitudes among the investigators didn't also improve: "There were times during the separate investigations of the Scarborough rapes and the St. Catharines rapes and murders that the different police forces might as well have been operating in different countries."

Or planets.

Just reading the report's Table of Contents confirmed the litany of woes that had plagued the Bernardo investigations:

- "Analyzing the Delays"
- "The Belated Unearthing of the Stalking Incidents"
- "Investigative Jurisdiction"
- "Bernardo's Suspect Rating Discrepancy"
- "The Media Leak"
- "The Interview Failure"
- "The Right to Counsel Problem"
- "The Recording Bungle"
- "No One in Charge, No One Accountable"
- "Continuing Hostility"
- "Were the Tapes in the House?"

What could easily have been a hatchet job, destroying careers and reputations, was instead a reasoned analysis that concluded that any tragic consequences spawned by human error were eclipsed by the ineffective case-management and information-sharing systems that had plagued investigators dating to the Scarborough rapes. Those systemic deficiencies were further complicated by the sheer volume of tips and possible suspects and the brutality of the crimes. Quite simply, years had passed before anyone had looked "outside the box" at the big picture and linked the cases.

The cops who had vainly tracked Bernardo all that time weren't stupid or lazy. There was no lack of dedication, motivation, or investigative skill. Indeed, there were clearly men and women from all departments who pushed themselves to review one more file, pursue one more tip, question one more suspect, walk one more mile for the sake of the victims and their families. There were just too many possibilities, too few hours in the day, and too little hard evidence.

The Metro investigators who first tracked the Scarborough Rapist were also swamped with several other serial-rape cases, signalling a rise in "stranger" attacks that were the most time-consuming and difficult to solve. Each attack in Scarborough led to a vigorous and determined response, but it simply could not be sustained because the dozen investigators—half the number requested by the Sexual Assault Squad, created from the original Scarborough task force— handled an estimated 2000 sexual assaults every year and solved 70 percent of the cases. The system was understaffed, overworked and stressed to the breaking point. The failure of what had proved to be ineffective case-management and information systems further hampered the separate Bernardo investigations by failing to link what, in hindsight, were clearly key incidents:

- Metro Police awareness that Bernardo, a suspect in the Scarborough rapes, was moving to St. Catharines
- The striking similarities between the Scarborough and Henley Island rapes
- Bernardo's residence within a mile of the Henley Island rape

- Repeated and insistent tips to look at Bernardo again
- Appropriate followup investigation on these tips
- The stalking incidents earlier reported to the Niagara Regional Police.

What had seemed random incidents at the time showed, in hindsight, clear patterns: "All this information was readily available, but there was no system to put it together and it got lost in the overall mass of investigative information. What is clearly needed is a systematic case management approach that taps into every available technique and resource and source of information and organizes the information in a way that it can be recognized and used effectively by investigators."

Two of the major aspects of Campbell's review were to answer lingering questions about what had been portrayed by the media as major screwups: Bernardo's untested DNA samples and the search of his home at 57 Bayview Drive which had failed, despite extensions running to 71 days, to find the damning videotapes, hidden in the bathroom ceiling, of him and Homolka abusing their young victims.

The Metro investigators had eventually come to believe that the Scarborough rapes would be solved by a match linking the rapist to his victims. Bernardo was among the many suspects interviewed, and one of the few asked to provide blood as well as hair and saliva on the "gut" hunch of an investigator.

The problems that delayed testing and matching were many. The Centre of Forensic Sciences (CFS) had just opened its lab in July 1990 and had neither the budget, staff, nor resources to cope with the flood of samples submitted by Metro investigators. At that time, their tests could not identify an assailant but could, with other evidence, exclude suspects. Those limitations were compounded by the fact that the cops had attached no priority to the samples. Lacking a prime suspect, they gave no direction to the lab as to which samples they wanted tested first. Instead, they went "fishing," playing the odds that the more samples they submitted, the more suspects they could exclude, narrowing the field from possibilities to probabilities. They were right—eventually. Campbell's report stated:

"Although samples of Bernardo's blood, hair and saliva were submitted to the CFS on November 21, 1990, the first test was not completed until February 1, 1993, over two years later. This first test showed a one probe match. . . ."

Prior to that, in 1987 and 1988, when the horror was just unfolding, conventional serology tests had been instrumental in eliminating some suspects, but results were still confusing as the unknown assailant was judged to be "either a B secretor, an O secretor, or a non-secretor." A trip to a private New York lab proved no more helpful. Finally, in January 1989, improved testing was able to confirm the Scarborough Rapist was a non-secretor, one of only 20 percent of the male population. That break allowed the cops to rescreen their suspects and eliminate many. By July 5, 1990, they had reduced their suspects to a pool of 40, and, on July 27, samples from the May 26 rape—Bernardo's last in Scarborough—were tested and reduced the non-secretor grouping by one-third, lowering the matches to 13 percent of the male population.

At a meeting on September 25, the "case scientist"—the sole qualified analyst then performing the tests at the CFS—had reportedly asked the Metro investigators to prioritize their suspects to avoid wasting valuable lab time or plugging the system by massive testing of all the remaining suspect samples. Everyone apparently left the meeting with a different understanding of what had been agreed upon and what would happen next.

Although Bernardo's original blood test, performed on November 21, 1990, confirmed that he was a non-secretor, and therefore a candidate for testing—one of five on the Metro shortlist—a written request from the cops on December 13 formally requesting the test "went into a black hole" according to Campbell. "Despite this request for testing, effective December 13, 1990, Bernardo's sample was not analyzed until February 1, 1993. It appears that Bernardo's submission went into a black hole at the end of 1990, from which it only emerged a year and three months later on April 2, 1992 when the police requested their request for testing [on 5 of the remaining 79 suspects]."

The sample was not logged into the system for testing until July 12—a further three-month delay—by which time the lab had already accepted another 26 cases. That same day, three more homicides and a sexual assault unrelated to the serial attacks in Scarborough were also logged in. The total delay for testing Bernardo's sample had now risen to 15 months, but Campbell laid no blame at the feet of the cops doing the grunt work: "The important fact is that little had changed since 1990. Although the CFS was waiting for the police to narrow down the suspects before testing, there were still five suspects, including Bernardo, submitted. . . . The fifteen month delay at the CFS cannot be attributed to police investigative work."

By April 1992, the CFS was so backlogged, still with only two qualified analysts (one technician, one scientist, and one trainee), that conventional "turnaround" times of between six and seven months from the time police submitted samples to getting results—increasingly, key evidence for rape and murder trials—became meaningless and seemed to be judged from the time it made it past the logjam of cases. If overload was a legitimate problem, Campbell didn't consider it absolution: "It is at the very least ironic that the CFS had developed the profile of the Scarborough rapist by early 1991 but never compared it with what we now know to be the other half of the puzzle, the Bernardo sample already in the possession of the CFS, submitted by the police for testing in 1990."

Campbell's frustration didn't stop there: "On December 13, 1990, Bernardo was one of five suspects who had the right serology. On October 17, 1991, Bernardo was still one of five suspects who had the right serology. Nothing had changed."

During those ten months, Nina de Villiers, Tammy Homolka, and Leslie Mahaffy died, Jane Doe was drugged and raped twice, and another girl was raped at Henley Island. Bernardo was involved in all but the first. Kristen French was still alive. The testing finally began six months after her abduction and murder.

When testing on the Scarborough rape cases finally began on October 29, 1992, the CFS advised the police that the samples from the four suspects besides Bernardo were "insufficient." The cops obtained and submitted new samples on November 12. Five days later, new test results showed there was still not enough to proceed with the testing of two of the suspects. Memories conflict as to whether more samples were requested, but none were resubmitted before testing resumed in January 1993. On February 1, tests excluded the other four suspects and linked Bernardo to three of the Scarborough rapes. The delay of that happy result stemmed, according to Campbell, from systemic chaos:

> The fifteen month delay was a black hole. For a year and three months the police waited for the CFS to do tests and the CFS waited for the police to do investigative work. There was no management or supervisory team in place in the Metro force or the CFS to ensure that the case was pursued vigorously. . . . The entire period from April 2, 1992 to October 29, 1992 was spent waiting for the Scarborough rape cases to get to the top of the queue because there was no system in place to ensure that serial predator cases got to the top of the queue right away.

Those failures were made worse by the investigators' awareness that rapists didn't just stop and that this one was escalating and likely to start killing.

> Yet there was no system in place to drive this case forward to the top of the priority list or to leapfrog it ahead of other serious sexual assault and murder cases. There was no case management system in the Metro force to supervise this cold case and drive it forward vigorously. There was no strategic co-ordination of the work of the different agencies involved in the investigation. No one assumed the responsibility to push Bernardo's DNA test ahead because there was no system to prioritize and urgently drive forward the investigation of this violent escalating mobile serial predator.

Campbell capped his recommendations for specific systemic changes with an imperative that all politicians can understand: money.

"From a financial point of view, the Bernardo case demonstrates that delays in DNA testing can cost millions of dollars in the investigation of offences that could be prevented by timely DNA testing."

Failure to act to correct the systemic problems could also heighten the risk of lawsuits and could cost governments millions of dollars to defend themselves in court for failing to provide the reasonable protection to the public guaranteed by the Canadian Charter of Rights and Freedoms:

> Again from a financial point of view, there is a rapidly developing body of law around the potential liability of government for failing to provide a reasonable standard of public protection, an area of liability which could prove very expensive to the government if reasonable standards are not met. . . . [T]he Bernardo case demonstrates that delays in DNA testing can imperil personal safety and cost lives. Any reluctance to continue to spend the public funds necessary to maintain a reasonable turn-around time for DNA tests must give way to a consideration of the financial and human cost of failing to do so. . . . [T]he Bernardo case, in terms of the government's obligation to provide a reasonable standard of public protection, demonstrates that the public will remain at unnecessary increased risk from violent serial predators unless a reasonable turnaround standard is maintained for DNA testing.

Without specific reference to the Charter, Campbell seems to be basing his point on Section Seven: "Everyone has the right to life, liberty and security of the person and the right not to be deprived thereof except in accordance with the principles of fundamental justice." Now that he had alerted the government to systemic failures in desperate need of repair, it was very possible, in fact probable, that any failure to act would lead to legal action by victims or their families in future.

The Charter was also a vital consideration in the search of Bernardo's home at 57 Bayview Drive.

It must be remembered that the Green Ribbon Task Force had

absolutely no grounds, aside from Homolka's "paper-thin" uncorroborated testimony, for a warrant to search Bernardo's home for evidence of murder. Only Metro, with its long-delayed DNA evidence, had reason to suspect him of a crime—the Scarborough rapes. After a prolonged 71-day search by specialists failed to recover the damning videotapes—later retrieved by Bernardo's lawyer Ken Murray following his client's instructions and a hand-drawn map, and surrendered much later to the prosecution by his second lawyer, John Rosen, under threat of having his office searched—the cops were again the target of public outrage. Why, the press and public and an awful lot of cops wondered, had they not just "trashed" the house or at least cut a hole in the ceiling where the tapes were hidden? Campbell answered both with five words: The Canadian Charter of Rights.

The meticulous preparations of the 1000-page search-warrant application, including "behavioural" aspects for the first time on a high-profile case, had had to comply with Bernardo's Section Eight Charter guarantee "to be secure against unreasonable search or seizure." The cops hadn't written the law, but they were bound by it. The fact that Bernardo rented the house did nothing to simplify matters.

While no one was happy that they had missed the tapes, their later admission as evidence—the evidence that ultimately convicted Bernardo—would be open to a Charter challenge and legal interpretation by a legal system obsessed with protecting the rights of the accused. If the warrant was a wondrous example of dotted i's and crossed t's, the cops who executed the search complained it was "difficult" and "tied our hands" and was "so restrictive it became unworkable." Whether, as many lament, "Charter chill" has spawned an era and mindset that "deters Crowns and police from doing sensible things," the inescapable overriding concern on this case, given its horror and lack of evidence, was, according to Campbell, to "court-proof" the search by applying "the highest and strictest Charter standards."

> The short answer to this criticism ("they did an awful search")
> is that the warrant did not authorize the police to tear the house

apart. . . . The Charter principle of minimization restricted the
amount of damage the police could do during the search.

The same applied to cutting a hole in the ceiling:

> Like the needle in the haystack, hidden things are easier to find
> when you know where they are. But at the time, there was no
> reason to cut a hole in the ceiling beside that potlight in particu-
> lar or even in that room in particular. There was no more
> reason to cut a hole in that ceiling than there was to cut a hole
> in every ceiling in the house where there were potlights . . . but
> to cut holes in every similar place in the house . . . [would be] no
> different from tearing the house apart.

Campbell applauded what was probably the "longest residential
search in Canada" as "generally a model of painstaking and detailed
thoroughness." Normally loath to speculate on "what ifs" throughout his report, he does raise one creative question whether conventional crime-scene investigators and the Criminal Code are the best
options in cases like this:

> A drug squad officer might be more predisposed than an identi-
> fication officer, by reason of experience and mindset, to consider
> a more intrusive and necessarily more destructive search than
> the search conducted for the tapes and more prepared to make
> out a case for legal authority to do so. . . . [D]rug officers are
> given by law, much more extensive search powers than officers
> investigating criminal offences like murder. Under Section Four-
> teen of the *Narcotic Control Act*, an officer conducting a drug
> search has the power to break a building apart. . . .

The priorities seem skewed but the fact remains that homicide
and sexual-assault investigators don't have the power under the
Criminal Code that a narc has under drug-enforcement legislation
to rip out walls and tear out ceilings. But at least no aspect of the
search was ever challenged in court. (Ironically, the owner later

tore down the house the cops had taken such pains not to destroy.)

The Charter also played a role in the one issue that Campbell addressed outside the literal terms of his mandate: media relations. As the investigations wore on, particularly after the abduction of Kristen French, animosity and outright hatred between the cops, guardians of public safety, and journalists, guardians of the public's right to know, "bordered on the disastrous," according to Campbell.

The problem began when Niagara Regional Police Chief Grant Waddell named Bevan as both head of the Green Ribbon Task Force and the sole source of information to be released to the media. It was a hopeless position. No one could do both jobs well. Whether Bevan lacked the time or the inclination to disclose relevant information in a timely manner, the press grew restive, then resentful at feeling shut out and obstructed in the performance of their duties. Bad blood rose further when the reenactment of the French abduction was limited to the local television station. Many excluded reporters turned aggressive and demonstrated just how deeply nature abhors a vacuum. As one newspaper reporter explained:

> Very early in the investigation, the cops did something to the media that is the worst thing you can do in a case like this: they gave them nothing to lose. They cut them off from information so completely that the media said, "Well, fuck you. I'll go get the story myself."

Campbell seemed to understand that anger and motivation and, conceding he had no mandate to investigate or critique the media, took the opportunity to remind journalists that police-media relations are a two-way street, citing the earlier Colter review of the issue: "The police are frustrated by what looks to them like a lack of accountability in the media. The police see no sanctions imposed against journalists for over-zealous reporting that obstructs the investigation. . . ." The perceived obstructions included:

- Interfering with witnesses
- Broadcasting answering machine messages so as to jeopardize voice identification procedures

- Printing photographs so as to jeopardize identification lineups
- Tailing officers and interfering with their work as they went about their jobs
- Threatening to release leaked information so as to put arrest plans at risk
- Harassing victims and families
- Cruelly printing a sketch of a victim/witness that identified her and exposed her to acute embarrassment at school.

The cops, and even some "real" journalists, had been especially disturbed by one aspiring author's allegedly confronting the French family with an ultimatum to tell him everything he wanted to know or he'd just make something up. At the very least, it was a cruel and unprofessional tack that might have been resolved with a phone call to the author's publisher (or mother!) to ask the point of bullying a family already drowning in pain and sorrow. There had been lots of bitching about this incident, but no one had done anything. Why? Campbell opted this one time for the middle ground:

> The sanction of arresting a journalist for the criminal offence of obstructing justice, is a very extreme step that police are most reluctant to take. It is too blunt an instrument except in the very clearest of cases and it is therefore ineffective as a practical sanction against media conduct that interferes in a practical way with the conduct of police investigations without clearly infringing on the Criminal Code.

Having defined the police's reluctance to obstruct a free press, a guild that fancies itself a profession, Campbell stepped beyond his mandate to make his only request in a 369-page review and 27 recommendations: "It would be a significant public service for the media to develop a set of professional standards to guide the conduct of those who cover criminal investigations."

At the same time, he made no effort to whitewash the behaviour of the police in the Bernardo investigations. Bevan, who headed the Green Ribbon Task Force, was commended for doing "what he could with the systems available to him," amid the destructive frictions between Niagara and Metro Toronto investigators and the differing agendas of their superiors that hit rock bottom in the botched Bernardo interview after his arrest:

> [I]t began badly, degenerated into an argument, continued badly, and ended badly. Nothing of value was ever gained from the interview. . . . if there was ever an abject example of how things can go wrong when police forces do not co-operate and no one is in charge or accountable, this is that example. . . . if there was ever an abject example of why it is necessary to develop a co-operative approach among police forces and a system to ensure such co-operation and accountability under a unified leadership structure, this is that example. . . . Communication and co-operation between agencies at all levels must be accepted, encouraged, directed and, above all, practised. If not, every other measure, effort, venture, and joint force operation is doomed to failure.

No one was surprised to learn that the Bernardo investigations had been plagued with fractious personalities but few may have known just how deeply the hostilities ran. Campbell cited the facts, but did not dwell on them. The report, while it "names names and kicks butt," never goes for the jugular. Every condemnation is generally balanced by another quote or finding that seems to hint that no matter how bad something was, it could have been worse. For example, his scathing judgment of the botched interview, with the blame falling on Metro's shoulders, also notes in passing that Bevan was absent at a crucial time and no one seemed to be in charge. He also takes great pains to praise the efforts of two Metro sergeants, Mike Boyd and Tony Warr, for their tremendous efforts in improving relations between investigators from all departments. Both were later promoted. Boyd must have been especially remarkable, for he catapulted over a half-dozen ranks to deputy police chief of Canada's largest police force without any apparent resentment from those he shot past or the rank and file. Mick Riddle, the

Niagara Regional sergeant in charge of disclosing evidence to Bernardo's defence attorneys, deemed Boyd a "consummate professional" who taught him more in 20 minutes than he had learned throughout his career. High praise indeed, considering the source.

Not every peacemaker made the report. Riddle was painfully aware of the friction between investigators. Despite all the public denials to the media that the investigation was suffering from jurisdictional jostling, those on the inside knew better. (It was Riddle's opinion that anyone who claimed that there had been no friction or animosity between the investigators—and it seemed to escalate with rank—should never walk within 100 yards of a polygraph machine for fear of setting off alarms.) Feeling he had survived too many scrapes to let a major investigation falter over personality conflicts, he had worked hard to keep all sides working together. He never realized his impact until a chance encounter much later with Tom Atkinson, a lawyer with the Toronto Stock Exchange, whom he had first met as a Scarborough Assistant Crown Attorney working with the Green Ribbon Task Force. As they reminisced about their experiences, Atkinson stunned Riddle by confiding, "The only time I felt safe was when you were there." This unexpected tribute nearly reduced the grizzled veteran to tears of gratitude.

But if interagency cooperation had bordered on abysmal at times, Campbell also found a shining example for bringing cops together: ViCLAS.

In his bid to end the pattern of deadly mistakes that had been repeated so many times in so many manhunts for serial predators, Campbell made 27 recommendations for systemic improvements. Beyond the evident changes required for DNA testing, better training, better media relations, and a uniform, province-wide case management system for major investigations and future task forces, he also urged the Ontario government to amend the Police Services Act to make it the law for *all* police forces in the province to submit their ViCLAS cases in a timely manner, noting:

At the time of the Bernardo investigations, there was no automated system in place to link violent predatory crimes. Use of the
system now in place, ViCLAS, is not mandated by regulation
and its power to link these crimes is greatly diminished by under-
use. It is likely that Bernardo would have been apprehended
much sooner had ViCLAS been in place at the time and fully
operational through centrally mandated reporting requirements.

After reviewing the Henley Island assault, Campbell saw what
MacKay had seen as soon as he had been called in for his behavioural expertise. That case could have, should have, and, if ViCLAS
had been up and running, likely *would* have linked the two investigations—the rapes in Scarborough and the murders in the Niagara
Frontier. It could have marked the end of Bernardo's lethal trail,
ended the horror right there, before the murders began. ViCLAS
would not have been deceived by the apparent differences in MO—
late night in Scarborough, early morning in Port Dalhousie—that
might have misled some veteran investigators into believing they
were dealing with two different predators. ViCLAS would have
linked them on the basis of the inner ritual, what was said when,
what was done how, during the attack. Instead, nearly two years—
plagued with false leads, time wasted rousting known sex offenders
who provided alibis, wrongful identification from a photo lineup,
and absolutely no responses from any outside force to a CPIC zone
alert sent out by Niagara Regional Police—passed before the investigators put the pieces together. Even then, they needed Karla.

Citing its growing international reputation for excellence, Campbell could not understand why ViCLAS seemed so little valued and
used, at home:

[I]t is ironic that ViCLAS, despite its international reputation
and accolades as the best crime linkage system in the world, is
used in Ontario to a small fraction of its capacity, in part
because there is no regulation that requires police to use it. . . .
The underlying premise of ViCLAS, amply proven by the
Bernardo case, is that repeat offenders follow similar patterns

and that homicidal and sexual offenders exhibit identifiable and often predictable characteristics and motivation.

To his credit, Campbell also stressed that ViCLAS could never replace the investigators in the field nor substitute for a thorough investigation: "ViCLAS does not solve cases; it tells police forces about similarities between crimes, particularly predatory crimes of sexual violence, and gives them the tools necessary to investigate and develop the links between offences committed by the same serial predator." And he cautioned that even a revolutionary investigative tool like ViCLAS wasn't much good to anyone if investigators refused to use it. "ViCLAS has little chance to work unless investigators enter all violent predatory crimes into the ViCLAS system. . . . The power of ViCLAS to link violent predatory sexual offences is greatly reduced because it is underused. In 1995, under thirty percent of Ontario's murders and under six percent of Ontario's Level One sexual assaults were captured by ViCLAS."

Campbell understood that busy investigators would rather spend time tracking the criminal than spend 45 minutes to complete a ViCLAS booklet, but seemed to consider the latter to be time well spent:

> Experience shows that it is not enough merely to encourage ViCLAS reporting by means of the standard policies and procedures of individual forces. Encouragement is not enough. Unless the entry of information into ViCLAS is centrally mandated and enforced throughout Ontario, and its operation supported through training and strong reinforcement of the reporting requirement, its power to link predatory serial crimes is greatly weakened.

Campbell admitted that it might well require "some additional resources" to expand existing ViCLAS units in the OPP and Metro Toronto, neither of whom was submitting anywhere near their potential cases, to handle the increased reporting that legislated compliance would produce. He saw it as money well spent.

The extra effort and resources are a small price to pay for the early linkage and resolution of serial crimes when compared with the enormous financial cost of a continuing major investigation, to say nothing of the human and social cost of delayed resolution during the time a serial predator continues at large.

Four years after the carnage had ended, Campbell was intent on making sure no one forgot the financial and emotional toll that had accompanied the lost and shattered lives at the hands of Bernardo. He was determined not to allow such suffering to have been in vain if this could be done by something as simple as making the cops complete one more form.

I therefore recommend mandatory ViCLAS reporting by all Ontario police forces of crimes that fit the ViCLAS submission criteria by way of regulation under the Police Service Act [*sic*] and the reinforcement of ViCLAS reporting by way of training and auditing.

It was total vindication for MacKay and ViCLAS.

Campbell left no loopholes. The law would require investigators to submit their cases or pay the consequences. His reasoning seemed simple enough for anyone to grasp:

- A proven need existed
- A proven solution existed
- ViCLAS was the solution
- Use it!

Although it was only one of 27 recommendations, the mandatory ViCLAS compliance, more than any other, made the Campbell Report a defining document in Canadian jurisprudence, a virtual Magna Carta espousing enhanced efficiency for the police, greater public safety, and lower political costs. All benefited, but particularly those most at risk—women and children.

But only in Ontario.

14

Turning the Tide

Bernardo wasn't the only sexual sadist stalking Canada at the time—nor was Olson the sole deadly predator a decade earlier, as evidenced by the unexpected body count of the Kamloops "Highway Murders"—his threat had merely overshadowed all others in the media. Sexual sadists, the rarest breed of serial killer, are also the most prolific. FBI profiling pioneers Robert Ressler and John Douglas counted 127 known victims among their early interviews with 26 jailed killers. Roy Hazelwood surveyed 30 serial rapists; 22 had escalated to murder and had killed at least 187. MacKay estimated there were as many as 20 serial killers stalking Canadian women and children—and God knows how many serial rapists. The sexual sadists in Quebec and Manitoba and virtually every other police jurisdiction nationwide were just as brutal, just as lethal as Bernardo. But, stalking remote killing fields far from Toronto, home of the English-language media in Canada, they remained largely unknown beyond the handful of grieving families and frustrated cops caught in their wake. Campbell had sounded the alarm about an invisible threat; had championed ViCLAS as a viable response to an unacknowledged horror stalking the land.

The solution would not come cheap, but no one was going to argue about spending money that would make cops better able to catch the next Bernardo. The Ontario government's response was as immediate, in bureaucratic terms, as it was edifying, giving MacKay an early Christmas present and total vindication for ViCLAS. On December 2, 1996, Ontario announced it had taken the major step to legislate mandatory compliance for all police officers in the province to submit their cases within 30 days. OPP headquarters in Orillia would house a new provincial ViCLAS centre that would eventually also house other behavioural disciplines—profiling, geographic profiling, polygraph, threat assessment—and become home to forensic psychiatrist Collins, who was seconded from the Clarke Institute to work with the OPP full time.

ViCLAS was set to be fully operational by January 1, 1997. Startup and operational costs were pegged at $3.2 million annually—little more than the estimated $1 to $2 million to pursue Olson and pay his wife, roughly half the $5.2 million bill to operate the Green Ribbon Task Force and prosecute Bernardo, and a drop in the bucket compared to the $8.2 million total for the Bernardo case when estimated associated police costs were added in. And that didn't include the bills for the Scarborough Rape Task Force in Metro Toronto. The highest public estimate was the $25 million that Senator Ann Cools said had been spent as she denounced the Crown deal with Homolka.

Mandatory compliance was legislated under the Police Services Act, and it was estimated that ViCLAS would soon be processing 17,000 reports a year as Ontario reached 100 percent compliance. The OPP initiative was not to be an exclusive domain, as senior criminal investigators would be seconded from the Metropolitan Toronto, Niagara, Durham, Peel, and York police services to work alongside the provincial police. Total staff was estimated at 22 uniformed officers (15 OPP and 7 secondments) and 19 civilians.

Nothing makes a computer user-friendly like legislation that compels compliance. Those who argued that the additional time spent filling out forms was cruel and unusual punishment depriving investigators of valuable time they could better use knocking on doors and canvassing neighbourhoods were now told, not asked, to spend the 45 minutes to complete the ViCLAS booklets which, at the very least, would serve as a useful checklist and case summary.

The government line was simple: "Every Ontarian has the right to feel secure in their own communities." But the Charter of Rights and Freedoms extended that claim to all Canadians, and Ontario, by going it alone, by raising the standard for public safety in central Canada, has perhaps unwittingly and certainly unintentionally increased the risk from serial predators elsewhere.

While Ontario will continue, certainly in the short term, to be plagued by serial predators and pedophiles, the "organized" rapists and killers and sadists—the brightest and hardest to catch, whose only fear is detection, whose every "success" fuels their delusion that they will never be caught—will eventually realize they are at much lower risk of being caught anywhere outside Ontario. Mobile by nature, the most cunning will eventually move on to safer hunting grounds where they will find the women just as tempting as the women in Ontario. The children just as vulnerable, the teens just as trusting and job-hungry. In time, Ontario may have to contend just with the "disorganized" predators—the least clever and easiest to catch. Then those across Canada who boast "it can't happen here" may learn more quickly and more often how easily and ruthlessly it can.

ViCLAS' unique program allows the specialist to create specific search queries for any case to determine if similar behaviour exists between any of the more than 140,000 cases in the database. So why doesn't everyone use it? Admittedly, no one likes the "paperwork" of any job, but, if Vorpagel, the pioneering FBI profiler, is correct that we are waging a war, ViCLAS adds an element of "brain" to "brawn" just as the code-breaking machines Enigma and Magic helped shorten World War II by revealing every step the Axis forces were about to take, saving millions of lives and cutting years off the most lethal conflict in history. But it was the grunts in the field, at sea and in the air, who won it, based on how the human analysts interpreted the data. Similarly, the cops in the field will always be the ones who stop the serial predators.

ViCLAS does not predict, it tracks and links and gets cops talking and exchanging information—all the things Campbell found wanting on the Bernardo investigations. How much better it is for us all if the cops can catch one serial predator, close dozens of cases, and gather enough evidence to put him away forever. Not a treatment for violent crime, but a cure. That is the gift of the investigators. ViCLAS offers them inexhaustible memory. As Thomas Müller, the

Austrian criminal psychologist who helped track serial killer Jack Unterweger across three countries on two continents, said, "ViCLAS never forgets."

Yet nearly six years after Campbell saw ViCLAS' power, only Ontario has legislated its use or comes closest to 100 percent compliance. However, there are encouraging signs: the Mounties made "significant" strides in improving compliance rates across Canada in 2001, and Quebec has mandated compliance to begin in 2002 and is expected to copy the OPP all-in-one centre, as did the RCMP before them.

In 2000, Gerry Séguin of the SQ studied the unsolved murders of young women age 18 and older to help push the need to create a "Cold Case" squad akin to those springing up across Canada. In Quebec, primarily in and around Montreal, he determined that 225 adult women had been murdered over the past 25 years, with no one being charged. The chilling statistic was ample proof to him of the dire need to make profiling and ViCLAS mandatory.

In 1995, largely due to Séguin's incessant lobbying and the success of the Brochu profile a year earlier, the SQ had agreed to adopt ViCLAS (SALVAC in French) and put him in charge. He had no budget, no staff, not even a computer. He used all his powers of persuasion just to find himself an office, then had to find a department to belong to. And that was the easy part. The rest was a constant, wearing uphill battle that he fought with such passion it probably consigned him to retire a sergeant. By the time Séguin had finally landed his first computer, monitor, and printer from the federal government, he had already received 500 completed forms from investigators across the province.

Continuing to chip away at bureaucratic indifference, he found an invaluable ally in Martine Fourcaudot, the only woman in SQ senior management, who managed to get him a temporary secretary to enter the cases into the database. That was just the beginning. Fourcaudot shared Séguin's passion for justice. She lobbied hard and, when the position of assistant director was created for her, brought her full political clout to bear to make Quebec the first province in Canada to legislate, without benefit of a formal review or inquiry, mandatory compliance for all police to complete and submit their SALVAC forms.

In any language, *c'est bon*!

The new legislation, "Projet de Loi 19," was passed by the Quebec National Assembly in June 2001 and was to have been enacted and put in force on January 1, 2002. It's not clear if the politicians or the police were aware of what they had agreed to. There is no profiler in Quebec. Séguin has been trained informally by MacKay, but the SQ never replied to a written offer from Plomp to have a member train as an ICIAF Understudy with MacKay as his sponsor and with the full support of the FBI, despite the fact that all that was required was a written commitment to share their candidate's expertise with other forces across Quebec.

Although Séguin plans to retire in the next few years, he is still the logical candidate if the new law comes into force as scheduled at the start of 2002. But the truth is that he has fought to create a position to be filled by those who follow him. His fight was no less lonely than MacKay's; he dodged some of the same bullets, survived lost skirmishes, and won a war with a seemingly invincible ally: Four-caudot. And women and children across Quebec are a little safer because of them.

Good intentions aren't enough. If Vorpagel is right, the annual murder rate in America is eight times the total loss of life in the destruction of the World Trade Center in Manhattan. The murders continue year after year after year and the body count by home-grown terror soars to the millions. Even if you divide by 10—the standard math to derive Canadian from American statistics—it is a chilling prospect. The sad truth is that more of us die at the hands of strangers and neighbours here than from any foreign threat. Why is so little done to change that? Where is the declaration of war?

If voluntary compliance doesn't work, the next step clearly belongs to the politicians. Protecting those most at risk is the peacetime equivalent of fighting for mom and apple pie; there is no safer political platform in good times or bad. Most decision-makers are parents or grandparents with a vested interest, a personal stake, in this issue. They should legislate compliance if only to protect their own children and grandchildren.

Otherwise, who must suffer or die next before the politicians avail themselves of what Ontario has and Quebec has promised? How many dark paths and cold trails must the police wander aimlessly before accepting that ViCLAS may offer the shortcut they so desperately seek? Why won't the federal government, responsible for the Mounties and the Criminal Code of Canada—one of the oldest criminal codes and arguably one of the worst written statutes in the world—make ViCLAS the national standard it can be? What safer issue could there be for backbenchers to push forward? What about the Opposition and the media?

Where are the headlines and editorials? Why do puppy farms elicit more public outcry than women and children at risk?

The issue cuts across party lines, police jurisdictions, gender, race, and religion. It is the ideal cause for backbenchers in Ottawa demanding a greater voice in government; the ideal forum for those "tough on crime" politicians of all political stripes to go beyond whining and bitching about the soft treatment of convicted felons at "Club Fed." There is no downside to protecting the vulnerable; that is the job of government and an equal-opportunity crusade. They need only follow Ontario's lead, using software that exists and has been distributed, and do their job by making the cops do theirs. It seems to be what Greg Johnson would call a "no-brainer."

If moral suasion is not enough, Campbell provides another compelling argument. In his review of the delays in testing Bernardo's DNA, he warned that hesitation by the government to fix those systemic problems could leave them open to a Charter suit. Section Seven does not proclaim "Everyone *except women and children* has the right to life, liberty and security of the person." By proceeding alone to legislate mandatory compliance for ViCLAS,

Ontario raised the bar and put all other provincial and territorial legislatures, and the federal government, in the legally vulnerable position of offering less protection to their citizens than Ontario offers its.

Yet one person can make a difference. One man. One woman. One child.

On April 12, 2000, the Ontario legislature enacted "Christopher's Law," named for Christopher Stephenson, the Brampton boy abducted in 1988; it requires convicted pedophiles and sex offenders to register their current address and report their whereabouts to the local police after release from prison or while performing community service. A provincial Sex Offender Registry (SOR), the first in Canada, was formally launched at OPP headquarters in Orillia on April 23, 2001, amid praise that lessons had been learned and applied, mistakes corrected and systemic cracks closed. Other children were now believed safer because of the terrible price Christopher and his family had paid.

In August 2001, the provincial premiers unanimously petitioned Ottawa for a national registry. The response was lukewarm at best, prompting Ontario Premier Mike Harris to declare he would lead the battle for a national registry, at one point offering to fund registries in other provinces to be set up with the Ontario software.

It seems a noble crusade, providing prompt data to police who know that, statistically, nine out of ten children abducted and murdered by sexual pedophiles are killed within the first 24 hours. Of those, 44 percent were killed within an hour of their abduction, 74 percent within three hours, and a horrific 91 percent within the first day. No one can dispute that anything to save those children should be attempted.

But is a national registry the right fight? Olson had no conviction for sex crimes—such charges were stayed in British Columbia and never pursued in earnest in Nova Scotia. Bernardo had no criminal record at all. So neither of Canada's two most deadly child rapists and killers would have been in the registry. How many more like them are there, just starting out on their rampage free to roam while the cops spend their time checking a registry that will have no record of them?

Perhaps the media blitz that accompanied the Campbell Report has blinded the politicians into believing that just because ViCLAS exists in their province or territory the cops are using it because they said they would. If they check, most will find another road to hell paved with good intentions. While compliance is better, it is still poor. Every unlogged case creates a gap in the trail through which a serial killer or rapist or sexual sadist can slip. The only exception is Ontario, but let a predator cross a bridge or highway out of the province and "poof!"—they vanish.

As Campbell warns:

> There must be a public recognition that these problems are not just problems for the police and law enforcement communities. They are problems for the community as a whole. A commitment to correct them is necessary in order to guard against another case like this.

Campbell and Bain and Dinneen had done their job. Something good had emerged from the tragedies in southern Ontario. Unable to turn back the clock or undo what had been done, they had crusaded to ensure the innocents had not suffered in vain. From that tragic past came a brighter, safer future. Hopefully the surviving victims and the families who had lost their daughters would find some solace in that.

Because of what they had lost, other women and our children are safer.

But only in Ontario.

The wisdom and clarity of the Campbell Report led to swift adoption and implementation by the Ontario government. As a defining document, a virtual Magna Carta enhancing the right to life, liberty, and security for women and children, its single glaring irony was easy to overlook, and overlooked easily by those affected.

In urging the government to legislate mandatory compliance, and duly noting that the system had been developed "largely through the initiative of [RCMP] Inspector Ron MacKay," it would be the OPP, not the Mounties—Ontario, not Canada—who would be first to benefit.

In the process, OPP Inspector Kate Lines became a force to reckon with. Lines, the second Canadian profiler, and the first woman profiler in Canada and one of a handful worldwide, was able to bring every aspect of behavioural science under one roof at the new OPP headquarters in Orillia, surpassing even the Mounties' efficiency. It was the most consolidated, coordinated, and powerful behavioural centre in the world. No one doubted Lines was up to the task.

Probably more than any other force in Canada, the OPP are considered the "polite" police. Best known by most as a highway patrol investigating traffic accidents and lurking along highway shoulders and turnaround lanes with radar guns trained down the road for unwary speeders, they are the "country cops" who seem unflappable, ingrained with maddening courtesy as they ticket you and wish you a good day. Though dubbed (Premier Mitchell) "Hepburn's Hussars" for its violent response to union pickets during the "Dirty Thirties" (perhaps unfairly, as that private army may have consisted of more University of Toronto students than cops), the OPP long ago shed that tarnished image and survived a Royal Commission investigation into alleged links to organized crime to be recognized for investigative and forensic excellence dating back to its creation in 1909.

The OPP was, for example, the first force in the world to use laser testing in criminal investigations. This was the result of senior forensics expert Brian Dalrymple's chatting over the fence in 1976 with his neighbour—who happened to have a doctorate in chemistry and enough clout at the Xerox research centre in Mississauga to provide the equipment and expertise needed. Dalrymple got his own laser a year later. In the first case in which it was used, it revealed a fingerprint in an offshore crime that proved police had arrested the wrong man and led to the arrest and conviction of the real criminal. In 1988, at the height of the Scarborough rapes, Dalrymple helped identify the dismembered remains of violinist Selina Shen, who had disappeared from that city, by footprint impressions in her shoes; he also helped convict her former boyfriend Rui-Wen Pan of her murder when the laser revealed Pan's partial thumbprint on a knife recovered from Lake Ontario.

Now, in the wake of the Campbell Report, and the legislated blessing of the Ontario government, Lines had a golden opportunity to extend the OPP reputation for excellence with a behavioural science section that was the largest in Canada and second only to the FBI's NCAVC worldwide.

Kate Lines has come a long way from her sheltered rural roots in Ennismore, north of Peterborough, Ontario. After joining the OPP in 1977, she worked her first four years patrolling the highways near Toronto followed by four years working as an undercover "narc" and "trusted" buyer, all capped by five years with anti-rackets, busting the "suits" and CEOs in ivory towers. It was a good education for a small-town girl in how the real world worked from the back alleys to the boardrooms. At the time she was picked for Quantico, she had 13 years' investigative experience and a degree from the University of Toronto where she also studied criminal deviance.

Lines' courage is legendary. But, as with many legends, she admits there's an element of myth in her best-known, most told, tale of valour. MacKay is fond of telling the story, as are others, of the time Lines endured a painful root canal without freezing to be able to make a major presentation later that day without slurring. Grown men cringe as they visualize this brave woman gripping the arms of the dentist's chair and toughing it out. Lines confirms the story is true—to a point. The freezing didn't take, waiting any longer would have made her late for her presentation, so she told the dentist to go ahead. Courageous lady? Yes. Did it hurt? Oh, my, *yes*! Hopefully the presentation went well.

That experience underscores their profiling experiences, with Lines and MacKay reaching identical conclusions time after time, but often seeing something at least a little differently. That's probably due at least in part to their different backgrounds, but also likely partially to their genders which MacKay and Lines both jovially dismiss as a "guy" or "girl" thing. No matter how well and how closely women work with men, there is no denying they can see things differently. That's not necessarily a bad thing. While studying crime-scene photos at Quantico, the men in Lines' class were stymied by visible but unfamiliar injuries under a female victim's breasts. A female classmate, viewing the same "evidence," concluded she had worn an under-wire bra, adding one more tenuous span to the always shaky bridge between Mars and Venus.

After Lines collaborated with MacKay on several early profiles soon after graduating from the FBI Academy, both were pleased, and possibly relieved, to see that their independent profiles were almost word-for-word identical, as were Ressler's and Vorpagel's when they profiled the Sacramento Vampire case years earlier. It was even more remarkable considering the major differences between the Canadian profilers that simply didn't exist for the FBI legends: age, gender, investigative experience. On the other hand, it seemed plausible that two people who hailed from Moosomin, Saskatchewan, and Ennismore, Ontario, would find something in common and professional respect evolved into personal friendship. In any event, their confidence grew with each joint opinion. It mattered less whether their conclusions were reached for different reasons than that they were proving to themselves, and hopefully others, what Lines termed "the ultimate strength of the multi-experience, multi-disciplinary approach to behavioural science support services."

As head of the OPP Behavioural Services Section, the first in the world to house profiling, geographic profiling, polygraph, forensic psychiatry, ViCLAS, threat assessment, and eventually the Ontario SOR under one roof, Lines was respected and seemed genuinely liked by those who worked with and reported to her. She got the same kid-gloves treatment as Collins, nicknamed "George" and "Rain Man" by his fun-loving police colleagues. Historically, transfer into the OPP from another force was said to be limited to constables, but when Kate Cavanagh married Detective Bob Lines after her return from Quantico, he retained his higher rank when he transferred in from the Metro Police biker squad. OPP wags began advising their friends that they now had a choice: get busted down to constable . . . or marry Kate. Everyone found it amusing, although no one volunteered to share the humour with Biker Bob.

What threatened to be less of a laughing matter was the sense that ViCLAS coordination would be the sole domain of the OPP, with the exception of Metro Toronto Police, which was so big it could, and would, do what it wanted. Devising the system, Greg Johnson had urged that it be decentralized to make it much easier to sell to investigators and police brass. He saw the FBI obsession with control as a needless source of friction. The RCMP had indeed posted ViCLAS coordinators in virtually every division across Canada, as it had done earlier for profiling. The OPP, it seemed to many, were less willing to share.

As with Lines' experience in the dentist's chair, there was more to the story. Lines did not run a closed shop. She had asked Mick Riddle, the disclosure officer on the Green Ribbon Task Force, to help set up the SOR, but he had declined, as its fate was in the air until after a pending Ontario election that he wasn't convinced the government would win. ViCLAS was centralized in the Behavioural Sciences Section to take advantage of the other disciplines under the same roof. Metro Toronto did not have these services to support ViCLAS in a "best fit" multidisciplinary setting. For example, ViCLAS analysts often consult about potential case linkages with members of the Criminal Profiling Unit. Such dialogue would surely expand with the rising number of cold cases accumulating across the country.

From June 17 to 26, 1995, four RCMP and two OPP profilers convened in Prince George, British Columbia, to review seven murders in Project Exclude. An all-Canadian show for the first time, Exclude also marked a reunion for MacKay and his longtime friend and colleague, Fred Maile, who had been saddled with the primary responsibility of lead investigator on the Olson murders and had paid dearly for the honour. Maile had retired and was a founding partner in CanPro, a private security company. Among his clients were Child Find, who had an interest in one of the missing-children cases being reviewed at Exclude. Despite the tragic circumstances that brought them together again, the reunion was a welcome bright spot to the dark cloud of unsolved cases of murdered and missing women and children.

In 1996, Lines hosted a four-day sequel to Project Eclipse at the OPP Academy in Brampton but the workshops remained the exception, not the rule. Most days were spent profiling individual cases. It helped that the investigators were now completing a ViCLAS booklet as a condition of getting their case profiled, but the caseload never seemed to get lighter or simpler. That frustration would prove minor, however, compared to what lay ahead in British Columbia.

The most complicated, though not always the most difficult, cases to profile are those in which the behaviour suggests that a cop or someone in a cop's family is the likely suspect.

Not that all cops are above suspicion or exemplary in character. Gerard John Schaefer, a onetime Florida cop, used to take young women he'd picked up hitchhiking or had arrested, depending on which version is told, to the swamp, then force them to strip, climb a ladder he'd placed under a tree, and put a noose around their neck. Plying them with liquor because he enjoyed watching his victims urinate, he'd eventually toss the rope over a tree limb, tie it to the front bumper of his car, and slowly back up until he'd pulled them off the ladder, then watch them hang until they died.

But if you're going after someone on your side of the Blue Wall without the evidence they finally amassed against Schaefer, you had better be pretty sure you've got the right guy.

At 12:30 a.m. on October 14, 1995, Tanya Smith and her friend, Misty Cockerill, both 16, were attacked by a bat-wielding man on a street in Abbotsford, British Columbia. Smith died during the ensuing rape; Cockerill was badly beaten and left for dead. The random crime paralyzed the Lower Mainland with fear. The terror only heightened when taunting phone calls were made to the police by a man claiming to be the killer. He vowed to strike again.

MacKay, asked to profile the crime within a month, offered only a verbal profile: he believed the killer was too familiar with police procedure not to be somehow connected to law enforcement. He could be a cop, or related to a cop. A month later, he was still reviewing the case, as well as a double homicide in New Brunswick and a murder and a series of suspicious fires in Ottawa.

He returned to Abbotsford in the new year. From February 23 to March 3, 1996, MacKay reviewed the troubling case, which had grown to involve 75 investigators who interviewed 9400 suspects and would eventually cost more than $2 million. It was Olson all over again. There were fewer victims, but no one knew when he'd strike again. Few people believed it was a question of "if."

MacKay was accompanied on his second trip by Mounties Glenn Woods and Keith Davidson, both fresh from a profiling seminar with Roy Hazelwood at Trois-Rivières, Quebec, where they had learned the same three-step procedure—what, why, who—he'd taught MacKay at Quantico in 1989. The message then, as now, was that you can't get to point B without finishing point A.

The difference, of course, was that MacKay's accumulated experience since then allowed him to do points A, B, and C at once. He was anxious to move ahead, but realized he had to allow Woods and Davidson to catch up at their own pace. They were good students, progressing exactly as the master had instructed them. Slowly. Carefully. Step by step. It drove MacKay crazy with frustration, but he allowed them to take all the time they needed. As the next generation of profilers, they had to satisfy themselves that they had accumulated all the information they needed to analyze the behavioural aspects of the crime.

When they ventured their profile, MacKay agreed with their analysis, adding only that their suspect would have red hair. Now it was Woods' and Davidson's turn to express their frustration. How the hell did MacKay know that? Elementary, my dear Mounties, a victim from a related crime had reported that her assailant had a freckled arm. That meant he had fair hair, likely red, or that a parent did.

There was no shortage of help in Abbotsford. Collins, the forensic psychiatrist, happened to be in Victoria lecturing at a course that had ended the day MacKay returned on his second trip with Woods and Davidson. MacKay also suggested to the local authorities that they bring in Rossmo for a geographic profile that could help tell them where their quarry lived or worked.

Rossmo was quickly briefed on the facts: Smith's body had apparently been taken by her killer and dumped in the Vedder River about 12 miles from the crime scene; Cockerill had managed to stagger to a nearby hospital despite her serious head trauma. The Abbotsford Killer, as he had been dubbed by the media, had made several taunting calls to the police from local pay phones, that investigators were unable to identify. The police were certain it was the killer calling because he described injuries to Smith's body that had never been made public.

Even before MacKay had returned to Abbotsford, long before Collins or Rossmo had arrived, the terror had continued to mount. Someone had picked up Smith's headstone from the local cemetery, transported it to a midtown radio station, and dropped it on a car's hood in the parking lot, defaced by the scrawled threat: "She wasn't the first and she won't be the last. One day, Misty." The police took the threat seriously and moved their surviving witness and her family into witness protection, worried that the killer would indeed come after her.

On another occasion, the suspected killer had tied a newspaper clipping around a wrench and hurled it through the livingroom window of a home he had apparently picked at random. The article was about Project Eclipse, the first international murder workshop MacKay had helped Davidson host back in October 1991, set up to review the 25 unsolved murders of young women in the lower British Columbia mainland. On March 2, MacKay met with investigators from Abbotsford, Richmond, Burnaby, and Vancouver City Police, all sharing jurisdiction for the attack or where the 25 victims had been found, to assure them that this killer had nothing to do with those cold cases.

MacKay said the clipping was part of the killer's collection and that he had likely thrown it through the window in response to a local television broadcast—not because he'd killed any of those women, but because he wished he had. This killer, MacKay explained, was a classic fantasy-motivated offender, collecting stuff on crimes he wished he'd committed. Such killers were as predictable as the sexual sadists like Bernardo. Interviewed long after their crimes, all related almost an identical story, as did their wives and/or girlfriends if they were involved. It was as though those guys had all studied Sexual Sadism 101.

The locations of the pay phones became the critical sites for a geographic profile. Rossmo had soon reduced a vast search area to roughly one-half a square mile that would contain both the home and the workplace of the Abbotsford Killer. The area was sparsely populated, so the police had a local radio station play a taunting tape they had received from a man claiming to be the killer, and it wasn't long before a woman called to say the voice sounded like her son.

At the time of his arrest, Terry Driver, a printer by trade, was married with two children. His father was a retired cop. Like Bernardo, he had no previous criminal record. He would not have been found in any SOR or any other registry.

The police at first lacked the evidence to charge Driver with murder, but his smug air of superiority landed him in the soup when he agreed to let the police take his fingerprints. He was sure he'd left no prints anywhere. He was wrong. Driver's print was on the tape from the wrench he'd thrown through the livingroom window. He was charged with murder.

At trial, Driver denied killing Smith. He claimed he had seen a mystery man run off and, seeing Smith lying there naked in the street, couldn't resist having sex with her. When she quit breathing during the act, he had assumed she was dead, taken her body to his favourite fishing hole, and set it adrift. The court didn't buy it, and the judge sentenced him to life in prison. Charges for several other sexual assaults were added later by other departments.

There seemed to be a lot of "mystery men" terrorizing western

Canada back then. On November 1, while running an international training conference in Victoria for 10 aspiring profilers, including three Mounties, MacKay got a call from Saskatchewan profiler and ViCLAS coordinator Henry Derkach in Regina (co-conspirator with Séguin on the Australian wine presentation to MacKay back in 1993). Derkach was seeking advice on the brutal murder of a young woman, turning to MacKay to help him understand, not solve, the crime—a crucial difference still not grasped by many investigators. MacKay listened intently as Derkach described the crime over the phone.

Gayle Exner, 16, had been kicked and punched black and blue. Her naked body had been dumped into a school window well. Her clothes had been tossed in after her, but the T-shirt was missing; it seemed possible that it may have been used to strangle her. An Indian man had told police he'd been sitting on the front step after fighting with his girlfriend when three guys walked past bragging they'd just killed someone. Heading in the direction they'd come from, he'd found Exner's body and reported it to the police.

Offering a "threshold analysis" over the phone, MacKay said to take a long, hard look at the guy who said he'd found her; he likely knew more than he was telling. Derkach passed the advice along to the investigators—Regina City Police with support from the Mounties—but they had already found a guy who claimed he'd been there. Under pressure, he named two others. At first, it all seemed to fit.

The three men all seemed to revel in the attention, but none wanted to go to jail. Each said he'd been there, but insisted the other two had raped and killed the girl. Without evidence to link them to the murder, the story no longer fit so neatly. But the Regina cops arrested and charged the trio, apparently believing they'd find the evidence to make the charges stick. They didn't.

They asked MacKay for a full analysis. He insisted that the three men hadn't murdered Exner, that they were just "wannabes" who had done nothing with their lives, and suddenly found themselves the focus of attention and loved it. MacKay again urged them to talk to the Indian fellow.

But by then he'd gone home to Ontario on a "sudden urge." The police who had searched his Regina residence recalled seeing a

T-shirt similar to Exner's under the couch, but it was never seen again. Interviewed in Ontario by Regina investigators, and told that his DNA matched trace evidence found at the scene, the man abruptly changed his story. Now he claimed Exner had been dying when he got there and had begged not to die a virgin. He said he'd simply accommodated her—a common story of chronic liars caught by evidence placing them at the scene alone.

The cops didn't buy it and neither did the jury, who convicted him of murder. He was sentenced to life in prison.

As Christmas arrived, MacKay's 35th as a Mountie, he turned introspective, toasted the successes of 1996, and, believing it time to pass the torch, vowed to be a civilian in the new year.

15

Passing the Torch

On January 7, 1997, MacKay returned from annual leave to immerse himself in work, profiling cases one day and public speaking the next to such diverse groups as university academics, cops, the media, and writers. Profiling and promotion, promotion and profiling. There weren't enough hours in the day for what seemed endless demands on his time and expertise. Between assignments, he accommodated increased requests for media interviews and foreign delegations interested in adapting ViCLAS to their needs. While Canadian cops, at least those outside Ontario where the Campbell Report led to legislated compliance in that province, were still too busy or too lazy to submit their cases to the database, international law enforcement proved keenly interested.

The Netherlands and Austria were the first to formally commit to using ViCLAS back on February 9, 1995. Four days later, MacKay declined an offer from FBI profiling pioneer Bob Ressler to promote ViCLAS at an international conference in China. While flattered, he didn't want to go looking for more international attention before achieving all he could in Canada. But foreign interest continued: Australia and Sweden came aboard, as did several U.S. states, and Hungary was interested. FBI analysts wanted it, but Washington wouldn't let them have it. In most jurisdictions in America, as it was across Canada with the exception of Ontario, it remained "women and children last." There was only so much one man could do.

For 35 years, MacKay had fought the good fight on many fronts as a savvy investigator, canny administrator, and, ultimately, as a visionary convert, prophet, and promoter. He had waged war against brutal serial killers and rapists, and was working with the

National Research Council in Ottawa to try to find a way to use ViCLAS to link serial arson. As trying and emotionally draining as those violent crimes could be, it was the internal fights with some peers and superiors that MacKay found most wearing. He had expected resistance from investigators to profiling because it was new and not "real" police work, and certainly to ViCLAS because it involved more paperwork. He'd have probably been disappointed, perhaps worried, if they hadn't been skeptical. He had once sat on their side of the table, dismayed to have a brass hat arrive from headquarters claiming he'd come to help. That was a sure sign of more paperwork, increased frustration, and less productivity while the street cops were forced to try out the latest harebrained notion that had impressed some senior officer or focus group in Ottawa but was surely doomed to fail in the real world of the grunts in the field. Now *he* was the brass hat come to help them. Outside the Force, he was the "Horseman" brass hat, which was no better. But he also knew they would come around when they saw that the new tools he offered actually worked.

Such logic held less sway at national headquarters. On the surface, MacKay enjoyed breathtaking success in Ottawa. A new section was created for him amid grievous government cutbacks soon after he returned from Quantico. That was expanded to a branch by a major RCMP reform in 1994, eventually staffed by two inspectors (MacKay and Woods), a sergeant (Johnson, later jumped directly to inspector), and a civilian assistant, Nancy Noel. Per capita, it was probably the most top-heavy unit in the entire federal public service, among the smallest, and certainly one of the most productive. But it was only after Assistant Commissioner Joop Plomp arrived after the reorganization that things began to truly move forward. A welcome breath of fresh air, Plomp not only approved but actively encouraged recommendations from MacKay that had been stalled on his predecessor's desk for more than a year; Plomp also became both mentor and guardian angel to MacKay. Without him, there may never have been a ViCLAS for Campbell to trumpet, for the world to adopt, and for many Canadian cops outside of Ontario to ignore or access as the whim struck them.

But if Plomp made all things possible, MacKay remained the catalyst, driving things forward, with an uncanny knack for finding the right people for the job. It went beyond Davidson and Johnson, or suggesting times when investigators should call in Lines and Collins and Rossmo. One of his proudest coups was Nancy Noel, the Quebec farm girl he felt lucky to find in November 1994 to be the administrative assistant for the Violent Crime Analysis Branch. Noel had all the necessary skills—she was bilingual, computer-literate, organized, motivated—and could handle the graphic written reports and photos of sexual violence crossing her desk without being traumatized or voyeuristic. Noel was a fixture there, and would be the last of the originals long after MacKay and Johnson moved on.

Always an investigator at heart, MacKay loathed the politics of policing but, by necessity, learned to play that game well enough to win approval to create a special section for profiling soon after his return from Quantico. The reorganization expanded that section into a branch—a breathtaking accomplishment in bureaucratic terms. He won more battles than he lost, but the skirmishes raged on both sides of the Blue Wall in a war that never seemed to end. If it was wearing and grinding and lonely, he would be the first to insist that he had accomplished nothing alone. As class valedictorian at Quantico, he had quoted Charles Brower, noting "few men are successful unless others want them to be," constantly acknowledging back in Ottawa that he had been helped tremendously by those around him and Plomp, his guardian angel, above. But time after time, he was first through the door; on every engagement, year after year, he was the point man. The mental stress of reviewing the details of the most horrific crimes across Canada, the lonely battles waged, won, and lost, the constant need to convey his vision to others who would not see or hear or act, exacted a toll. Not every incident, individually and combined, can be totally compartmentalized, internalized, or drowned in an occasional medicinal tumbler of good Scotch whiskey.

It is a marvel that MacKay survived his experiences intact. The physical exhaustion of his demanding schedule, crisscrossing the

country, constantly starting over on each case with a new group of
skeptical investigators who are so desperate they'll try anything to
solve their case, rarely a break in the carnage to draw a clean breath.
That he had achieved so much, either alone or as the man leading
the charge to reform and progress, cannot be overstated. The
emotional toll of his job was well documented. John Douglas, lionized by Hollywood and publicly thanked at the Oscars, made no
secret of the fact that he had burned out on the job. Had drunk
more. Had collapsed. Was partially paralyzed. Had nearly died.
When Lines had arrived at Quantico for her profiler training in
1991, four FBI profilers were off work on stress leave, incapacitated
by the physical and psychological toll of the volume and horrific
details of the incredibly savage and heart-wrenching murders they
had profiled. Yet, in their darkest moments, Douglas and the others
had an identifiable peer group, a sympathetic ear from those who
did the same work, suffered the same emotional toll, understood
what it cost to look into the shadows—down dark paths and cold
trails—and watch monsters emerge.

MacKay was alone. Not just in profiling heartache and tragedy,
but in fighting entrenched police traditions, opening closed minds,
preaching a new gospel to battle-scarred men and women who do not
embrace change, do not welcome intrusion, hate surprises. Yet, in
many ways, that was the easy part. MacKay was a proven investigator who knew the ropes, knew what to think, what to expect when he
entered a room with all eyes blazing "show me." But nothing in his
personal or professional life could adequately prepare him to cope
with the bureaucratic battles and blunders that will eventually wear
down the feistiest spirit. Nothing kills an idea faster than a committee
and Ottawa was too often a place where ideas went to die.

The war envisioned in MacKay's youthful dreams, fought in the
skies as a jet fighter pilot, he had waged on land as an unlikely revolutionary. But even the bravest and most battle-hardened warriors
become war-weary and succumb, no matter how great their physical
and psychological stamina, when time becomes the foe. After three-
and-a-half decades, and what seemed an eternity since he and Maile
had sat in on Mather's FBI lecture about "stranger" homicides in

1979 (a time when only grunt tactics, hard work, and good intentions solved major cases—or didn't), MacKay knew it was time to pass the torch to his handpicked successor, Inspector Glenn Woods.

The two men had met at a promotion party in Ottawa in 1994. Woods' older brother Mike had been with MacKay that long-ago night when they apprehended the two young bank robbers and recovered the stolen cash and one well-used vulcanized vagina. Mike had been unavailable to join MacKay when he was looking for a seasoned investigator to help design his then-unnamed crime-linkage system, but, with Plomp's blessing and active support, the hunt continued. In the end, there just seemed no escaping the Woods boys. At their first meeting, Glenn, the younger brother by 15 months, had impressed MacKay as a keen, intelligent, bilingual, and experienced major-crime investigator. A few phone calls to trusted friends assured MacKay that Glenn was highly qualified. He was also available; his scheduled posting, and position, had disappeared, abolished by cutbacks.

Woods joined the Violent Crime Analysis Branch on January 16, 1995, and immediately began training as a profiler. Almost exactly two years later, he reviewed one of MacKay's profiles and found two things his mentor had missed. The student had caught the master and MacKay was satisfied that he could move on and leave his cherished creation in good hands. If he hadn't seen it all, he'd seen enough, perhaps too much. He advised his superiors he planned to retire that summer. But first he took steps to provide for those he would leave behind, and those who would follow them.

MacKay's immediate priority was to honour those who had fought the good fight at his side. Olson had proved the need for change; Bernardo and a score of others had confirmed the need. Their murderous sprees bore grim testimony to the unlimited mayhem and tragedy one person can inflict on so many innocents and their loved ones. Now, less than two decades after Mather and Bianchi, a new generation of cops had matured, better armed and educated than ever before, to crack the tough cases using the tools that came into prominence in the 1990s—psychological and geographic profiling, forensic psychiatry, ViCLAS, DNA labs.

Cases flooded in for profiling and linkage faster than ever, a testament to MacKay's success. The investigators in the field still solved the cases, but had a better arsenal now. It was still a war, but now it was a fairer fight.

In a detailed formal submission running to several pages, he requested that Davidson and Johnson, as well as computer whiz-kids Ripley and Leury, be awarded the prestigious RCMP Merit Award for their heroic efforts to make ViCLAS what was being universally hailed as the best serial-crime linkage system on earth. He scored a major coup, with Plomp's help, by having RCMP Commissioner Phil Murray agree to present the coveted award—and the accompanying $10,000, to be split among the four recipients—and praise the two uniformed and two civilian members of the Force for their "tremendous innovation and ingenuity." As a further tribute to the two young college students who had spent their final semester learning about serial rapists and killers from Johnson, Davidson, and MacKay, and who had then applied their rather unique education to devise a better way to stop them, the presentation ceremony was held at the Woodroffe campus of Algonquin College in Ottawa.

No college or university graduates in any field had likely done more, or more quickly, than Ripley and Leury, whose ability to "think outside the box" hastened the replacement of the ill-fated Major Crime File with ViCLAS, a system that so rapidly had become the envy of the world. (Praised in Canada, they found their reward in America, joining the brain drain south to Texas in search of new challenges and more money.)

The merit awards also qualified the quartet for the ultimate award in the federal public service, the Award of Excellence, presented by the Treasury Board of Canada on behalf of a grateful government. Cops and college kids are rarely, if ever, considered for this award, ranking second only to the Order of Canada in bureaucratic prestige. MacKay, it seems, was a hell of a writer and talker when it came to recommending those around him for awards and kind words.

And promotion. Everyone around MacKay, often at his recommendation, was promoted. Davidson rose to staff sergeant and trained to be a profiler; Johnson jumped to inspector in charge of staffing and recruiting for Ontario's O Division; and Woods rose to superintendent in 2001, backdated to 2000, when all behavioural functions—profiling, geographic profiling, ViCLAS, and polygraph and statement analysis—were grouped under his command in one place, as the OPP had done earlier with Kate Lines.

In other words, MacKay's successor virtually entered the position at a higher level than he was leaving—one final bureaucratic coup for his department. Why?

Mainly because that's the way MacKay wanted it and what he had lobbied for. If it seems strange that the man behind it all, the first non-American profiler and ViCLAS visionary, was the only one never promoted after being commissioned for Quantico, it wasn't for lack of offers. But as each opportunity arose, MacKay refused it, and finally put out the word that he did not wish to be considered for promotions. Quite simply, he believed that what he was trying to do was too valuable, and too vulnerable, to leave to others. In the past, MacKay had left other projects before they were completed—a routine occurrence in government—and watched his successors let them die or kill them off. The best of intentions could not survive career aspirations and he considered profiling and ViCLAS too important to abandon to the trust of others who lacked his vision, zeal, or staying power.

It wasn't ego or naked ambition. Quite the contrary. While promotion sometimes seems a reward for putting in your time without screwing up or making waves, it also acknowledged jobs well done. With his proven track record, can-do attitude, and Plomp watching over him, it seems a certainty that he would have been promoted on the basis of his ability, quite possibly more than one level. But he wanted to finish the job. The Campbell Report had changed everything. If its recommendations for mandatory compliance could be adopted and applied across Canada, so many lives could be saved, so much needless suffering avoided. No one could protect all the potential victims from serial predators, but MacKay was determined to help save as many as he could. He wasn't going to abandon them to others who had demonstrated by their inaction that they were willing to accept "women and children last." He refused to let that happen. Not on his watch.

But his dedication to enhancing public safety, particularly for women and children most at risk, came at considerable personal and professional cost. Not every casualty was a stranger in MacKay's war on violent crime.

In 1962, at his first posting in Fort St. John, B.C., fresh out of the training depot at Regina, MacKay and another Mountie took a teenage woman who had attempted suicide by slashing her wrists to the local hospital emergency department. Just 23 at the time, he was entranced by the emergency room duty nurse as she bandaged the bleeding wrists and soothed the unhappy teen. An amazing number of cops seem to fall in love with nurses and teachers, and MacKay was, in his words, "smitten on the spot." There wasn't much time for personal chitchat, but he was able to memorize the nurse's name tag before leaving. Luckily, MacKay's corporal was married to a nurse who worked at the same hospital and MacKay asked him to ask his wife to ask "S. Williams" if she'd be interested in going out with the Mountie who'd brought in the attempted suicide the other night. Word filtered back that Sandy Williams was indeed interested in seeing the Mountie socially.

MacKay was delighted. All seemed well with the world. Until Sandy opened the door. It seems she thought she'd agreed to go out with the *other* Mountie. But she was surprised, not disappointed, and it would take more than a little misunderstanding to deter a smitten Mountie. It just upped the challenge. MacKay persevered and, to their delight and surprise, they found they had much in common. Both were working their first jobs in their new professions. Both came from out of province (she from Edmonton, he from Moosomin). Love conquered all.

The date became a romance became a marriage became a family. Eventually.

They decided to get married in Edmonton on July 31, 1965, but there was a bit of a glitch. Back then, a Mountie still had to get permission from the Force to marry. Just as the bureaucracy would later screw up their later forced relocation to Ottawa, the RCMP subdivision clerk lost his request for permission to marry. But again it would take more than that to stop a love-struck Mountie, and his now equally smitten nurse-bride. The permission finally arrived weeks after their wedding. The happy couple moved into their new home in Prince George until 1970, then relocated to his new posting at North Vancouver with their two young sons, Cameron, 3, and Craig, 1. Once again, all seemed well with the world.

That world fell apart the day MacKay and Brian Sargent realized they were the likely targets of the murder contract allegedly put out by Connie Gunn. Forced into hiding, they tried to resume their normal lives, to get the boys back in school and among their friends, but their fear of the unknown never eased. The heartache of parents who lose a child, and had no idea it was coming, is terrible; but there is a particularly gnawing fear that afflicts mothers and wives who believe their loved ones are at risk and feel helpless to do anything to protect them. Every time they watch their kids head off to school, their husband walk out the door to go to work, they can't help but worry that it may be for the last time.

The relentless dread took its inevitable toll. With her husband setting out his handgun within arm's reach every night before coming to bed (and checking under his car every morning for a bomb), Sandy fought the deep depression engulfing her, carried on, did what had to be done.

But when they arrived in Ottawa and encountered the chaos of an RCMP headquarters that didn't have a clue what to do with them, her world collapsed. The anxiety and depression became so severe and sustained that the vibrant wife and mother who had driven all over the Lower Mainland and beyond without a care in the world has never gotten behind the wheel of a car since. To this day, though some days are better than others, the funk never totally lifts. Her psychiatrist likens her condition to the suffering and post-trauma stress of a person taken hostage. MacKay likens it to being a passenger in a high-speed car chase: the driver has some control and can anticipate events, but the passenger can only sit tight and hope to survive the ride. Sandy remains under psychiatric care, taking each day as it comes and savouring the good ones, suffering through the bad. Her courageous struggle is at least in part what motivates MacKay. This time the crime's personal.

In the end, MacKay was honoured with a "letter of appreciation"—his superior had nominated him for a Commissioner's Commendation a year earlier but it had apparently sat in someone's basket for a while—for getting Gunn off the streets. Appropriately, it was signed by E Division Assistant Commissioner Tom Venner, who had also chased Gunn as a young cop in Alberta years earlier.

There should be more. If the Award of Excellence, presented at MacKay's recommendation to all who worked to make ViCLAS a reality, is indeed second only in prestige to the Order of Canada, it's obvious how a grateful nation should bestow its thanks on the man who has done more than any other to put Canadians, particularly women and children, less at risk. And when they drape the Order around his neck, Sandy should be close by, sharing the moment and the honour for what she has endured.

His family's ordeal brought MacKay to Ottawa and thence to Quantico. It is questionable whether anyone else would have had the stamina, perseverance, and vision, would have sacrificed what he did, to accomplish what he has. Parents across this fair land should remember that and whisper a heartfelt "Thank you, Ron" every night as they tuck their children safely into bed. If Olson and Bernardo and countless others have taught us nothing else, we have learned that the fine line separating life from death is often a question of time and space. If those who suffered or died had been able to steer clear, it would have been someone else and another family grieving a lost child.

MacKay has made the world a safer place, a lesson not lost on a kindred spirit south of the border.

• • •

Steve McCarthy joined the Massachusetts State Police in 1986, working Research and Development and plainclothes, being promoted to sergeant in 1997 and inheriting the new Massachusetts VICAP from its original program manager, Sergeant Michael Kalmbach. Aside from attending a few homicide seminars and visiting the FBI VICAP centre, McCarthy was starting at ground zero. As a computer science major, his technical background uniquely qualified him to run the State Police VICAP, derived from the FBI national database; but, with ingratiating Boston Irish charm and self-deprecating humour, he claims he got the prestigious job for being the "resident geek."

McCarthy was dismayed almost immediately, finding FBI VICAP underused, disorganized, and outdated. Quite simply, it was not performing at its peak, and had no hope of doing so unless major changes were made and the proper resources in almost every conceivable category were forthcoming from Washington. When he enquired about their "established operating protocol," he learned that they had no team or model in place to help get him up to speed. They did offer to send him some VICAP forms.

McCarthy retraced the steps taken earlier by Davidson and Johnson to review the existing state systems. Everyone, it seemed, was doing it differently. During his research, he discovered that the New Jersey State Police was using ViCLAS to analyze and link sexual assaults, under the command of Detective Sergeant James McCormick, a former Quantico classmate of MacKay's. What was confusing was that he was also using FBI VICAP for homicides. That seemed odd since the Canadian system would do both, until he realized that by using VICAP, New Jersey got free computers from the feds.

Compared to ViCLAS, McCarthy judged VICAP to be "fairly primitive." It just made sense to him that it would be far more productive to pair homicide linkage and analysis with rapes and sexual assaults. The FBI didn't agree, and, in fairness, didn't have the staff, budget, or resources to make it happen even if they had agreed. They couldn't even provide adequate training to the states who adopted their system or devised their own on the FBI model.

McCarthy redirected his research to mapping crime trends and patterns, and charting time lines—hard data that he could submit to the federal government to kickstart them into giving better support to VICAP. And he questioned why the FBI would not adopt, or at least interface with, ViCLAS—exactly what MacKay had asked in a memo to the FBI several years earlier. Did it not make sense for two close allies like the Bureau and the RCMP to share information and resources? Apparently not. McCarthy seriously considered going with ViCLAS, the demonstrably superior product, but still thought the better plan was to get the Canadian system talking to FBI VICAP, and through it to the state and city systems that could plug into the U.S. national system. Why split the pot, he asked, when we could be working together through fat and lean times?

The deafening silence out of the FBI and Washington prompted him to take two steps. First, he persuaded the northeast states to band together into a larger regional lobby group that would have a louder voice. The resultant North East Regional VICAP (NERV)—New Jersey, New York, Pennsylvania, Connecticut, Rhode Island, Vermont, New Hampshire, Maine, and Massachusetts—expected to be much more effective at getting across their concerns and opinions and getting some clearly required action.

The second step was the unprecedented step of drafting a letter to Janet Reno, then the head of the federal Justice Department, and FBI Director Louis Freeh signed by 13 major law enforcement agencies from across America to express their concerns and offer suggestions directly to the top. A catalyst for that letter was McCarthy's dismay at finding the FBI VICAP was maintained by a skeleton crew of seven or eight analysts who seemed paralyzed by Bureau policy. While visiting the national VICAP centre to educate himself, McCarthy had spied an unopened box of MapInfo software that had been sitting at the foot of a desk under a quarter-inch of dust for a couple of months while the analysts awaited the arrival of a computer technician to install it and teach them how to use it. Each package cost $1500 U.S. and there were 10 packages in the box.

In frustration and disbelief, McCarthy had ripped open the box, probably violating a dozen federal statutes, installed the software, and asked the analysts to download their information on how many states were sending their cases to VICAP. He had then used the software to create a colour-coded map that clearly showed where VICAP was working and where it was not. The analysts had gasped in awe at the visual evidence; their supervisors had gasped with glee at how pretty the map was.

McCarthy had come away very disappointed. When he had called back six months later, the only copy of the software installed was the one he had set up.

But he had no quarrel with the analysts. He realized what they were up against and respected them for accomplishing what they had with the resources at hand. Washington moved at a glacial pace, as though rating VICAP less highly than major cities changing street lights and filling pot holes. In his letter to Reno on October 27, 1998, he expressed the collective concerns of the 13 signatories with the national VICAP program and inquired "how we may work together to address these issues." It began:

> The Violent Criminal Apprehension Program (VICAP) is undisputedly a worthwhile program that is long overdue. It provides investigative support, analysis and coordination to law enforcement agencies in their efforts to investigate, identify, track, apprehend and prosecute violent serial offenders. With approximately 16,000 law enforcement agencies in the United States, and more than 20,000 homicides, the services of VICAP are direly needed.
>
> Unfortunately more than a decade has passed since its inception and VICAP is still far short of its potential. Only half of the states currently participate in some fashion and the Federal VICAP program is understaffed and under-funded, even in light of this year's proposed enhancements. This situation adversely affects the performance of the program and its ability to fulfill its mission. This fact also compromises the effectiveness of the participating state agencies. While some states have achieved remarkable success, as a whole the VICAP program has not thrived to the degree that it should. It is incumbent upon

the Federal government to devote the necessary resources to this valuable program. Therefore we are writing to ask for your aid in aggressively supporting the VICAP program.

The successful analysis of violent crime requires information, equipment, training, coordination and resources. With its current resources the FBI program is hard pressed to provide these components. By way of a comparison, consider that the Canadian ViCLAS program, Canada's equivalent of VICAP, has ten times the staffing of VICAP, for a country with a fraction of the population and caseload of the United States.

The letter concluded that for VICAP to be the national success it could be, it required more money for state training, conferences, and equipment, better efforts to educate the politicians and the law enforcement community to its benefits, and expanded staff, services, and expertise to make it a national state-of-the-art data collection system, or risk more states adopting ViCLAS or devising their own systems.

A response eventually came from Roger A. Nisley, FBI Special Agent in Charge, Critical Incident Response Group. It didn't really commit to anything, but it had been signed by a high-ranking official. In bureaucratic terms, that meant someone was listening.

In January 1999, NERV discussed capturing sexual-assault information at the regional level since the FBI was opposed to incorporating it into VICAP. They devised a form and, after lengthy review, presented it at the FBI National VICAP conference in Quantico in February 2000 to mixed reviews. While some were all for it, other regions of the country just weren't ready to address sexual assaults.

Curiously, the strongest opponents seemed to be FBI agents with a profiling background. But any concern that the new form or ViCLAS would encroach on their turf was unfounded. VICAP was limited to homicides with no survivor to question. The surviving victim was the heart of the sexual-assault form, as he or she could relate what had been done, what had been said, and in what order, during the attack. This was vital to analyzing and linking serial rapists and especially sexual sadists like Bernardo. Offender behaviour was a vital clue you just didn't get from a serial killer's victims.

The objections lost some of their force when the FBI brought in Roy Hazelwood. He pointed out the obvious: behavioural experts should be capturing all the information that the NERV and ViCLAS questions were asking. The disputed questions were retained by a split vote.

The North East was convinced it would just have to strike out on its own. McCarthy, perhaps anticipating that, already had a prototype Web-based system up and running to collect sexual-assault information. To his surprise, the FBI asked him to bring the new form to the National Advisory Board meeting in Las Vegas that December. The ensuing FBI review was sharply critical of some of the questions drawn from ViCLAS and debate turned tense.

But there was also an increasingly vocal VICAP minority championing the need to capture sexual assaults. In fact, New York State had, like Ontario, legislated mandatory reporting of homicides and sexual assaults to their state VICAP. New York City Police, affectionately dubbed the "Crown Jewel of VICAP" or the "800-pound gorilla" of American law enforcement depending on who was telling the story, was accustomed, like Metro Toronto Police, to getting what they wanted, and certainly what they needed. Now they needed a system to capture that information to comply with the law.

That was enough to prompt the FBI to reassess their stance on the sexual-assault form, but the debate was revived about the ViCLAS behavioural questions. Arguments grew heated but, by a split vote, it was agreed to retain them. The FBI later confirmed it would make it a priority to incorporate the forms into their VICAP software.

Finally, years after ViCLAS was offered to the FBI for free, they are taking steps, not to adopt it, but to duplicate it. While it seems a waste of millions of dollars, it may ultimately move all existing systems closer together in a continental security blanket that can help track down serial rapists as well as killers across most of North America. If it does, it is a tribute to NERV, despite the fact that in most states compliance remains voluntary, and Mexico, a free-trade partner of both the United States and Canada, is excluded.

The battle to adopt geographic profiling went less well. While McCarthy and the state police saw its merit after a demonstration by Kim Rossmo, MacKay, and OPP geographic profiler Brad Moore, there was no money to buy the system. A request for a grant from the National Institute of Justice was rejected, in part because the Institute was critical of the evaluation method which McCarthy had asked to have done by several local academics at Harvard and the University of Massachusetts. Interestingly, another objection rested on whether the caseload in Massachusetts justified "more" geographic profilers. Rossmo had to chuckle at that, because there were only three geographic profilers in North America at the time and all of them were in Canada. The ATF was the first to buy the program in America, but, at this writing, it has yet to designate anyone to learn how to use it. NERV may still be first to make it operational. If not, odds are still good it will be up and running there before the FBI which can use it to national advantage.

Things seem to be improving. The new guard at the FBI seems more receptive and case submissions to VICAP have risen dramatically. Alaska, like New York State, has legislated mandatory compliance for VICAP, but just for homicides. In the other 48 states, voluntary compliance continues to allow the trails of serial predators to end abruptly at state lines, reducing investigators and analysts to reliance on "SWAG"—a "scientific wild-assed guess."

Until law enforcement agencies in America comply in tracking serial rapists as well as killers, they will, like Canada, outside of Ontario, abandon those most at risk, placing "women and children last."

There just seemed no getting around the FBI. If it was true in America that Washington giveth and taketh away, there was no denying that whatever the FBI did, or did not do, impacted heavily on profiling in Canada. In 1994, MacKay and Lines were still the only two handling an increasing flood of cases from across the land, and most of Lines' efforts were concentrated in Ontario. The pace and workload were becoming severe. Then, after Lines' class graduated in 1991, the FBI suspended the Fellowship Program at Quantico for one year. Training would continue for FBI agents, but the door was barred to outsiders. In 1992, the program was suspended indefinitely. When MacKay retired, Lines would be alone and profiling would cease, or be greatly reduced, outside of Ontario. There was simply no one in the wings to be passed the torch.

The FBI continued to offer support to the 32 profilers it had trained from outside agencies across America and in Canada, the Netherlands, and Australia. At their annual meeting at Quantico in 1992, MacKay grabbed the brass ring, recommending that the Fellowship, which had become known as the International Criminal Investigative Analysis Fellowship (ICIAF), form an Education committee to train the next generation of profilers. His suggestion, and his election as its chairman, were approved unanimously, giving him a mandate to determine course content, selection criteria, and a host of lesser issues to ensure they attracted the best and brightest "understudy" candidates. One of the first to grasp that the FBI had lost its cherished tradition and monopoly for training profilers was John Douglas, head of the NCAVC, who later confessed to MacKay, "We dropped the ball."

Indeed. MacKay had spied the opportunity the void created, recovered the FBI fumble, and was scampering to daylight in the finest Lombardi tradition. He had first learned of the suspension in a phone call on February 11, 1991, and immediately tried to interest the Mounties in taking over the training of profilers. That plea fell on deaf ears. But he wasn't going to let the opportunity slip away twice, and faxes were soon flying across the country and around the world, as committee members in such distant locales as Ottawa, Amsterdam, Australia, Florida, Illinois, and Los Angeles hammered out the framework of their new Understudy Program, partly on suggestions from Hazelwood, who had been instrumental in setting up the FBI Fellowship.

Meeting again at Quantico on September 23, 1993, the general membership of the ICIAF and several FBI agents voted unanimously to adopt the freshly drafted program. For two years, candidates would combine academic study with operational applications of what they had learned under the supervision of a fully qualified member of the ICIAF. Their training would conclude with a month studying a wide range of cases working with FBI agents at Quantico before being tested by a three-person examination board of certified profilers.

A year later, the FBI suspended its in-service training for its Fellowship graduates. The upstart ICIAF was on its own. It was up to the task, graduating its first two profilers in 1995: Sergeant John Yarborough, of the L.A. County Sheriff's Office, and Special Agent Wayne Porter, of the Florida Department of Law Enforcement. In 1996, Texas Ranger Inspector G. W. Hildebrand joined the Understudy Program and attended his first class in Quebec. A year later, working with MacKay with no budget, on their own time and nickel, and with a kind offer for free accommodation and meeting rooms from his friend, a Texas millionaire who had hosted the state governor when Hildebrand was in charge of her security, they set up an eight-day conference at the 4S Ranch near Wimberley, Texas. In early October 1997, 42 members of the ICIAF and FBI profilers gathered for intensive training and socializing and to celebrate the graduation of four more profilers who faced their final exam boards there. All of them were Canadians—Woods, Urbanoski, and Davidson from the RCMP, and Jim Van Allen from the OPP—raising the total since 1993 to seven from five agencies in two countries. Eleven more were enrolled in Canada, the United States, and Australia. As a capper, OPP profiler Kate Lines was elected president of the ICIAF.

The successes were earned. The course was no cakewalk; Davidson had seen to that. He had pushed for an association of analysts when ViCLAS was first launched and, with some legal advice, had authored the CAVCA Constitution. Then, with what must have seemed incredible timing to others, he rewrote the already demanding understudy criteria, making them even more stringent, *before* he and the other Canadians entered the program. Their graduation marked the first time candidates were examined en masse in person by their three-person rating board. With training and testing spanning half the globe, testing was usually administered by telephone conference call or computer e-mail chat. With no budget, working on their own time, it was the only way a candidate in one continent could be tested by rating-board members based in another.

How tough was it? Hildebrand, who had earlier earned a Master's degree in justice administration, considered MacKay's program "10 times harder." By mid-August 2001, eight years after the first candidate had registered in the program, one-quarter of the 32 candidates that had been enrolled—the same number trained by the FBI—did not finish the course for various reasons. Twelve had graduated as Full Fellows, another as an Associate. Eleven were in training, three of them at the exam phase.

And one had retired.

On June 18, 1997, MacKay wrote his final profile, for a murder on Cape Breton Island. Two days later he cleaned out his office and, on June 25, he turned in his badge, handcuffs, and revolvers. He had never been issued a new 9 mm because he knew he'd never need it. The last time he'd drawn his gun was to lay it within arm's reach of his bed to protect his family if anyone burst into the house to claim the alleged murder contract on him nearly a dozen years earlier. It must have seemed longer.

Beyond protecting his family, the only time MacKay had drawn his gun in the line of duty had occurred in Prince George a few years after joining the RCMP in 1961. On that occasion, he was one of several Mounties to respond to a "trailer dweller" shooting up his neighbour's barn. The neighbour happened to be Ben Ginter, a brewery owner and British Columbia's minister of highways, infamous for getting speeding tickets. The gunman had been ticketed by a local Mountie and took his frustrations out on Ginter's barn. The police were quickly summoned.

MacKay had arrived in an unmarked police car, which may have been a good thing as the marked cruiser that pulled in behind him soon had a bullet-riddled driver's door. Lying in the grass watching the trailer on a nearby knoll while .303 rounds dropped leaves on his head, he slowly inched close enough to the trailer to drop tear gas inside through a small bathroom window. The gunman quickly surrendered and just as quickly dropped his pants when ordered to by MacKay to ensure he wasn't concealing a gun. A freelance photographer commemorated the moment on the front page of the local newspaper.

The gun battle had lasted about a half-hour and the gunman had been wounded in the arm. While others prepared the man to go to hospital, MacKay watched the man's trailer catch fire and incinerate from a misplaced round of tear gas that had missed the window and gone into the wall. With order and public safety restored, and believing there was nothing he could do, MacKay headed to the local Legion branch for a cold beer.

Although his final day with the RCMP was technically September 4, MacKay was now, for all intents and purposes, a civilian. It had been a hell of a ride for the Mountie from Moosomin.

Perhaps the best way to judge just what MacKay accomplished, to show just how much he was a man for his times and how much the times had changed, is to compare him to a legendary Mountie who was also a man for his times. Sam Steele is a virtual god in Mountie history and there are those who consider it heresy to compare him with any mortal. MacKay would be the first to cry out, blush, and beg off. But there is no better benchmark for excellence and daring, for perseverance and results. Both are classic examples of how Socrates thought a life should be lived: "The unexamined life is not worth living." Both Mounties could look back on a life well spent, and see that they were leaving the world a little better and safer than they had found it.

Contemporaries of Steele no doubt considered him a dashing figure, never more so than on that historic day he dragged himself off his sickbed, barely able to stand, stared down a mob alone, read the Riot Act, and threatened to shoot the next person who stepped forward. Few are so bold today, perhaps because of the paperwork involved when guns are drawn. On the other hand, those who know MacKay best consider him "decent" and "realistic" and "a hell of an investigator." But both are obviously men with the courage to act on their convictions, whatever the cost. Steele, a "man's man" in every sense of the term, was instrumental in bringing "peace, order, and good government" to the unsettled prairies of a young Canada in a career highlighted by the Red River Rebellion, the Canadian Pacific Railway, and the Klondike gold rush. More than a century later, MacKay, an "investigator's investigator," profiled virtually every major, high-profile, complicated, or bizarre case in Canada, in a career highlighted by profiles for the Green Ribbon Task Force, the Toronto Transit Rapist, and the Yellowknife Bomber.

Similarly, Steele saw action in the Boer War (MacKay's grandfather served with the 17th Strathcona Light Horse, part of the unit raised by Steele) and World War I; the dark paths and cold trails MacKay travelled were as shadowy as the former and as gruesome as the latter. Steele protected the most vulnerable on the Northwest Frontier—the settlers from the Indians, the Indians from American whiskey traders, and everyone from Ottawa; MacKay devised innovative new ways to protect the most vulnerable in contemporary society—women and children—from sea to sea, to sea, across the continent, and around the world.

Steele's funeral in 1919 rivalled that of presidents and prime ministers. The body was returned to Winnipeg and escorted through the streets at the height of that city's violent General Strike. As his flag-draped casket rolled past, the cursing and the clubbing stopped, as if on cue, as combatants on both sides of the protest lines doffed their caps in respect at his passing and his passage.

Steele would be bewildered to see how lawless and violent we have become, but it's a safe bet he would look with greater favour on MacKay's efforts for the public good and the image of the Force than those who contracted that image to the Mickey Mouse marketing of a foreign corporation. Both men would be first through the door or into the fire again and again and again. Neither would wait to let things happen; both would act to make things happen.

The facts speak for themselves. In 1989, when MacKay left for Quantico, there were no profilers in Canada, no ViCLAS, questionable collaboration among jurisdictions. When he retired, he left behind a network of profilers across Canada; a serial-crime linkage system that is the envy of the world; and an understudy program more demanding than that pioneered by the FBI. Perhaps the true measure of his success is that in the spring of 1998, the year after the Wimberley success, the FBI sponsored a six-day ICIAF in-service session—its first involvement in training "outsiders" since 1994, issuing diplomas to Woods, Urbanoski, and Davidson.

It was an encouraging sign for future cooperation, but the cases kept pouring in. In May 2001, Woods called MacKay back to work as a consultant to help clear the logjam of cases that needed to be profiled and to help train the next generation of profilers.

Much had changed. When Sergeant Larry Wilson joined Johnson, and later worked under his replacement, Inspector Derek Ogden, as the system development coordinator in 1996, he was struck by just how deeply and widely the system was resented by investigators in the field; it was possibly the most hated system among cops that he'd ever seen. Some of their bitterness may have been justified. To some extent, ViCLAS was a victim of its own success. The original system was capable of handling the thousands of cases that were initially input to the database, but not the tens of thousands now flooding in. In its third year of operation, ViCLAS had logged roughly 20,000 cases. Investigators had linked roughly one-third of them using traditional police techniques; ViCLAS increased that by 7 percent and listed another 10 percent as potential linkages that detectives had not suspected. All this with only partial compliance.

The database soon climbed to just over 47,000 cases from across Canada. It was only a fraction of the 140,000 cases that would represent total compliance; still, it was enough to identify more than 3100 series of two or more crimes representing over 9200 individual crimes—meaning the cops can now solve, on average, three crimes for every serial criminal they arrest. With full national compliance, be it legislated or voluntary, the extrapolated numbers are 9000 crimes series comprising more than 27,000 crimes. Linking serial predators to all, or at least many, of their crimes increases the chance they will be designated Dangerous Offenders and never return to the streets to kill and rape again.

Wilson was an ideal choice to help steer ViCLAS to its next level.

A "poor country boy" who hailed from near Saint John, New Brunswick, son of a lighthouse keeper and youngest in a family of nine sisters and two brothers, married to a wife with nine sisters and two brothers, he was just naturally good at dealing with people. He was progressive and he was bright. As the first, and for a long time the only, Mountie seconded to Green Ribbon, his main job as a case manager was to track "persons of interest" and rate the suspects.

His instincts were pretty good: a review of that investigation pointed out that while Metro Police had rated Bernardo a 3C (low) suspect, Wilson had pegged him 1C (high). He had devised a method of timeline analysis based on credit cards, phone calls, border crossings, and police checks, almost anything that could put a suspect at a certain place at a certain time. Afterwards, when Bernardo was arrested, Wilson had been able to translate the data to show that after each abduction Bernardo had gone into a "hibernation" period followed by heightened activity. This corroborated what MacKay and the other behavioural experts had claimed all along about serial offenders in general on the basis of their behaviour.

Voluntary compliance nationwide rose steadily from the first 124 cases in 1992, the year before ViCLAS was officially launched at the OPP Academy, to more than 5000 by 1995, the year it had been projected to be up and running and fully operational. It grew by more than another 1000 the next year, then exploded, nearly tripling in the single year after the Campbell Report led to legislated mandatory compliance in Ontario. Any politician who wonders what is the difference between letting the cops do their job, and making them do it, need only scan the stats:

YEAR	CASES
1992	124
1993	218
1994	2,135
1995	5,543
1996	6,940
1997	15,138
1998	20,285

1999   21,592

2000   25,121

2001 (to September)   120,362

In its first decade, ViCLAS submissions have soared from roughly 120 to 120,000! Of the 141,635 new and historic, solved and unsolved cases entered into the database by early January 2002, analysts have identified 12,297 series of crimes and linked a total of 43,089 cases to these series, or 30.4%. If there was mandated compliance across Canada, the increase in case submissions, and in the identification of crime series and case linkages could be equally breathtaking. But until then, to encourage further voluntary compliance across the country, Wilson oversaw the entire reengineering of the system and, mainly by amalgamating similar questions, lopped nearly one hundred off the form (from 263 to 168)—and got rid of the short booklet, which dissuaded investigators from ever completing the longer, more detailed booklet.

A quantum leap occurred in autumn 2001, when the Metro Toronto Police Sexual Assault Squad leapt at the chance to test the prototype ViCLAS Electronic Submission Project (VESP). It's a reunion of sorts, as Metro ViCLAS coordinator Constable Jim Moores first worked with Wilson on the Green Ribbon Task Force, analyzing details and tracking suspects, and is credited with first uttering what became the ViCLAS slogan: "Created by Canadian police for Canadian police."

If VESP works as planned, it can replace the booklets with an on-screen program that is much faster and easier to complete—just point and click—allowing an investigator in Victoria to complete and transmit an electronic file to the main database in Ottawa that would be immediately accessible by a ViCLAS specialist in St. John's analyzing a similar case, just by hitting Enter: instantaneous communication across the country for investigators who remain reluctant to cross the hall to share a lead with a colleague. It marks a breathtaking advance in interagency cooperation, demonstrating how it can work and how it should work, but, sadly and inexcusably, has so rarely worked, often with tragic consequences.

There are other rays of hope. In Ottawa, where Vince Bevan, former head of Green Ribbon, now heads that city's police force, ViCLAS coordinator Sergeant Ralph Heyerhoff is beating a different path to the same goal of reducing the time and effort required for investigators to complete and submit their cases by linking their Records Management System (RMS) to ViCLAS. From details that are always entered early into the RMS, he hopes to be able to cull the information ViCLAS needs, then enable the immediate electronic transfer of those applicable electronic files. If it works, it will virtually eliminate the current time consuming, labour intensive, duplicative effort required to retype that information manually into ViCLAS.

A veteran investigator whose career spans undercover work and witness protection, Heyerhoff is applying the common sense he mastered on the streets to the computer lab, while retaining the common touch that makes others eager to get involved. When he was investigating break-and-enters years ago, Heyerhoff met regularly with colleagues from his own and outside forces working similar crimes and facing identical problems, to wit: "A kicked-in door, a ransacked home, and no fucking evidence." He has hosted, and helped others set up, similar gatherings for ViCLAS analysts from across Ontario, a social forum that allows strangers on a common mission to put faces to names, compare notes, share problems, and swap ideas, believing, like MacKay, that those who "buy in" work harder, and that a little communication can save a lot of legwork, frustration, and heartache.

The importance of all these efforts is heightened by the fact that cops across Canada are set to retire by the thousands in the next few years. The new breed of investigators is better educated, more computer-literate, and, without the guiding wisdom of the old guard, hopefully creative and open to new ideas, anything that will help clear the growing number of cold cases. ViCLAS is one key weapon in the war FBI legend Russ Vorpagel declared and MacKay and others waged. The potential for victory, for savings in money, misery, and human life, is breathtaking.

If it's used.

MacKay's gifts, all that he fought for, sacrificed, accomplished, created, and bequeathed—alone or with others—are owed the thanks of a grateful nation and parents across the land. And his gifts just keep on giving.

In early January 2001, four years retired, MacKay sat at his breakfast table, sipping coffee and reading about the prison escape of the murderous "Texas 7." He viewed each escapee as a candidate for an Indirect Personality Assessment (IPA). Roy Hazelwood and FBI colleague Dick Ault had designed the first IPA questionnaire to cut through masked "persona"—how everyone, including violent offenders, project themselves to others—to reveal core personality traits most likely to emerge under any circumstance and learn what really "makes them tick." MacKay and Davidson had refined and expanded the original 69 questions—aware that there were no "cookbook" solutions, that the IPA varies with each situation—stamped their new form with the ViCLAS logo, and used it to focus on specific offender types such as sexual predators, to help assess threats and prepare interview or trial strategies.

Costly and time consuming, IPAs are not to be used lightly, but when needed and done right they have proved their worth in homicides, rapes, arson, bombings, stalkings, threats, and even civil suits. By examining past behaviour, a profiler can accurately predict the most probable current and future actions under any circumstances. MacKay had, in retirement, fine-tuned it to 103 questions in eight categories and saw no reason why it wouldn't help predict what to expect from seven escaped killers. He e-mailed his revisions, its cover page stamped with the ViCLAS logo, to Hildebrand, who promptly reviewed the fugitives' files to help predict what they would or would not do under the pressure of the manhunt. Woods, Collins, and the OPP sent copies to the FBI, who input and analyzed the data while the investigators prepared a media blitz, including a segment for the popular television program *America's Most Wanted*. Although their plans were cut short when the Texas fugitives were recaptured, the leader was the first to surrender when cornered and another shot himself rather than go back to prison, just as Hildebrand's IPA had predicted. It was widely assumed to be an FBI coup by the Americans until Hildebrand pointed out the ViCLAS emblem on the cover page. It was a rare moral victory for MacKay; another notch in the belt for Canadian ingenuity built on an FBI base.

But accolade is not legacy. The enduring value of what MacKay had bequeathed to Canada and the world was clinched in 1999, two years after he retired . . .

. . . when he was no longer a cop . . .

. . . on a case he had nothing to do with.

From half a continent away, ViCLAS pointed an accusing finger at the man who murdered a little girl named Alison in Toronto in 1986.

Epilogue

Alison

On January 15, 1996, almost exactly six months before the Campbell Report publicly vindicated ViCLAS, if only in Ontario, and MacKay as its visionary, RCMP Corporal Christine Wozney capped her ViCLAS workshop for Vancouver Police with her standard "hard sell." She had extolled the virtues of the system, and now invited her audience of city cops to bring her any case, anytime, and she would do everything she could to help them solve it by using ViCLAS to analyze and hopefully link it to other crimes from other times and places. At the end of her presentation, she was approached by a young beat cop, Constable Doug Fell, who in 1989 had been tipped off to a man whom he and his partner, Constable Mark Wolthers, considered a strong suspect in the disappearance and murders of dozens of downtown prostitutes. Fell was impressed with Wozney and her presentation and wondered what ViCLAS could do with seven-year-old information.

Fell and Wolthers had become friends at the training academy and partners on the street. Each stood six-foot-four, but their presence on the street went far beyond physical stature. If not exactly caped crusaders, they were truly a dynamic duo. Fell was the outgoing talker, Wolthers was the meticulous record-keeper and son of Detective Harry Wolthers who had prompted "Project 28"—named for the number of officers working the case—after identifying a local man as a "soldier" in the New York Carlo Gambino "family" by his photo inside the back flap of the cover of *Murder Incorporated*, a book on organized crime. After he had threatened to go over the head of a doubting inspector, his information had led to the first major operation in the infancy of the Coordinated Law Enforcement

Unit to combat Organized Crime, in those long-ago days when it was properly equipped, staffed, and allowed to do the job.

Harry Wolthers had taught his son the two "gets" of good police work: get off your ass and get an informant. Unlike many street cops, both men treated their sources with respect, had reduced some to tears of gratitude just by expressing their thanks after a successful bust with a crate of fruit or a bottle of hooch. Not surprisingly, information kept pouring in to them, although every source knew they'd be busted if caught committing a crime.

Over coffee in the headquarters cafeteria, Fell had recounted to Wozney how they had parlayed a chance run-in with a parolee caught shoplifting a brick of cheese into information on Frank Roy, a parolee from Ontario with a record of brutal sexual assaults on young women, some of them left for dead. Believing it more important to investigate a plausible lead in the serial disappearances of local hookers than to make a cheese bust, they heard the man out. He was talking fast, anxious to avoid going back to jail. With a little legwork, and a look at Roy's parole file, they learned that Roy had also been interviewed and cleared by Metro Toronto Police for the murder of a young girl in 1986. Her name was Alison Parrott.

Their informant was a member of Roy's sexual-deviance support group. Probably no cop anywhere anytime had scored such a coup; Fell and Wolthers thought they'd died and gone to police heaven. Troubled by the alarming rise of missing and murdered prostitutes, discouraged by the lack of progress in identifying what some whispered was a serial killer and the lack of follow-up with Roy, they had been open to anything. The abductions and suspected murders had occurred on their beat; they had known several of the victims. Now, on the basis of information from their informant, and their own research into Roy's past, pulling up whatever files they could from police and parole computer systems, they considered him a prime suspect among hundreds.

Fell and Wolthers duly passed along their insider information to Vancouver homicide detectives. They insisted on meeting their snitch, and brought heat to bear when told he refused to talk to anyone but Fell and Wolthers.

It reminded Wolthers of his first encounter with an elite unit. A snitch had alerted his father to a pending Asian drug deal, and his father had passed the information to Wolthers, who had alerted the drug cops. But the cops had dismissed him: how could a street cop know about the drug deal if they didn't? When Wolthers had returned later bearing nine grams of heroin as evidence, they had investigated *him*.

But their source on Roy relented and met with a detective and his sergeant who were investigating unsolved murders. The meeting was apparently a disaster, and their informant vanished after the meeting. Apparently, no action was ever taken on their information. Wolthers had quietly set aside the file he'd accumulated, believing it would be valuable some day down the road.

Now, seven years later, they drew Wozney into the case. Wolthers turned over his four-page brief on Roy to her on February 5. Wozney had never heard of Roy. He wasn't in the ViCLAS database but, reviewing his violent past, she knew he should have been. Of all the rapists and killers she had chased over the years, Roy may have come closest to pure evil.

Francis Carl Roy, born September 18, 1957, had a reputation for violence and a rap sheet for rape. Wolthers and Fell's informant, who knew Roy well, said he was dangerously kinky, the type of pervert even other deviants avoid. First jailed for brutally raping two teens in Ontario in the early 1980s, he was a ripple lost amid the waves of national outrage directed at Clifford Olson's murders on the west coast and the "blood money" deal that took him off the streets forever. Paroled early, Roy had arrived in Vancouver in mid-1988 with a woman he claimed was his fiancée and soon talked his way into a city job as a youth counsellor, claiming a fictitious psychology degree from the University of Toronto. No one apparently checked that out. Nor his criminal past.

Poring over Roy's parole file, comparing his record with the details of hooker deaths and disappearances during the time he had been in Vancouver, pursuing other information on her own, Wozney agreed with the street cops that Roy may have abducted and murdered some, perhaps several, of them. Everything he did and said spoke to his hatred of women in general, and prostitutes in particular. He had confided to another parolee that he would drive any hooker who ripped him off into the mountains and strangle her with wire. But the best the cops could come up with was a parole violation. When Roy called the cops to report that someone had left a knife under his porch, the cops hadn't bought the "someone" and busted him, citing the weapon as a parole violation. Fell and Wolthers had the privilege of escorting him back to jail to serve the final few months of his sentence for the 1979 and 1980 rapes in Toronto. On another occasion, an informant told them he had seen Roy take a prostitute into the bushes in Queen Elizabeth Park. The cops found a rape kit—a sheet, leather ligature cord, and knife—hidden under a nearby rock, but as it hadn't been used, and the hooker was unharmed, no elite unit saw grounds for charges and no action was taken. Suspicion was not evidence. Roy had walked free once more, just as he had in Toronto almost a decade earlier.

There was no doubt that Roy was a hard man to catch. Literally. He ran like a bat out of hell—hard, full out, wind blowing past his ears—for hour after hour. Fell guessed that he ran more than 60 miles a week. Roy had the stamina of an Olympian, the strength and agility of a boxer, and the nasty temper of a bad drunk. He fled Vancouver in 1991 after allegedly bludgeoning a man with a chunk of wood in a vicious bar fight. His fiancée's father had reportedly bought his one-way ticket cheerfully just to see the back of him.

Back in Toronto, there were suspicions that Roy had picked up where he had left off. In addition to being a suspect in the murder of Alison Parrott in 1986, he had been questioned a year later by Metro Toronto Constable Edward Everson, a member of the High Park Rapist Task Force, in connection with that series of sexual assaults, but another man was eventually charged.

Roy's criminal record dated back to 1976, escalating from possession of stolen property to theft, fraud, and break-and-enter with intent. In October 1979, he made the leap from petty punk to predator, sodomizing a 19-year-old woman. He was sentenced to six years in prison in early 1981 for that attack; another five were tacked on, to be served consecutively, for raping a 14-year-old girl in August 1980. On appeal, the latter was cut in half, reducing his total sentence to eight-and-a-half years. He was out on parole for those two rapes when Alison Parrott disappeared on Friday, July 25, 1986. His alibi cleared him as far as the investigators were concerned. The paperwork that showed he had been questioned and excluded as a suspect was processed, stamped, and filed.

On July 27, the day Alison's body was found, Roy turned himself in to police, confessing that he had assaulted a 20-year-old woman—lured her to his apartment, and beaten and tried to smother her with a pillow—all less than 48 hours before Alison disappeared. In hindsight, it seemed a calculated ploy, a tactic often used by bad guys to remove themselves from police interest regarding another crime. In this case, it was Alison's murder. And, in this case, it worked.

Roy pleaded guilty to the July assault in October, was sentenced to five weeks in jail—the equivalent of time served—and fined $200. His parole officer's recommendation to revoke his day parole was ignored although he was briefly returned to a halfway house. It was his third conviction for assaulting young women, but that may have just been the brutal tip of the iceberg. He had also been charged with past offences ranging from assault to abduction, but, like the sex charges Jim Hunter had laid against Olson, they were stayed by the Crown and he was never prosecuted for them.

In the fall of 1989, the missing and murdered Vancouver prostitutes became the focus of international attention as MacKay helped Davidson host Project Eclipse, an attempt by Canadian and American profilers to analyze 25 unsolved murders of hookers and young women to see if any could be grouped to one or more serial predator. Several were linked behaviourally, but no one was ever charged. As the alarming toll continued to rise to 50 missing women, public sentiment grew more vocal that the cops weren't doing all they could to solve the disappearances and the deaths, certainly not making the effort they would if scores of housewives or "nice" girls vanished and turned up dead—or not at all. Wozney agreed with Fell and Wolthers that Roy seemed a logical place to start looking. He lived near where the missing prostitutes had worked, had a record of violent sexual assaults, and had been fingered by their informant as a very danger-ous predator. If only someone would listen.

Wozney was familiar with investigator arrogance from her years working serious crimes, knew it could undermine or cripple an investigation, and strongly suspected that was the case here. Fell and Wolthers had assembled an impressive dossier on Roy, but they were street cops, so far down the police food chain they wouldn't even register on the radar of senior brass and homicide detectives who seemed more intent on discrediting them and their informant than checking out their lead. Roy was never questioned about anything by anyone.

Wozney wrote a detailed report on Roy and sent it downstairs to Serious Crimes, her old unit, to have them investigate and find the evidence to charge him. If it was a no-brainer to her, Roy still had little to fear from the cops. Her report was "filed" in a corporal's desk drawer. Just one more setback for Wozney, a free spirit too often dismissed by too many cops since basic training as "blonde fluff," an unlikely candidate to investigate, let alone solve, major crimes like rape and murder.

But no one was more amazed than Wozney that she was a cop.

Christine Wozney grew up a small-town girl in Prince Rupert and Prince George, B.C., wanting to be a journalist, crusading or other-wise. She won several national creative-writing awards in high school—most notably the Leacock competition for humour at age 14—and was snapped up in Grade 12 as a copywriter by a local radio station impressed with her press clippings and awards. She loved her job but, after two years, the party-hearty lifestyle of the 1970s was exacting its toll. Casting about for less self-destructive employment, she applied to the Mounties as a secretary. To her shock, they considered her overqualified and suggested she apply for police training; it was her first inkling that women could be cops. On August 31, 1976, four weeks past her 20th birthday, Wozney joined the Mounties and went to Regina for basic training. It proved challenging for all.

Wozney warmed to physical conditioning as Goldie Hawn embraced forced marches as the hapless army recruit in *Private Benjamin*. She just never saw the point of climbing that long rope dangling from the ceiling beam. What if she mussed her hair? Split a nail? Wouldn't it be safer and simpler to talk the rope into coming down with its threads in the air? Her instructors persisted, she relented, climbed the rope, graduated, and was posted to North Vancouver, where MacKay was her training officer as sergeant in charge of the General Investigations Section.

Wozney quickly warmed to police work as she never had to basic training, greatly relieved to learn that her job primarily involved talking to people, listening to them, showing compassion, empathy and, most importantly, common sense. No need to leap a tall building or climb a single rope. If she didn't look the part of a stereotypical homicide or sexual-assault investigator, she played the role well. There were always male cops who resented her promotion opportunities as a woman, but there were also those who appreciated talent. She was mentored by "the best" and few could deny her results. Bad guys liked her. Told her things. Snitches sought her out to eagerly rat out others. Rapists and murderers confessed to her as she played along, feigning sympathy or assuring them she understood. Men she sent to prison kept in touch. Like Maile with Olson before her, Wozney would do whatever had to be done to rid the streets of a predator.

It all took a toll. In time, Wozney edged toward burnout. Weary of the endless carnage and human suffering, she asked, then begged, for a transfer to the new ViCLAS section, not because she believed, or even cared, that it could do what it claimed, but as a haven to "zone out" and avoid confronting the horrible aftermath of violent crime up front and personal. Her boss initially objected, arguing she was too good at what she was doing, that she would be bored silly working with a computer. She persisted; he relented. The rest is history.

Soon after transferring, the ViCLAS bug bit Wozney. Originally one of four corporals, she was promoted to sergeant in May 1996, and eventually staff sergeant in charge of the ViCLAS unit 13 months later. Once she realized just how well it worked, she was a convert, then its champion to all who would, or, like Fell and other city street cops who had been ordered to attend her presentation that day, had to listen. It was time well spent. If Fell and Wolthers were the catalyst to spark interest in Roy, Wozney was the fire, a torch-bearer to warm and shed new light on a 10-year-old cold case. She passed the information on to Metro Toronto Detective Sergeant Victor Matanovic, a one-man cold case squad known affectionately as the "Mad Russian" to colleagues whom he entertained by belting out Kenny Rogers tunes, or, on lonely surveillance stakeouts, by recounting "Little Red Riding Hood" with exaggerated accent, dramatic, and comedic flair. The last to join the pursuit of Roy, he soon led the pack, blazing down the final leg of the chase . . . and caught him.

On Thursday, February 22, 1996, Wozney phoned Matanovic to advise him that British Columbia was starting a Historical Homicide Review of cold cases and, on the basis of what Fell and Wolthers had discovered, that she considered Roy a good candidate for further investigation in the missing and murdered Vancouver prostitutes case. Matanovic, sick at home, got the message four days later. He had first discussed the need for a cold case unit at Metro with his mentor and good friend Robert Montrose in 1989, actively lobbied for it in 1994, and was given the OK in April 1995. Matanovic, never having heard of Roy, checked him out with Steve Irwin who had been reassigned from the Sexual Assault Squad to the Intelligence Bureau, and with mentors Steve Marrier and Steve Ressor, would soon be cited publicly in the Campbell Report for the interview debacle with Bernardo.

Irwin told Matanovic that Roy had been questioned and cleared in Alison's death in 1986. Matanovic persisted, and got Irwin to send him Roy's file. Reviewing those yellowed documents, he found the suspect's original statement to police riddled with deception.

The apparent inconsistencies and contradictions leapt off the page. Admittedly, being a liar didn't mean you were a killer, but the more closely he read—and Matanovic was meticulous—the less things jibed. His curiosity was piqued. Poring over the file that weekend, he was left with one unsettling question: How had they cleared this guy? On March 4, he got a copy of Alison's post- mortem report and 10-year-old crime-scene photos from the Metro file. The next day, Wozney called and left a message that she had read Roy's file at the parole office after their chat on February 26. She had been blown away by a detailed report submitted to Metro investigators by Roy's parole officer, Shelley Hassard, urging them to interview him again in July 1987. Other nuggets of information that had been collecting dust for 10 years were Roy's initial statement to police in 1986 and information gleaned that same year and again in 1987 from convicted cop killer Herb Archer, who informed the cops that Roy had been a prison photographer and had bragged about using a camera to lure women.

The accumulated evidence, all of it in the file, convinced Matanovic that Roy should never have been cleared as early and as easily as he had been. In his mind, he should never have been cleared at all. The familiar adrenaline that surges through investigators when they sense a break in a case began to pound. Over the phone, Matanovic offered to mail Wozney a copy of Roy's file and asked her to send him whatever information she had generated so far on him. When she noted that she planned to attend the Metro Sexual Assault conference in Toronto on March 18, they agreed to meet and exchange files then.

On March 12, 1996, Jim Moores entered Alison's name into the Metro ViCLAS system. A week before meeting Wozney at the crime conference, Matanovic was reassigned and put in charge of six detectives investigating "fresh" homicides. He continued reviewing the Parrott case at home in his off hours, thanks in no small part to having a very understanding wife. When he and Wozney met as planned on March 18, 1996, she found the encounter an emotional rollercoaster. Crushed to learn that his cold case pursuit had been shut down as a full-time operation, she was elated moments later to hear him confirm his interest in Roy, that, from what he had read to date, he no longer considered him "cleared" and would continue his followup. They exchanged files. Neither contained any new evidence. What had changed was how the information was being interpreted after sitting in Roy's file for a decade. On the train ride home, Matanovic was stunned to read what he considered the most intelligent report in the file: Hassard's chillingly detailed alert to the Metro investigators in 1987, "Reasons Why Frank Roy Is a Good Suspect in the Alison Parrott Murder."

Among Roy's former parole officer's key facts were that he and Alison had trained at the same athletic club, that he knew track jargon and cameras, giving him the means and opportunity to abduct the young girl, that he had done it before, twice luring young women to an isolated spot to rape and sodomize them. It hadn't stopped there. Hassard pointed out that Roy knew the west end of Toronto—where Alison had lived and was found dead—having attended school (in fact, Roy and Matanovic had attended the same high school), worked, and run about 10 miles a day in the area. Alarmingly, he had scored "sadistic" to sexual-response testing in Kingston Penitentiary, was diagnosed with an antisocial personality, and loved boxing. He could be as happy gauging how many punches it would take to knock out a victim as he was raping and sodomizing—and now, she believed, likely killing—unconscious or bound women and girls with no fear of detection:

> Roy is a convincing liar and is not threatening in appearance. He is small of stature, has a boyish enthusiasm and winning smile. He is likable, has the gift of the gab, is reasonably articulate and is confident. . . . He also thinks he's a good criminal and would not get caught. . . . In my opinion, the MO is similar to the Parrott case. I know that Roy was previously investigated and cleared, but I think he is worth a second look.

As for motive, that was simple. Roy *liked* it. He brutalized women, not for the sex, but the thrill he got from his power to inflict pain and terror on his young, helpless victims. Hassard had no

doubt he'd do it again, was sure he had done it again, this time escalating to murder. When she heard nothing from the Metro investigators, she phoned them, begged them to interview Roy again.
Nothing happened. As the Campbell Report would soon lament, the
same mistakes just kept happening over and over again. It was as if
Bernardo and Bundy and all the others who had taught such deadly
lessons had never existed. As a result, no young innocent who
strayed—or was lured—into the path of a predator like Roy had a
ghost of a chance for escape. What made this case worse was that all
the information had been there, that it had taken a decade to deci-
pher its uncoded contents, written in plain language, to relearn the
same lesson yet again. How many more had died at Roy's hands
over the past 10 years? How many more would die if they didn't get
him off the streets quickly? Who had to die before someone would
read the signs and stop him?

The unofficial investigation into Roy began to heat up behind the
scenes. In Vancouver, Wozney liberated her report on Roy from the
corporal's desk drawer, blew off the dust, and packed it off to a
ViCLAS conference in Ottawa, waving it under as many noses as
possible to persuade Metro and the OPP to enter Roy into their
database. No one paid her much mind. In Toronto, Matanovic was
encountering similar resistance, and overcoming it with the help of
an equally determined investigator, SAS Detective Ruth Schueller.
Matanovic was having trouble locating the files on Roy's two earlier
convictions and turned to Irwin in Intelligence for help. Irwin came
up with nothing. On May 29, 1996, Matanovic brought Schueller
into the investigation to help locate the missing files. She found them
stored in the Sexual Assault Squad, Irwin's former unit. Finally, fully
armed with the information from Fell, Wolthers, Wozney, and at
long last his own force which had conducted the initial investigation, Matanovic geared up for the final leg of the chase—a cop
driven to stop a predator dead in his tracks.

Working at home on his own time, Matanovic pored over the files.
He was painstakingly meticulous, dissecting data, reading and reread-
ing every report, digesting every interview, every scrap of paper, every
photo and map. Analyzing. Questioning. Double-checking. On June

10, he asked Wozney to interview Karen Pudwell in Vancouver to get more background on Roy from his former fiancée. Wozney passed his request to her former supervisor in Serious Crimes and, after repeated entreaties, two Mounties interviewed her in August 1996. Matanovic had Roy in custody by then.

Matanovic arranged to have Roy put under surveillance and, on July 10, Metro surveillance officers Detective Constable Lou DiLorenzo and Detective Constable John Angus obtained castoff DNA samples from a coffee cup and two cigarette butts. The DNA evidence would either exclude or confirm Roy as the killer when it was compared to evidence swabbed from Alison a decade earlier. On July 25, 1996, 10 years to the day that Alison had been lured to her death, Pamela Newall called Matanovic from the Ontario Centre of Forensic Sciences to say they had a match.

Two days later, Saturday July 27, Matanovic contacted Collins, the forensic psychiatrist seconded to the OPP from the Clarke Institute, to help prepare psychological collateral material for a search-warrant application as he had when the two men had collaborated on the only Metro cold case ever solved to that point, the 1982 murder of Argonaut cheerleader Jenny Isford and the conviction of fetishist stalker and serial rapist William Brett Henson, condemned by his DNA. They agreed to meet and, at Collins' suggestion, with OPP profiler Jim Van Allen. The Metro cop had never heard of Van Allen or Kate Lines, and was admittedly skeptical of profiling, but the lunch yielded some good ideas. Matanovic particularly liked Van Allen's suggestion that he have the other investigators call him "Boss" in Roy's presence. To further rattle Roy, it was agreed he should be arrested by a petite blonde policewoman—he hated women, having grown up in an all-female home headed by an abusive and very domineering mother—and a Mountie to make him wonder what they had on him. Wozney filled the bill on all counts, and was Matanovic's first consideration, but in the end he opted for local talent: Metro Detective Sergeant Jane Wilcox—brunette, taller than Roy, and a good cop who would follow Matanovic's instructions to the letter—and Mountie Corporal Harold O'Connell, who was on secondment to Metro Homicide.

In the final hours before closing his trap, Matanovic held his cards close to his chest. He briefed each group of the arrest team separately, none knowing what the other was doing. Many expressed surprise at this late hour to learn that their target was Alison's suspected killer. No one but the surveillance team leader knew the actual time of the arrest nor where Roy was to be taken to avoid any possible media frenzy that could impact on his interview with the suspect. Matanovic stayed out of the picture, preparing to interrogate Roy.

At 7:00 a.m., July 31, 1996, Collins went on standby alert as Matanovic went over the final details of his game plan with those who would apprehend Roy. Surveillance confirmed the man was at home. Satisfied that his quarry had nowhere to run, and ready to run his own gruelling marathon in the interrogation room at 41 Division, Matanovic ordered the arresting officers: "Take him." Wilcox and O'Connell arrested Roy without incident and charged him with the 10-year-old first-degree murder of Alison Parrott.

For the next several hours, Collins and Van Allen monitored the Mad Russian's brilliant interrogation. As he had 10 years earlier, Roy denied any involvement in Alison's death. He changed his story when confronted by the DNA evidence against him, but Matanovic, who by now knew the crime, the area, and his suspect, kept trapping him with his own lies. At 3:00 the following morning, Collins and Van Allen walked out of the police station, confident that Matanovic had caught Alison's killer.

On August 1, Matanovic called Wozney and left a one-word message on her telephone voice mail: "Bingo!"

In mid-September, Matanovic travelled to Vancouver to track Roy's movements while he had lived there. In the process, he unearthed background information that Roy was fired from his job as a city youth counsellor in early 1989 for allegedly fixating on a 14-year-old girl and telling her he wanted her to have his baby. His fiancée dumped him and Roy began frequenting prostitutes. Matanovic was able to trace the young girl to Hawaii. Denied permission to travel there to interview her by his boss, one of the original investigators on Alison's murder, he passed the information on to Vancouver Police and the local Mounties hoping it might help their probe into the string of prostitute homicides which had first brought Roy to the attention of Fell and Wolthers.

Despite advance notice that he was coming west, and offering to meet with Vancouver homicide detectives and Mountie investigators to discuss how his expanding investigation could impact on their probe into dozens of disappeared and dead hookers, no one met with him except the two street cops who had so long ago set the wheels in motion, unleashing Matanovic like a runaway train—a man on a mission with enough apparent zeal and integrity that Fell and Wolthers were able to unearth their original informant and persuade him to meet with the Metro detective to discuss Roy. Matanovic knew all about investigator resistance and turf wars, and didn't expect homicide investigators to check their ego at the door—you needed a strong ego, the self-confidence to believe you'd catch the perpetrator, to do the job—but he hadn't expected them to check their brains at the door either. Yet the only guys who'd help him try to catch a killer were two street cops and their informant. No matter. Nothing would stop him now. Roy's days of roaming free were numbered. He had no clue of the train bearing down on him or that the Mad Russian was angry and had him in his crosshairs.

Back in Ontario, there was no rush to judgment. Roy did not stand trial until 1999, when after prolonged deliberations— Matanovic's "Six-Day Nightmare"—a jury convicted him of the premeditated murder of Alison Parrott on April 13, 1999. Justice had come at last, after 13 years—two years longer than Alison had lived. A decade after MacKay went to Quantico to become the first Canadian profiler, six years since ViCLAS was unveiled at the OPP Academy in Brampton, the young girl with the haunting smile had been avenged and with that came, if not celebration, then, hopefully, a sense of closure.

•   •   •

The media flurry that followed Roy's arrest and conviction worsened already bad feelings as agendas surfaced and the case became proprietary. Everyone, it seemed, who hadn't sought or had a piece of the action now wanted a slice of the glory. Roy's arrest came in the immediate wake of the Campbell Report being made public, allowing Johnson a new opportunity to promote ViCLAS. Wozney ducked the publicity, booking off work, avoiding the media, refusing even to answer her home phone, allowing free rein to others to bask in the limelight. When she finally spoke publicly, after Roy's conviction three years later, she took great pains to extol Fell and Wolthers and Matanovic as the heroes she truly believed them to be. She minimized her own role, deflecting all credit and glory to ViCLAS, and publicly lamented the lack of recognition for Fell and Wolthers by their own force.

Matanovic crossed swords with Johnson, arguing that good old-fashioned investigative work, not ViCLAS, had cracked the case. That was true. Roy wasn't even in the database before Matanovic got involved. Wolthers and Fell and Wozney provided no new evidence. ViCLAS had *not* solved the case. ViCLAS would *never* solve a case. That was, and always would be, the realm of the investigators. But ViCLAS got the cops talking.

Ron MacKay had argued from the beginning that ViCLAS was much more than a high-tech database, that it went to "state of mind." A tool to help solve crimes by analyzing and linking their behavioural components was also a catalyst to get cops talking, sharing information, swapping theories and leads. The ViCLAS "system" was a network of computers *and* people, neither half able to do its job without the other, both equally vital if it was ever to realize its potential. That applied to mentality as much as to technology. How well it worked depended on the people who were involved. In the aftermath of Roy's conviction, the signs were not encouraging.

Fell and Wolthers had refused to talk to the media about their role in the case until they got the OK from Matanovic. After Roy's conviction, they finally got their press conference. No senior brass attended from their force to show support for a job well done. The lone exception was their sergeant, Ken Frail, who happened by and stopped to chat, curious what was going on. Proud to learn that two of his own were the focus of the media attention, he promptly submitted both men for a Chief's Commendation. No response. Only when Johnson, at Wozney's urging, sent a formal note of thanks and congratulations was a "Good Job" note attached from Vancouver Police Chief Terry Blythe. Aside from the occasional passing "attaboy," that was it. The common sentiment among their colleagues seemed to be that Fell and Wolthers had benefited from "dumb luck" more than any investigative prowess or initiative.

Matanovic was disappointed by the heavy ViCLAS spin in the media, his recognition in Metro limited to a "Thanks, Vic," and a bear hug from Detective Rocky Cleveland, the original lead investigator on the Parrott murder. He was further upset to learn belatedly that Crown prosecutor Paul McDermott had sent letters of commendation to then-Chief David Boothby acknowledging "key" individuals in resolving Alison's murder. As he did not receive one, he was curious who had. No one would tell him, citing "confidentiality" as their reason. On April 24, 2001, he wrote to Metro Police Chief Julian Fantino, recounting the details of his investigation and concluding:

> The following are the individuals that provided a piece of the puzzle that contributed in bringing to justice Alison Parrott's killer, albeit thirteen years later. The Toronto Police Service and the community are indebted to the following persons: Police Constable Douglas Fell, Constable Mark Wolthers, Ms. Shelley Hassard, Corporal Christine Wozney, Detective Ruth Schueller, Constable Edward Everson (Posthumously), Detective Constable Lou DiLorenzo, Detective Constable John Angus, Detective Sergeant Jane Wilcox, Corporal Harold O'Connell, members of Intelligence Bureau Mobile Support Services and the two inmates who will remain anonymous.

As of this writing, there has been no response. One of the unnamed informants died in 1999. The other, due largely to the efforts of parole officer Hassard, who wrote the detailed report urging the police to reinvestigate Roy, was paid a $10,000 reward.

Many other pretenders basked in glory they did not earn, rose to rank they did not merit on this case, and ingratiated themselves falsely to those who trusted and relied on them. Their absence on this very short list speaks volumes. To paraphrase MacKay, there is shame enough for all.

But if Fell and Wolthers and Matanovic were unjustly overlooked, Wozney was a target for the wrath of officialdom, bullied and pilloried for suggesting it should never have taken so long to solve Alison's murder in a *Globe and Mail* article. That did not sit well with those who had spent so many years not solving the case. They resented the implication that they had not done all they could— although the fact that the 10-year-old homicide was solved within months by four cops on three forces in two provinces working half a continent apart, three of whom had had nothing to do with the case, seemed to offer some evidence of its truth. It was basic training all over again for Wozney, dangling once more in midair, but this time the rope was looped around her neck.

Mussed hair and split nails were the least of her problems until Johnson intervened and saved her career, citing all she had done, the glory she had brought to ViCLAS and thus to the Force, and raising the likelihood that she had been misquoted, the standard ploy when all seems lost.

The fallout from Roy's conviction was not policing's shining moment. Never in the annals of crime were so few so abused by such multitudes for accomplishing so much with so little for so many. Glory, like gold, does strange things to people. The bickering at the lower levels had much to do with clashing egos and personalities— people who thought the Battle of Britain was an overblown air show because they weren't there. It was equally simple in the upper ranks. As with Olson and Bernardo and dozens more who never made the national news, political agendas rear their ugly heads during and after every major police investigation as the battle for turf becomes a bid for headlines that can translate into more staff, bigger budgets, and larger egos. MacKay had always said there was enough glory for everyone when a major case was solved, but not everyone thinks like MacKay—certainly not those chasing promotion.

Wozney survived, bruised but breathing. Still, it seemed an odd expression of gratitude for helping to rid the streets of one of the most cunning and lethal serial predators to ever stalk the land. Her "sin" was to speak the truth within hearing of those who can't handle the truth and are embarrassed by it. She never claimed to have solved the case, never claimed that ViCLAS solved the case, never once cited Fell or Wolthers, Matanovic or Hassard, without praising them as the heroes who cracked the case rather than herself. True, the case was clinched by DNA tests that did not exist in 1986. So what? Bernardo had given DNA samples two years later and they sat, and sat, and sat . . .

Systemic failure cannot be set right by four cops, no matter how skilled and dedicated. This case was solved as much by character as clues, and the courage to do one's job when others wouldn't or couldn't and certainly didn't. Justice for Alison hinged on a simple formula:

$$\text{Tenacity} + \text{Passion} + \text{Commitment} = \text{Conviction}$$

Had any element in that equation failed or faltered, the puzzle would never have been finished. Had Fell not asked Wozney for help at her ViCLAS workshop, had Wolthers not kept meticulous seven-year-old records, had both partners not excelled at cultivating informants, had Wozney not distilled their findings with her own and forwarded it all to Matanovic, and had Matanovic been less meticulous or relentless, there seems little doubt that Frank Roy would still be stalking young women today.

That possibility was particularly distressing to Wozney, no longer just a cop who'd seen the worst, but a new mother who, like all moms, can at times fear the worst. It was an unhealthy combination, yet her daughter, Jessica, born in December 1996, sustained her through the darkest moments of the frustrations encountered chasing Roy, and the ensuing fallout after his conviction. With Roy off the streets, a Christmas gift to all women everywhere, she had time to reflect on what had been accomplished by so few for so many. As she rocked her infant daughter to sleep, feeling at peace with the world and as one with Jessica, her mind would wander to Alison. Not once or twice, but night after night, each time raising the same anguished question: "How could anyone hurt a little girl like that?" And in that moment, she would clutch her own precious daughter a little tighter, shed the last vestige of her cop persona, and cry for another young girl she never met, couldn't save but, by God, had helped avenge.

As a mother Wozney sensed, more clearly than she ever had as a cop, the grief of those whose child is stolen, their lives and dreams shattered in an instant of horror and madness. As a cop—that harsh world where tears and fears and even compassion can be mistaken for weakness—she has rededicated herself to protecting her own and as many others as possible. In a job that she loves, but fears too easily bends to mediocrity, she refuses to sit back and take the easy way that appeals to so many, stays the course, does whatever must be done, whatever the cost, to make Jessica and those like her a little safer. Just one more rope to climb in the killing fields of dark paths and cold trails.

Sadly, the misdirected abuse heaped on Wozney was just another example of senior Mounties refusing to stand by investigators who drew heat or public notice for doing their jobs. Historically, when an outside force, particularly one with Metro's clout, barked "Jump!" the "Brass Stetsons" in Ottawa paused just long enough to ask "How high?" before pouncing with both leather boots on their hapless investigator. Anyone who actually read the entire *Globe and Mail* article would have grasped in an instant its focus on perceived foot-dragging by Vancouver police—who raised no complaint with Ottawa—while lamenting, almost in passing, the delay by Metro and the OPP to enter Roy and the Parrott case into ViCLAS. In fairness, Alison was a Metro homicide and the OPP were no more likely to ever bypass another force, certainly not a major partner like Toronto, to enter their case directly into the database than was RCMP Commissioner Phil Murray to deflect Metro Police Chief David Boothby's venom by telling the former major player in the early days of the investigation to quit whining and clean up his own mess.

Boothby and Metro faced far worse than Wozney. A year earlier, two years after Justice Archie Campbell had warned in his review of the Bernardo investigations that doing anything less than everything possible to protect *all* citizens may leave the police and politicians accused of violating the Charter of Rights and Freedoms, Madame Justice Jean MacFarland of the Ontario Court of Justice had slammed Metro police for violating *Articles* 7 and 15 by using women as "bait" for a serial rapist in the "Jane Doe/Balcony Rapist Case" in the summer of 1986 when Alison Parrott had been lured and murdered.

In October 1999, six months after she was reprimanded and disciplined by Ottawa, ViCLAS and presumably Wozney, were again vindicated by a scathing review that this time found that the Metro serial-rape investigation had been woefully "irresponsible and grossly negligent," that the cops had "failed utterly in their duty to protect women," based on an investigative strategy "motivated by . . . mythology and discriminatory sexual stereotypes" that women would become "hysterical" if warned there was a predator in their midst. Ensuing changes were dismissed as having more to do with protecting the image of the police than women at risk.

Nearly 10 percent of the Metro audit, and seven of its 57 recommendations, involved ViCLAS—what it is, why it must be used, how it can be improved—as it applauded the cops for changes to the Sexual Assault Squad and throughout the force, but warned "there is more to be done." It was once again, as the Campbell report had warned, history repeating. But the worst seems yet to come. No professional, legal or common-sense opinion seems to have changed political and police inertia as storm clouds gather over a pig farm in Port Coquitlam near Vancouver where the Mounties are scouring the landscape for evidence of the fate of 50 missing women dating back several years. The media is already reporting jurisdictional infighting, a stayed attempted-murder charge against a key suspect, ignored alarms raised by street cops and leads from the public.

Two decades later, politicians outside Ontario (and possibly Quebec) ignore their duty and Charter obligations and police hierarchies across the land stone their prophets and visionaries for demon-

strating the courage of their convictions. It's Olson all over again . . .
and Bernardo . . . and Francis Carl Roy. And so many, many others.

British Columbia, and the Lower Mainland in particular, is a
magnet for predators with its balmy climate and easy pickings. In
the aftermath of the murder of Melinda Sheppit, the 16-year-old
Ottawa prostitute whose death brought MacKay and Collins
together, two others were attacked. One of them survived and from
what she told police they believe, but cannot prove, they know the
killer. Their suspect left Ontario soon after for Vancouver. All
Ottawa police could do was pass along their suspicions. A man
suspected in the disappearance of a young girl walking home from
work in New Brunswick also went to Vancouver as, of course, did
Frank Roy. No one has arrested the Highway Killer(s) since Mike
Eastham's Kamloops meeting identified 40 victims a year after
Olson, a homegrown terror, was jailed forever. Nor has Roy or
anyone else ever been charged with the abduction or murder of
dozens of Vancouver prostitutes—the early number officially pegged
at 31 had soared to 50 (some say more) before police identified a
possible strong suspect in Port Coquitlam at the time of this writing.

Interestingly, perhaps coincidentally, ViCLAS compliance in
British Columbia soared from an embarrassing 10 percent to 89
percent after Roy's conviction—less than in Ontario, but apparent
recognition of ViCLAS' worth. In 1999, Langley Township Coun-
cillor May Barnard, who had first heard of ViCLAS when she was a
witness in a White Rock murder case six years earlier, and learned
later that the system was not being used as much as it could be,
raised the issue with the Union of British Columbia Municipalities
and won unanimous support for asking the Attorney General of
British Columbia and the Solicitor General of Canada to make
reporting violent offenders to ViCLAS mandatory. While rates are
voluntarily improving elsewhere, gaps still exist across Canada,
allowing serial and sexual predators to escape and resurface to strike
again. Hope springs eternal, but only Ontario, and possibly Quebec

if they have proceeded as scheduled, have taken all available steps to enhance public safety.

Much as we might like to think it, those sworn to serve and protect us are not always white knights who can protect us from all harm. They face a difficult task. It is impossible to slay all the dragons when dinosaurs roam the earth. Twenty years after Olson, there are still those who do not, will not, or cannot grasp the lessons learned so painfully. The controversial book *Where Shadows Linger*, by W. Leslie Holmes with Bruce Northorp, heralds two investigators in its opening chapters who allegedly "solved" the case while four of Olson's victims were still alive. It records, but buries deep in its pages, the sad fact that Jim Hunter had the killer in custody on sex charges with *ten* of Olson's victims still alive. In fact, one of those credited with solving the case lost Olson and the bloody shirt he was wearing. It changed the killer's MO; he burned his clothes after each later murder. And when he was devastated at losing a key suspect and critical evidence, who consoled him? Maile!

If the case was "solved," why were the investigators left chasing 10,000 tips? Why did the taxpayers of British Columbia foot the bill for the $100,000 deal for Olson's wife? Perhaps because there is a vast difference between *knowing* and *proving* whodunit. That requires evidence. Maile asked for it, didn't get it. The deal was struck. Maile did what he had to do to get Olson talking himself off the streets forever. As thanks, he got a free supper from the prosecutor and a torrent of hate mail and obscene calls from cops who did nothing to help solve the case but hated him for how he did it, oblivious to the fact that the alternative was to leave free a child killer who had already killed 11—one of which the cops didn't even know about until Olson confessed to it in court.

Not surprisingly, Maile wishes ViCLAS had been available in 1980: "I'm positive in my mind, if the system was up to date and used properly, that there could have been two or three lives, or even more, saved."

Bruce Northorp, the retired superintendent in charge of support services and "coordinator of the original RCMP investigation," was less charitable:

I don't know how [Maile] could have come to such a conclusion. . . . In my view, ViCLAS would have done nothing. Both ["solvers"] were faster than ViCLAS could have been. . . . In May 1981, only two of Olson's victims had been found. . . . It is sheer conjecture to consider if geographic profiling would have pointed to Olson as a logical suspect. . . . By July 1981, few of the bodies of Olson's victims had been found. In most instances, all the police had were the locations where the missing children had last been seen. Given these circumstances, it is unlikely that either geographic profiling or ViCLAS would have been of any real benefit had they been available in 1980–81.

In fact, geographic profiling and ViCLAS would not have solved the case. They would have identified a geographic area that told the investigators where they were most likely to find the killer—where he worked or lived—and identified and linked similar crimes to show where he'd been. But neither would ever identify a killer. Ditto for behavioural profiling, which identifies the suspect personality type, not who he is. No computer or behavioural system comes with a magical "SOLVE" key. It is still the investigators' job to figure out "whodunit" and produce the *evidence*—physical, forensic, circumstantial, survivor, or eyewitness testimony—to *prove* it.

The battle continues. The war rages on. Casualties mount. While world attention focuses on the revived threat of international terrorism, those with the power and the mandate to protect us at home ignore, outside Ontario (and presumably Quebec in 2002), a vital tool that already exists. This is akin to waging, and very likely losing, World War II by ignoring the intelligence from Enigma or Magic code-breakers. ViCLAS is only as good as the information it gets, and is undermined by every unfiled case or withheld piece of evidence. But—as the behavioural experts have stressed here repeatedly—even at its best ViCLAS will never solve a single crime. That has always been, and will always be, the lot of the dedicated men and women who beat the bushes for evidence and suspects, who knock on doors and resolutely perform what must clearly be the hardest job on earth—telling strangers that those they love most in the world aren't coming home again. It is not a job for the faint of heart or the unbridled ego.

Veteran police officers are set to retire across Canada in record numbers, taking with them the conventional wisdom of the streets learned through years of experience and hard lessons that have been passed from generation to generation of investigators. The new breed of cops are better educated and more computer-literate than any who have gone before. They have access to more and better tools than existed for those who preceded them. Much will change, hopefully improve, but success, and solving cases, will still rely on Fell and Wolthers' tenacity and street smarts, Wozney's passion, and Matanovic's meticulous attention to detail.

Finally convicting Frank Roy for the murder of Alison Parrott was a triumph for justice and those who avenged her. Interestingly, Fell, Wolthers, Wozney, and Matanovic collaborated to close the file on Alison and the prison door on Roy two years after MacKay, the well travelled, long-suffering Mountie from Moosomin, had retired. MacKay had nothing to do with that case and everything to do with a new tool and refreshing mentality that helped close it. He was the vision behind Keith Davidson and Greg Johnson, who drove the system forward.

Quite simply, and *no one* disputes this, ViCLAS got cops talking and sharing information. The pooled information led to a killer down a very dark path along a very cold trail. Investigators put one more killer, too clever to be caught, in prison for life. And women and children who may have crossed his path are just a little safer.

That is MacKay's legacy.

And Alison's.

Acknowledgments

Dark Paths, Cold Trails is my fourth book and by far the most ambitious to date. As always, no matter how lonely the task of writing seemed when the screen and brain were blank, there were many others unseen in the wings who helped me finish what I had started.

This book marked a reunion with editor Don Loney who was integral to my first two works, *Billion $$$ High: The Drug Invasion of Canada* and *Unkindest Cut: The Torso Murder of Selina Shen*, the latter in development with Alliance Atlantis as a feature film. Don saw the merit in this project immediately and moved quickly to make an idea a reality. I thank him for his infectious enthusiasm, patience, and encouragement that kept me sane through difficult times.

Similarly, I thank David Kent, President and CEO of Harper-Collins, who boosted my spirits at a crucial time by confiding to me his belief that this was one of those rare books that could "make a difference." His faith and kind words helped transform what began as an homage to a handful of men and women, who have made the world a safer place, to a crusade to spread their protection to women and children—those most vulnerable and at highest risk from serial predators—across Canada from coast to coast. If this book does spawn change, it owes much to his timely words.

Apologizing to any I miss, others at HarperCollins who come immediately to mind for my thanks are editor Karen Hanson and copy editor Rodney Rawlings, techno-wizard Roy Nicol who assumed responsibility early for the flood of photos and accepted my evident lack of organizational skills with good humour, my publicist, Felicia Quon, and the smiling sea of faces of editorialists and marketeers who treated me so well on my sojourn to the big city. Be assured that if names have slipped away, my appreciation has not. Thanks also to Ian Murray, he who cuts cheques so promptly. Go Sens!

Special thanks to my agent, Suzanne DePoe, at WCA Film & Television, Ltd., for negotiating me those cheques and other projects, and to her cohort Debbie Wood whose quick wit and ready laugh were often timely.

This book relied heavily on the cooperation of others starting a decade ago when Brian Sargeant walked me to Ron MacKay's door. I owe a debt of gratitude to the score of police officers across Canada and the United States who conjured up distant, sometimes painful, but always amazingly vivid memories to ensure I got this right. Special thanks to Ron MacKay, and to those inspiring men and women I met through him, for trusting me to tell their stories, many speaking publicly for the first time. I have made every effort to get it right. For errors made and missed, I apologize and take full responsibility.

Thanks to Millie for opening "Hotel Mom" and to good friends Bill and Mary Tannahill for opening their home when I was on the road.

And an appreciative tip of the surgical cap to Dr. Roy Masters and his talented team at the University of Ottawa Heart Institute for getting me this far.

As always, I thank my family who were there when the screen was blank, once again enduring my moods with patience and faith, their good humour, sustaining me through bouts of doubt, the long lonely days and endless nights of writing, revising and whining. I never forget that I am a writer because they let me. Any success is truly measured by their unflagging love and support.

Finally, to my Muse, the whirling *Terpischore* in graceful human form, whispering from the void later than ever before, Her flame forging a bolder writer, a wiser man, my profound thanks for a hell of a ride. Then, in a heartbeat, gone. A Muse is a terrible thing to waste.

DOUG CLARK
North Gower
February 2002

A Note on Sources

Much of what is written here is based on extensive interviews with the key players in this saga, taken from the public record, public documents and Internet sources. For more detailed material on the early days of "stranger murders," criminal profiling and serial-crime linkage, I recommend:

CANADIAN

Eastham, Sgt. Michael (RCMP ret'd) with McLeod, Ian, *The Seventh Shadow: The Wilderness Manhunt for a Brutal Mass Murderer*, Warwick Publishing, 1999.

Ferry, Jon and Inwood, Damian, *The Olson Murders*, Cameo Books, 1982.

Holmes, Leslie W. and Northrop, Bruce L. *Where Shadows Linger: The Olson Murder Investigation*, Hertiage House, 2001.

Leyton, Elliott, *Hunting Humans: The Rise of the Modern Multiple Killer*, Penguin Books, 1989 (first published as *Compulsive Killers*, New York University Press, 1986).

Mulgrew, Ian, *Final Payoff: The True Price of Convicting Clifford Olson*, Seal, 1990.

Rossmo, D. Kim, *Geographic Profiling*, CRC Press, 2000.

AMERICAN

Douglas, John and Olshaker, Mark, *Mind Hunter: Inside the FBI's Elite Serial Crime Unit*, Scribner, 1995.

Jeffers, H. Paul, *Who Killed Precious?*, Pharos Books, 1991.

Keppel, Robert D. with Birnes, William J., *Signature Killers:*

Interpreting the Calling Cards of the Serial Murderer, Pocket Books, 1997.

Michaud, Stephen G. and Hazelwood, Roy, *The Evil That Men Do: FBI Profiler Roy Hazelwood's Journey into the Minds of Sexual Predators*, St. Martin's Press, 1999.

Ressler, Robert and Schachtman, Tom, *Whoever Fights Monsters: My Twenty Years Tracking Serial Killers for the FBI*, St. Martin's Press, 1992.

Rosenthal, A.M. *Thirty-Eight Witnesses: The Kitty Genovese Case*, University of California Press, 1999.

Vorpagel, Russell, as told to Joseph Harrington, *Profiles in Murder: An FBI Legend Dissects Killers and Their Crimes*, Dell, 2001 (Perseus Books, 1998, reprinted by arrangement).

Index